THE LAST COURSE

THE LAST COURSE
The Desserts of Gramercy Tavern

Claudia Fleming

with Melissa Clark

PREFACE BY DANNY MEYER • FOREWORD BY TOM COLICCHIO

Photography by Dana Gallagher

RANDOM HOUSE

NEW YORK

Library of Congress Cataloging-in-Publication Data
Fleming, Claudia.
The last course: the desserts of Gramercy Tavern/Claudia Fleming with Melissa Clark.
p.   cm.
ISBN 0-375-50429-Xs
1. Desserts.   2. Gramercy Tavern.   I. Clark, Melissa.   II. Title.
TX773 .F596 2001
641.6—dc21   2001019075

Random House website address: www.atrandom.com

Printed in the United States of America on acid-free paper
2 4 6 8 9 7 5 3
First Edition

Book design by Esther Bridavsky

I'd like to dedicate this book to the memories of my father, James Matthew,

and my brother, James Patrick.

And to my mother, Elvira, the most creative person I know.

ACKNOWLEDGMENTS

There wouldn't be a Gramercy Tavern dessert book if it weren't for Danny Meyer and Tom Colicchio, the two visionaries behind the restaurant. To Danny, I owe gratitude for all of his sage advice and support over the years. And to Tom, my true mentor, many, many thanks for all his continued inspiration. Watching Tom's creative process helps me develop as a cook, and there's nothing more gratifying than that.

I couldn't have written this book without the help of my sous-chef, Christopher Albrecht, whose excellence, dedication, and hard work have allowed me to both look good and carve out the time to write a book.

Similar words of appreciation go to all the veterans in the pastry department of Gramercy Tavern, such as Michelle Antonishek, Vlademir Lopez, Jose Mora, Castulo Flores, Angela Batista, and everyone else who has passed through these doors. You've all taught me so much.

I must also gratefully acknowledge John Schaefer, Gramercy Tavern's chef de cuisine, whose organizational skills and steel-trap mind keep the kitchen running like a well-oiled machine and make my job easier in the process.

Many, many thanks to our sommelier, Paul Greico, for his brilliant wine and dessert pairings. The book has been greatly enriched because of them.

Without great products, my work would be impossible. I would therefore like to thank Modesto Batista for getting me anything and everything I need at a moment's notice. And thanks to my produce purveyors—Franca from Berried Treasures, Red Jacket Orchards, Samascott Farms, Locust Farms, Phillips Farms, Cherry Lane, and my favorite, John the Greek—for getting me the best of the best, every single day.

I also want to thank those I've learned from on the way to Gramercy Tavern, including pastry greats Pierre Hermé, Lindsey Shere, and Nancy Silverton. All of these brilliant chefs continue to stimulate my work with their unique, inventive visions.

The elegant look of this book is a direct result of three talented women: photographer Dana Gallagher, prop stylist Suzanne Shaker, and book designer Esther Bridavsky, who worked together to capture the essence of what I do and translate it, visually, to these pages.

Amy Scheibe also merits thanks for coming up with such a perfect title for the book, even before a single word had been written!

Thanks to my agent and friend David Black, who helped me believe that I could handle such a huge undertaking as this book.

Special thanks as well to Melissa Clark, who made writing a book both possible and *fun,* and has become a great friend. And to her recipe-testing assistants, Amy Shiu and Zoe Singer.

My gratitude, also, to my dedicated editor, Pamela Cannon, and to everyone at Random House for their exuberant belief in the project. It helped keep me going when it seemed like the end was hundreds of recipes away.

Thank you to my dear sister, Lauren Regan, who has since childhood supported me with unbridled enthusiasm no matter what I thought I wanted to do, and instilled in me an appreciation for all things fine and beautiful.

And last, I have to thank my sweet husband, Gerry Hayden, whose encouragement so many years ago helped me believe I could actually make delicious desserts.

PREFACE

It's easy to look at a winning bet in retrospect and then to proudly pat yourself on the back. I'd like to say that I knew from the start Claudia Fleming would be the perfect pastry chef for Gramercy Tavern, but actually, I'm not sure I had ever even tasted Claudia's desserts when we hired her.

I first met Claudia in 1987 when she was interviewing to become a server at Union Square Cafe. Even from half a room away, I could feel her warmth, poise, and intelligence. I knew we would hire her before I even sat down for the interview. During her time at Union Square Cafe, I grew to admire Claudia for her dancer's dignity, competence, and self-assurance. She has an extraordinary work ethic and is amazingly self-sufficient. She was one of the few servers I had ever met who wouldn't permit me to help bus her station! She is also passionate about learning new things. It didn't take long before Claudia's curiosity led her to the Union Square Cafe kitchen and into the pastry station. After several months, her passion for pastry carried her off to study in France, and we were sad to lose her.

In early 1994, when Gramercy Tavern was in construction, I heard that Claudia had returned from Paris and was working part-time as a consulting pastry chef in New York. Chef Tom Colicchio and I were looking for a talented pastry chef for Gramercy Tavern, but not one whose already established style would have to be melded with Tom's. We wanted to find someone who would have the flexibility, persistence, and innate ability to grow with us. When we made the decision to hire Claudia, it was based purely on my sense of her as a person and Tom's confidence that he would be entirely comfortable collaborating with her as a cook. We knew that Claudia's personality meshed perfectly with our approach to the restaurant, so we followed our instincts.

It couldn't have turned out better. Claudia's desserts strike a perfect balance between heart and mind, providing the ultimate close to the dining experience at Gramercy Tavern. Just as the restaurant strives to combine luxury with warm, down-to-earth hospitality, Claudia's desserts are based on purity, elegance, and grace, but omit fancified elements like pulled sugar or gold leaf. She creates outstanding combinations by treating perfect Greenmarket strawberries as if they're little jewels and making the most technically perfect chocolate tartlet you could imagine; then she has the confidence to toss those berries with tarragon, or to serve the tart with a miniature chocolate malted. Claudia's ideas never seem like whimsy for the sake of whimsy. They thoroughly demonstrate the knowledge, savvy, and technical expertise that she has been so determined to master. Just watching her amazingly strong, adept hands at work is enough to convince me that this is what she was always meant to be doing.

Over her years as Gramercy Tavern's pastry chef, Claudia has grown more confident and authoritative, and so have her desserts. They've become purer and more delicious, and, as always, they make sense. You can taste much pleasure in these desserts because they are conceived and prepared entirely for your enjoyment, rather than for the pastry chef's own edification. Claudia is an unusually empathetic person—how people feel matters a lot to her, and this makes her desserts even more satisfying to the soul. It also helps that she has extraordinary *taste*. But perhaps most remarkable is Claudia's rare combination of humility and excellence. I don't know many people who possess those two qualities in such harmonious abundance.

When you leave a meal at Gramercy Tavern, your last impression is a powerful one: you feel comforted in your heart and stimulated in your mind. Claudia's desserts are an essential component of this—and I just can't imagine how dinner at Gramercy Tavern could end on a more delicious note.

—Danny Meyer, owner, Gramercy Tavern

FOREWORD

People's taste in food is often divided into two categories: those who love salty, savory foods, and those who prefer sweets. There is, however, a specialized third category: those who work with savory foods, but who are done in by their sweet tooth. Throughout my workday I find countless excuses to amble over to the pastry station, where I help myself to handfuls of tiny pecan sandies, fingerfuls of candied kumquats, tastes of raw cookie dough. It's no accident that the sorbet and ice cream drawer are right next to my station.

When I opened Gramercy Tavern, Claudia was the only member of the kitchen staff with whom I hadn't worked before. And yet, before hiring her, I never asked her to cook for me, I tasted no sample desserts, and I never once asked her to design a pastry menu. I didn't need to. Over the years my intuition about the best people has served me well, and my intuition told me Claudia would be a star.

For one thing, I knew Claudia had technique. Her résumé boasted a stint at Fauchon, under the legendary Pierre Hermé. I knew that that sort of experience would ground her with impeccable skills, the kind of exacting technical ability necessary for the job ahead.

Second, I had a feeling based on Claudia's personal style—the way she carried herself, even the way she dressed—that she was a person of integrity and determination. I remember thinking that if her desserts resembled these outward cues, then stylistically we were in sync.

Finally, after one brief interview, I knew Claudia was the perfect fit for us because she convinced me that she "got it." Back then the style of the day was architectural desserts—confections that towered high above the plate, with rock-hard ice cream providing the supportive structure. When I had discussed the job with other candidates, I'd explained that I was looking for someone who was willing to forgo theatrics in pursuit of mind-bending flavor. I remember most people's reactions; in short, they didn't get it. Wasn't it important to dazzle the guests? But when I explained to Claudia that I wanted people to go "ooh" and "aah" *after* they'd tasted the dessert, she alone grew excited at the prospect. She immediately grasped that I wanted the desserts at Gramercy Tavern to have the same sensibility as the rest of the food—simple, straightforward, emphasizing intensity of flavor over flash.

During Gramercy's first year, Claudia would knock on my door with her latest desserts, asking for my input. I'd taste, we'd discuss, I'd make suggestions. Then one day something seemed to click. Claudia started coming to my office with complete desserts that required nothing from me, other than to lick the plate.

Her dishes just floored me with their ingenuity, their clean style, and, most important, their flavor. She'd nailed it. These wonderful desserts were cropping up with increasing regularity in magazine and newspaper articles. And why not? They were newsworthy.

What I most appreciate about Claudia's desserts is that in the smallest ways, each and every component is that much finer than everything else out there. Compare Claudia's short crust to anyone else's in New York—it's that much thinner, and, again (the only word that really works), *finer.* These are small distinctions, but in the world of pastry, they are everything. She constantly tests the limits—how light can she make puff pastry, how much more flavor can she give the ice cream and sorbet? Mostly, I think I respect her work because, unlike some cooks, who start with a heightened sense of presentation and then find food to "match," Claudia begins by making every element on the plate as flavorful as possible and then works to match the presentation to the food. Again, a subtle difference, but it neatly sums up what Gramercy Tavern is all about.

One of the highest compliments I can pay Claudia is merely the truth: after years of seeing her look to my food for inspiration, the tables have turned. These days I head over to her station and borrow liberally from her *mise-en-place* to inspire my cooking.

In this book Claudia's integrity and passion for flavor come through on every page. As I read it, I was reminded that first and foremost a great pastry chef has to be a great cook, and Claudia is. She has managed to take what she does at Gramercy Tavern and break it down for any level of cook; it's a book not just for pastry chefs, but for *cooks who want to make dessert.* It was both a joy to read and a torment—time and again, I found myself marking my place and heading over to the pastry department for just one more pecan sandy, another syrupy kumquat, one more spoonful of sorbet.

—Tom Colicchio, chef/owner, Gramercy Tavern

CONTENTS

HERBS AND FLOWERS

SPICES

INTRODUCTION

I've always loved desserts, for both their sweet flavors and their diverse textures, like the crunch of a chocolate-covered pretzel or the silky mouthfeel of homemade butterscotch custard. Growing up, I was the kind of kid who sometimes wouldn't eat dinner but ate ice cream and cookies instead. Or, if I thought I wasn't hungry, I could still be tempted by a slice of my mother's homemade chocolate cream pie.

Being a pastry chef, however, was not something I grew up fantasizing about. Instead, I wanted to be a dancer. I started taking ballet lessons at the age of six and turned out to be quite good at it, which was probably part of the reason I loved it so much. But there's another reason, too. As the youngest of three, I felt that dancing was something that was all mine. It was important, and it was special, and that made me want to keep doing it.

Working in restaurants (initially as a waiter) was a happy accident that occurred because I couldn't support myself as a dancer. The first real restaurant I worked in was Jams in New York City with chef Jonathan Waxman (and partner Melvyn Master). This was in the 1980s—an amazing time to be in the restaurant business. A food revolution was in full swing, and there I was smack in the middle of it. Jams was a huge change from the other places I had worked at (one of

which was an ice cream parlor); I saw tiny baby vegetables for the first time, and dishes like lamb tenderloins on a composed salad or black-bean cakes with duck confit. I saw chefs handling ingredients as if they were jewels. It was the beginning of New York's fascination with California cuisine, and I thought it was incredible.

After Jams, I moved on to work for Danny Meyer at Union Square Cafe. I knew that I didn't want to wait tables my whole life. I felt the time had come for me to make some kind of decision: what, *exactly,* should I do with my life? I asked Michael Romano, the chef (and now an owner) at Union Square, if he'd let me work as a prep cook so that I could see if I liked working in the kitchen. Being a prep cook is the lowest rung on a chef's ladder. You peel sacks of potatoes and onions, wash all the baby lettuces, shell crates and crates of fava beans, and generally learn your way around a professional kitchen. I also started attending Peter Kump's Cooking School in the evenings for a more formal education.

I was absolutely thrilled to be working in the kitchen, but I was at my happiest hanging around the pastry station. I'd pester the pastry chefs with scores of questions and follow them around, learning what I could from leaning over their shoulders and watching. When a pastry position finally opened up and was offered to me, I literally jumped at the chance. From that moment on I knew I was in the right place.

I learned a lot as an assistant pastry chef—so much, in fact, that it made me realize how much I still didn't know. I noticed that many of the best pastry chefs I'd met in New York had spent some time apprenticing in Europe (that is, if they weren't *already* French). I wanted to go, too, if I could figure out a way to get there. I had no connections, not much in the way of foreign-language skills, and little money. Still, I was determined. A Paris-trained friend, Maury Rubin of City Bakery, arranged for me to work with the people with whom he had studied. I drained my savings account, and two weeks later I was on my way to France. I worked at a shop called Rousseau et Seurre for a while, then went to work under the renowned chef Pierre Hermé at Fauchon.

Studying in Europe was an important career move in several ways. Most important, it gave me a strong, solid foundation in the art of pastry, laid out in a very codified way. As a former dancer, I deeply understood the value of mastering technique. When I was dancing in the studio, it was all about learning the steps and coordinating the music and the timing. I drove myself very hard so that when performance time came, I was confident enough to let go and just dance. This always shocked my teachers—how different I was onstage. But I felt that sense of freedom because I trusted my technique. It's the same with cooking. Thanks to my training in France, I feel confident enough to experiment. I know I've tried some wacky things (like the cilantro syrup on my coconut tapioca, see page 242), but I also know that my desserts work because they are all based on good technique.

After nine months in Europe, I came back to New York. I heard that Danny Meyer and Tom Colic-

chio were opening Gramercy Tavern, and a friend told me to call Tom, the chef. I was ambivalent at the time. I thought it was too high-profile for me, and too big. But once I talked to Tom, I was convinced that it was my next step. His enthusiasm was infectious, and I felt it would be a good fit. It was one of the best decisions of my life.

Although studying in Europe helped me feel secure in my technique, until Gramercy Tavern, I didn't really have my own style as a pastry chef. I knew that I had discipline, a good work ethic, and a certain measure of creativity, but I didn't know what I was capable of until Tom encouraged me to experiment, which I did in direct relation to him and his approach. One of our goals at Gramercy Tavern is to provide a seamless transition from dinner to dessert, and I feel we accomplish that easily, since my style and Tom's are so closely linked.

When I first started, I would come to work every day and just watch Tom. I saw his integrity and his honesty in handling the food. He really lets his ingredients speak for themselves and never tries to impose the latest trends or esoteric notions on them. The cuisine he prepares is made as good as it can be by just coaxing and tweaking the ingredients, but never by being manipulative. I learned that the most delicious foods are those that have been nurtured and treated respectfully. It was an important lesson.

In a way, it's what makes the whole dining experience at Gramercy Tavern special. It's where my style, Tom's, and owner Danny Meyer's overlap. We all have one goal at Gramercy, and that is to nurture people, simply and without pretense. It's a philosophy we take very seriously, and it extends to all facets of the restaurant, from the staff, to the purveyors, to the clientele, and of course to the food itself. We try to give our customers pleasure without overwhelming them with formality. It's certainly the way I feel most comfortable in a restaurant.

Giving people satisfying but unintimidating food fits in with this overall mission, and that's exactly what I try to do with my desserts. It's hard to describe one's own style, but I know that the basis of mine is flavor. First and foremost, everything I make has to taste absolutely delicious. But deliciousness can take many forms. For me, a successful dessert is one that combines clean flavors with a streamlined presentation and a variety of textures and temperatures. It makes sense to have something crispy and something soft sharing a plate with something hot and something cold, since it's the contrast that makes each experience complete. For me, striking a balance between these different components is the real challenge.

Another element at work in my desserts is the variety of ways in which I play with the main ingredient of each dish. Usually, I work within a theme, often revolving around one particular ingredient. When I come up with the dessert, I think about that ingredient in every possible permutation to try to figure out how I can get the most out of it. So while I'm combining textures and temperatures on the plate, I'm also taking into account the best way to showcase my main ingredient. If it's a pineapple, I might serve it raw and tart in a relish, cooked and highly sweetened in a sauce, churned into a snowy granité, dried to a crisp chip in the oven, or made into a buttery tart or airy soufflé. That way, the diner can really get to know the different personalities of a pineapple.

It may be because my training wasn't as structured as that of many other pastry chefs, or maybe it's just because of who I am as a person, but I'm very open to taking chances with my menu. In fact, I really love

taking risks—making that leap of faith with a dessert combination and hoping that it appeals to the person eating it as much as it does to me. Serving a miniature chocolate malted in a shot glass alongside a chocolate tart garnished with a scoop of extra-bittersweet chocolate sorbet makes sense, especially to the kid in me. The sorbet, like a slightly more sophisticated Fudgsicle, seems to cry out for a malted companion. In terms of balancing the plate, the malted breaks up the intensity of all the dark bittersweet chocolate in the tart and in the sorbet. Sometimes I wonder what some of my teachers would think if they came to the restaurant and saw what I am doing. I'm honestly a little afraid they'd be horrified, and I can imagine them thinking, "Claudia! You can't serve waffles with flan!" But to me, it works: a silky maple-syrup flan garnished with crunchy, freshly made waffles. Waffles topped with maple syrup and butter is a natural breakfast combination. All I did was translate it into dessert. The only time a dessert doesn't make sense is if it doesn't taste delicious.

I gain my inspiration from different ingredients as they come into season; from the homey desserts of my childhood; from skimming international food magazines; from my teachers; and from cuisines around the world. Reading a book on spices, I learned about *dukka,* a musky Middle Eastern nut paste used as a dipping sauce for bread. It usually contains hazelnuts, sesame seeds, cardamom, cumin, coriander, and salt. I decided to try adding sugar to the mix. Now I sprinkle it between layers of phyllo dough and serve it with sorbet made of labné, a thickened yogurt. It's a traditional grouping of Middle Eastern elements used in an untraditional way. Often an idea for something new comes from simply breathing life into an age-old combination. There's my apple tarte Tatin, for example, which I serve with a miniature goat-cheese cheesecake and golden raisins simmered in verjus (juice from unripe fruit, usually chardonnay grapes). I wanted to adapt a classic cheese course of cheese, bread, and fresh and dried fruit. It may seem slightly strange at first, but it is ultimately comforting and familiar. For me, it's almost like a game or a puzzle, to let my mind wander around an idea and think, "What if?" What if I made basil into ice cream, what would happen? The worst possibility is that it wouldn't taste good and I'd try again. Tarragon tastes like licorice, so why not combine it with anise meringues and strawberries as a twist on a classic vacherin?

When it comes to presentation, my style is fairly restrained, yet elegant and sophisticated. Personally, I hate when a dessert comes to the table looking like it just landed from Mars. When I worked as a waiter, I always thought it was a bit strange if, when I served a dessert, a customer would say, "Oh, this is so beautiful! I don't know whether I should eat it or take a picture of it." I don't want my desserts to be flashy or intimidating. I just want them to look harmonious and provide a few small, sweet bites after a wonderful meal.

And when I say a few bites, I really mean it. My desserts are definitely small. By the time people get to dessert, they are already pretty full. I think the ideal dessert is a few perfect, intense tastes filled with balanced flavors and textures. No one likes to leave a dinner table being overly full, but most people want to end with something sweet. Small portions satisfy both desires.

Describing my desserts makes them sound more fussy than they actually are. I once read an article about how a German fashion designer came up with her line of clothing. First, the article said, she'd take a concept, then strip away everything superfluous until the idea was as clean and simple as it could be while still making sense. I like to think I work in that same way. First I break each component of my desserts down to its very essence, and then I build the components back up again, changing the combinations to suit the seasons, my mood, or the feeling of the menu in general.

When using this book, please don't think that any of my recipes are written in stone. They all work as is, but that doesn't mean they won't work if you alter them to suit your own tastes or to accommodate a favorite flavor. When adapting or combining these recipes, if there's something you like, and you combine it with something else you like, chances are you're going to like the end result. You might want to change a recipe because you don't have a particular ingredient on hand. If a recipe calls for a combination of almonds and hazelnuts and you have only almonds, use all almonds. Don't hesitate to make variations.

The dessert may not taste exactly like it does at Gramercy Tavern, but it's going to taste delicious. And that's the purpose of dessert.

As a pastry chef, I try to make desserts that people would not make for themselves every day. I want my desserts to be extra-special, and I always try to give my customers more than they might even think they want. That's why when I compose a dessert, it usually consists of several elements that come together on the plate to form a new whole. But making several sweets to end one meal isn't practical for everyone, especially for a home cook who doesn't have an entire staff of assistants candying orange peel and curling tuiles. I've written this book with the home cook in mind. While the last chapter shows how I put the different components together to create my menu at Gramercy Tavern, each separate recipe can stand alone as a simple but vibrant and unforgettable dessert in its own right. Determine how much time and energy you have to devote to dessert on any particular occasion. Make one component or make several—then play with the different elements and come up with your own individual interpretations.

The most important thing to remember is that cooking, and I think especially dessert-making, is incredibly fun. I truly hope that you enjoy this book as much as I love eating dessert. After all, that's the best part.

A NOTE ON INGREDIENTS

For the most part, I discuss the ingredients central to each chapter in the chapter introductions. But there are some ingredients that span the whole book. Here are a few words on the basics:

Flour: I use both all-purpose and cake flour, depending on the recipe. All-purpose flour has slightly more protein than cake flour, and is suited to desserts and baked goods that require a little bit of structure, like cookies and tart crusts.
Cake Flour: Higher in starch and lower in protein, cake flour bakes up more delicately, giving cakes an especially tender crumb. Make sure to purchase plain cake flour. The self-rising kind, with its added leaveners and salt, won't work in these recipes.
Butter: I always use unsalted butter. We don't stock any other kind in the pastry kitchen at Gramercy Tavern. Try to find the freshest butter you can, and freeze any that you are not going to use in the next few weeks. This will prevent the butter from absorbing any off tastes from the refrigerator.
Salt: Although in most pantries a cylinder of iodized salt is the standard, I use kosher or fine sea salt, even in baking. I find it has a purer taste.

A NOTE ON FREEZING

While I don't freeze many of my finished desserts, I do freeze doughs and both baked and unbaked tart crusts. The trick to freezing is to wrap everything well in plastic wrap, then freeze it for no more than two or three months, and preferably just a few weeks.

For unbaked doughs (like cookie dough and tart dough), your best bet is to let them defrost slowly in the refrigerator rather than at room temperature. A baked tart crust can be defrosted at room temperature (it will take only 15 to 30 minutes), but you'll have to refresh the crust before using it. To do so, unwrap it and place it in a 350°F. oven for 5 minutes, then cool and use as directed.

A WORD ON THE WINE NOTES

Just as every course of the savory part of the meal deserves its own well-matched wine, so does the very last course: dessert. Pairing wines with sweets is just as challenging as choosing wines to go with dinner, so I enlisted the help of Gramercy Tavern's brilliant wine director, Paul Greico. Paul has carefully selected styles of wine to go with all the desserts in the book, and you will find his excellent recommendations at the end of each chapter introduction. For the composed desserts in the last chapter, Paul has suggested some of his favorite wines that are particularly well suited to the flavor combinations of each dish. While serving wine with dessert is optional, it does make for a harmonious and elegant presentation that will make your last course even more special.

THE LAST COURSE

BERRIES

Intensely flavored seasonal berries are probably everyone's favorite fruit. But unfortunately, like most good things, they are as fleeting as they are beloved. So during their short summer seasons, I always make desserts in which berries play a starring role, presented at their sweetest, freshest, juiciest best.

Because berries are fragile, soft fruits, I buy seasonal local varieties from the farmer's market. Out-of-season berries have been bred for durability and shipping, and the result is a sour and hard product with none of the fresh berry's enticing characteristics. Another benefit to buying berries at the farmer's market is the amazing assortment you can find there, including raspberries that come in white, black, golden, and pink as well as red. The different varieties all possess unique qualities that, when combined, achieve an unparalleled harmony of flavors.

Unlike that of apples, pears, or most other fruits, the flavor of berries becomes diluted when they are cooked. Heat seems to destroy their delicate taste and texture, making them watered-down shadows of their fresh selves. In this chapter the berries are used either fresh or barely warmed, so that they stay as intensely flavorful as possible. In the Raspberry–Lemon Verbena Meringue Cake, the berries are insulated by a layer of meringue, so that even though they are baked, they barely feel the heat, warming just enough to release their perfume but not enough to break down. To make berry compotes, I toss whole raspberries, strawberries, or blackberries with uncooked puréed fruit. This way, their flavors and colors stay bright and clear, without tasting cooked and dulled. This said, I do lightly simmer some of the berries for the blueberry compote. Blueberries are pretty hardy, and I find that cooking intensifies their flavor and releases the pectin in their skins, which provides a natural thickener for their sauce.

Berries are delicious with most of the produce that is harvested at the same time of year, so they combine beautifully with other summer fruits like apricots and peaches. I also like to pair berries with fresh summer herbs, such as tarragon and verbena, which bring out their natural qualities and highlight their sweetness.

Blueberries and strawberries should be rinsed right before they are used, then spread on a clean dish towel to dry. I don't wash raspberries and blackberries at all; I just pick through them to remove any leaves or twigs.

Buy plump, vibrant berries that retain their shape yet are fully colored and soft. Avoid mushed or moldy berries and use the berries shortly after purchase.

WINE NOTES: BERRIES

In general terms, one can make wine from any number of different fruits, including the family of berries. These wines can be incredibly fruit-forward and unctuous, and they taste perfect with a dessert employing the same berry. As a general rule of thumb, for a dessert wine to match a dessert, it must be sweeter than the accompanying dish. And in the case of berry wines, they are usually very sweet and contain slightly higher alcohols. Some of the berry desserts will demand a bigger, more robust wine with not only more alcohol, but some tannin to cut some of the sweetness. Recioto della Valpolicella is a sweet version of an Amarone that fits this description. (Reciota means "ears" in Venetian dialect, named for the ripest, sweetest grapes near the top if you hold a bunch up by its stem and imagine that it is a head.)

For the dark and sweet berries in the blueberry desserts, add a lightening spritz to the mix with an Australian sparkling Shiraz.

RASPBERRY–LEMON VERBENA MERINGUE CAKE

A giant, three-layer confection of vanilla butter cake, berries, and meringue, this dessert looks gorgeous when you pull it out of the oven with its lovely, caramelized top. As you eat it, you first encounter soft, creamy meringue, then tart berries in lemon verbena syrup that oozes into the soft, velvety cake below. The cake, berries, and meringue meld together to form something like a trifle or a warm summer pudding, with the unexpected spark of verbena, a lemony fresh herb.

Although this cake needs to be served straight from the oven, most of the components can be made in advance. Just before serving, whip the egg whites, assemble the layers, and bake for 15 minutes. It's a stunning dessert well worth the planning.

Yield: 8 servings

VANILLA CAKE
½   cup (1 stick) unsalted butter
¼   vanilla bean, split lengthwise, pulp scraped (see page 180)
3   large eggs, at room temperature
½   cup sugar
¾   cup cake flour
⅛   teaspoon salt
1½ teaspoons vanilla extract

LEMON VERBENA RASPBERRIES
⅓   cup sugar
1   large sprig of lemon verbena
2   half-pints raspberries

LEMON VERBENA MERINGUE
⅔   cup milk
1   large sprig of lemon verbena
6   tablespoons sugar
2   large eggs, separated
1   tablespoon cornstarch

1. To prepare the cake, preheat the oven to 350°F. Grease and flour a 9-inch springform pan. In a small saucepan over low heat, melt the butter with the vanilla pulp. Set aside to cool.

2. Using an electric mixer fitted with the whisk attachment, beat the eggs and sugar until thick and pale, about 5 minutes.

3. In a bowl, whisk together the flour and salt. Sift the flour mixture into the eggs in three additions, folding to thoroughly combine after each addition. In a separate bowl, whisk together 1 cup of batter with the melted butter and the vanilla extract. Fold into the remaining batter. Pour into the prepared pan.

4. Bake the cake until a tester inserted into the middle comes out clean, about 20 to 25 minutes. Transfer to a wire rack to cool. (The cake can be baked 1 day ahead; wrap well and store at room temperature.)

5. Release the sides of the pan and use a large serrated knife to trim off the top ⅛ inch of the cake (save for snacking). Lock the cake pan sides back around the trimmed cake and reserve.

6. To prepare the lemon verbena raspberries, in a small saucepan over medium heat, bring the sugar, ¼ cup water, and lemon verbena to a simmer. Cook, stirring occasionally, until the sugar dissolves, 1 to 2 minutes. Turn off the heat and let cool completely.

7. Strain the syrup, discarding the verbena. Brush a little of the syrup over the top of the cake and set aside. In a bowl, toss the raspberries with 2 tablespoons of the syrup. Use a fork to lightly crush one third of the berries so they release their juices. Set aside while you prepare the rest of the cake.

8. To prepare the meringue, in a small saucepan over medium heat, bring the milk and the lemon verbena to a simmer. Turn off the heat and let cool completely. Strain the milk, then measure out ½ cup, discarding the rest.

9. In a heavy saucepan, combine ¼ cup of the milk and 1 tablespoon of the sugar; bring the mixture to a simmer over medium heat. Meanwhile, in a large bowl whisk together 1 tablespoon of the sugar, the egg yolks, and the cornstarch. Whisk in the remaining ¼ cup of cooled milk. Remove the hot milk mixture from the heat and add a little to the egg yolk mixture to warm it, whisking constantly to keep the yolks from cooking. Pour the egg yolk mixture into the hot milk mixture, stirring the milk constantly as you pour. Return the custard to the stove and bring it to a boil, whisking constantly. Let boil for 1 minute, then strain the custard through a sieve into a large, clean bowl. Cover the surface of the custard directly with plastic wrap and set aside.

10. Preheat the oven to 350°F. In the bowl of an electric mixer fitted with a whisk attachment, whip the egg whites until they hold soft peaks. Continue to beat, gradually adding the remaining 4 tablespoons of sugar, until the whites form stiff peaks. Whisk about 1 cup of the egg whites into the custard to lighten it, then gently fold in the remaining whites in two batches.

11. Spread the raspberries and their juices evenly over the top of the cake. Using a spatula, spread the meringue over the top of the raspberries, being sure to spread it all the way to the sides of the pan. Bake the cake until the meringue is set, about 15 minutes. Turn the oven to broil. Transfer the cake to the broiler and broil for about 30 seconds, until the top is nicely browned. Be careful; it burns easily. Remove the pan sides and serve the cake while still warm.

SERVING SUGGESTION
• Serve with candied almonds (see page 261) and/or scoops of Raspberry Sorbet (page 20).

BLUEBERRY–CORNMEAL CAKES

Reminiscent of the crisp tops of blueberry corn muffins, these golden little cakes are absolutely irresistible. The cakes have a delicious sugary crust like a muffin top, but unlike muffins, the crumb is moist, buttery, and very tender. The blueberries are studded throughout the batter, and while they bake, they pop, becoming jammy and concentrated. When I can get them, I try to use tiny, intensely flavored wild blueberries or huckleberries, but regular blueberries are fine, too. Serve these rich cakes on their own for tea, or pair them with ice cream, sorbet, or fresh fruit for dessert.

Yield: 12 cakes

1   cup (2 sticks) unsalted butter
2⅔ cups confectioners' sugar
1   cup almond flour
½   cup plus 1 tablespoon cake flour
¼   cup coarse yellow cornmeal
1   cup egg whites (about 8)
Grated zest of ½ orange
1   cup blueberries

1. Preheat the oven to 400°F. In a large skillet over medium heat, melt the butter. Continue to let the butter cook until some of the white milk solids fall to the bottom of the skillet and turn a rich hazelnut brown. Strain the browned butter through a fine sieve into a clean bowl and discard the solids.

2. Sift together the confectioners' sugar, almond flour, cake flour, and cornmeal. Place the sifted ingredients in the bowl of an electric mixer fitted with the whisk attachment. On the lowest speed, add the egg whites and zest; mix until all the dry ingredients are moistened. Increase the speed to medium-low and stir in the browned butter. Increase the speed to medium and beat until smooth. Remove the bowl from the mixer and fold in the blueberries. (The batter can be made up to 3 days ahead and refrigerated.)

3. Butter and flour 12 muffin tins or 2-inch mini tart tins. Spoon the batter into the tins and bake for 18 to 20 minutes, or until the cakes are golden brown around the edges. Transfer to a wire rack and cool completely.

SERVING SUGGESTIONS
· Serve with fresh seasonal berries.
· For a composed dessert, add scoops of Sweet-Corn Ice Cream (page 127).

BLUEBERRY–CREAM CHEESE TARTS WITH GRAHAM CRACKER CRUST

These gorgeous little tarts are a fresh take on blueberry cheesecake. Instead of a crumbly graham cracker crust layered with dense cheesecake and a cooked berry glaze, they have a crisp graham cracker shell filled with soft, airy cream cheese custard, crowned by a juicy fresh berry compote. It's a lighter, more dainty dessert, with all the lush, sweet-tangy flavors of cream cheese and ripe summer berries.

Yield: 16 tarts

GRAHAM CRACKER TART SHELLS
1   cup (2 sticks) unsalted butter, softened
¼   cup firmly packed dark brown sugar
¼   cup granulated sugar
¼   cup honey
2   cups all-purpose flour
½   cup whole wheat pastry flour
1   teaspoon salt
½   teaspoon ground cinnamon

CREAM CHEESE PASTRY CREAM
1   cup milk
5   tablespoons sugar
4   large egg yolks
2½ tablespoons cornstarch
¾   cup (6 ounces) cream cheese, cut into cubes and softened
1   teaspoon vanilla extract
½   cup heavy cream, whipped to soft peaks

BLUEBERRY TOPPING
2½ cups blueberries
1   tablespoon sugar

1. To prepare the graham cracker shells, in the bowl of an electric mixer fitted with a paddle attachment, cream the butter and the sugars until smooth, about 1 minute. Add the honey and beat until well combined.

2. In a medium bowl, whisk together the flours, salt, and cinnamon. Add the flour mixture to the butter mixture in two batches, scraping down the sides of the bowl between additions. Mix until the dough is well combined. Scrape the dough onto a piece of plastic wrap and form it into a disk. Chill until firm, at least 1 hour and up to 2 days.

3. Preheat the oven to 325°F. On a lightly floured surface, roll out the dough to ⅛ inch thick, about a 13 × 16-inch rectangle. Using a 3-inch round cookie cutter, cut out 16 circles of dough and press them into greased mini muffin pans or 2-inch tart pans, trimming away any excess dough. (Alternatively, fit rectangles of dough into mini rectangular tart tins.) Prick the dough all over with a fork. Chill for 20 minutes.

4. Bake until golden brown, 18 to 20 minutes. Transfer to a wire rack to cool. (The tart shells can be made up to 1 day ahead and frozen for up to 3 months; see page xxv.)

5. To prepare the pastry cream, combine ¾ cup of the milk and 3 tablespoons of the sugar in a medium saucepan; bring to a simmer over medium heat. Meanwhile, in a large bowl, whisk together the egg yolks, cornstarch, and the remaining 2 tablespoons of sugar. Whisk the remaining ¼ cup milk into the egg yolk mixture. Remove the milk mixture from the heat and add a little of the hot milk to the egg yolk mixture to warm it, whisking constantly to keep the yolks from cooking. Pour the egg yolk mixture into the hot milk mixture, whisking constantly as you pour.

6. Return the custard to the stove and bring it to a boil, whisking constantly. Let the custard cook for 1 to 2 minutes, until it thickens. Add the cream cheese and vanilla extract and whisk until smooth. Strain the mixture through a sieve lined with cheesecloth into a clean bowl. Cover the surface with plastic wrap and refrigerate. When it is chilled, whisk the pastry cream until smooth and fold in the whipped cream.

7. To make the blueberry topping, in a medium saucepan, mix 1 cup of the

blueberries with the sugar. Cook over low heat until the berries have all popped and broken down, about 5 minutes. Strain the cooked berries into a bowl and discard the solids. Add the remaining 1½ cups whole berries to the cooked berry syrup and toss to combine.

8. To assemble, spoon the pastry cream into each tart shell and top with 2 tablespoons of the blueberries. Serve soon after assembling.

VARIATION
This recipe can also be made into 2 large tarts. Divide the dough in half and roll each piece into an 11-inch circle. Fit the dough into two 9-inch tart pans, trimming away any excess. Prick and bake as directed above, increasing the baking time to about 25 minutes. Cool the shells completely. Divide the filling and topping between the two tarts just before serving.

Alternatively, you can make one larger tart (10-, 11-, or 12-inch) and use the remaining dough to make graham crackers. Roll the dough out to ⅛ inch thick, cut into square or rectangular crackers, place on a baking sheet, prick with a fork, and bake at 325°F. for about 15 minutes.

SERVING SUGGESTION
• Serve with scoops of Honey–Lemon Thyme Sorbet (page 163).

BLACKBERRY NAPOLEONS WITH ORANGE SHORTBREAD WAFERS

This rich but summery dessert was inspired by a raspberry napoleon that I saw in one of the dessert books by the legendary Michel Roux. I like the simplicity of the presentation, which consists of shortbread cookies sandwiching fresh berries. In my version, I use blackberries layered between orange-scented shortbread wafers and garnished with a rich, tangy, orange-scented crème fraîche cream. The result is a dessert that is as bright and refreshing as a summer berry dessert should be, yet is satisfyingly creamy and crumbly at the same time.

Yield: 6 servings

ORANGE SHORTBREAD WAFERS

1	cup (2 sticks) unsalted butter, softened
¾	cup confectioners' sugar, plus extra for garnish
2	teaspoons vanilla extract
1½	teaspoons grated orange zest
2	cups all-purpose flour
1	teaspoon salt

BLACKBERRY FILLING

2	half-pints blackberries
1	tablespoon sugar
¾	cup crème fraîche
2	teaspoons orange-blossom honey
¼	teaspoon orange-flower water, or to taste

1. To make the wafers, using an electric mixer fitted with the paddle attachment, beat the butter and sugar until creamy and smooth, about 2 minutes. Add the vanilla extract and orange zest and beat well. Beat in the flour and salt until well combined. Form the dough into a disk, wrap in plastic wrap, and chill for at least 3 hours and up to 3 days.

2. Preheat the oven to 300°F. Roll the dough between two sheets of wax paper to 3/16 inch thick, about a 10 × 14-inch rectangle. Using a 3-inch round cookie cutter, cut the shortbread into 12 rounds and place them 1 inch apart on an ungreased baking sheet (do not reroll the scraps). Prick the shortbread with a fork and bake until pale golden all over, 25 to 30 minutes. Cool completely on a wire rack.

3. To prepare the blackberries, in a small bowl, combine a quarter of the berries with the sugar. Let the berries macerate for 10 minutes. Purée the mixture in a blender, then strain through a fine sieve, discarding the solids. In a bowl, toss the remaining blackberries with the purée and set aside.

4. In the bowl of an electric mixer fitted with a whisk attachment, combine the crème fraîche, honey, and orange-flower water and beat until the cream is smooth and holds soft peaks. Refrigerate the honeyed crème fraîche until needed, up to 2 hours.

5. For each serving, place a tablespoon of the honeyed crème fraîche on a plate, spreading it out into a 3-inch round. Cover the round with a layer of blackberries and then top with a shortbread wafer. Spread another tablespoon of honeyed crème fraîche on the shortbread wafer, then layer more berries on top. Place a shortbread wafer over the berries. Serve immediately, garnished with confectioners' sugar.

SERVING SUGGESTION

• For a composed dessert, replace the crème fraîche with Frozen Orange-Blossom Honey Mousse (page 156) and serve with scoops of Orange Sorbet (see Variation, page 93).

TARRAGON-MACERATED STRAWBERRY SHORTCAKES WITH TARRAGON CREAM

This has all the elements of a strawberry shortcake with an intriguing twist: the scent of tarragon in the berries and cream. It's a terrific combination. The bright, sweet taste of strawberries pairs wonderfully with the licorice earthiness of tarragon. Go out of your way to find ripe, in-season strawberries for this dessert. Franca of Berried Treasures at the Union Square Greenmarket in Manhattan provides me with these jewels from early June until the first frost, and the small, juicy red fruit really makes this dessert superlative.

Yield: 8 servings

SHORTCAKE BISCUITS

- 1⅔ cups all-purpose flour
- 3½ tablespoons sugar
- 1½ tablespoons baking powder
- ⅛ teaspoon salt
- 6 tablespoons cold unsalted butter, cut into ½-inch cubes
- ⅔ cup plus 1 tablespoon heavy cream
- 1 tablespoon turbinado (raw) sugar

TARRAGON CREAM

- ½ cup fresh tarragon leaves (about ½ ounce)
- ⅓ cup light corn syrup
- 1½ cups heavy cream
- 2 tablespoons confectioners' sugar

TARRAGON-MACERATED STRAWBERRIES

- 6 large sprigs of fresh tarragon (about ½ ounce)
- 2 pints strawberries, hulled and sliced lengthwise
- 3 tablespoons sugar

1. To make the shortcake biscuits, in the bowl of a food processor or an electric mixer fitted with the paddle attachment, combine the flour, sugar, baking powder, and salt. Pulse or mix to combine. Add the butter and pulse or mix until the flour resembles coarse meal. Add ⅔ cup of the cream and pulse or mix until the dough just comes together, scraping down the paddle and mixing bowl if necessary. Turn the dough out onto a lightly floured surface and gently pat it together into a 6-inch square, 1 inch thick, incorporating any stray crumbs. Refrigerate the dough for 1 hour.

2. Preheat the oven to 350°F. Cut the dough into 9 biscuits. Brush the top of the biscuits with the remaining tablespoon of cream and sprinkle with the sugar.

3. Place the biscuits 2 inches apart on a parchment-lined baking sheet. Bake until the biscuits are golden brown, 20 to 25 minutes. Transfer to a wire rack to cool.

4. Meanwhile, prepare the tarragon cream. Bring a pot of water to a boil. Fill a bowl with ice water. Plunge the tarragon leaves into the boiling water for 30 seconds, then drain and plunge into the ice water. Drain well, squeezing out any excess moisture. Combine the tarragon and corn syrup in a blender and purée. Let rest for 30 minutes. (The syrup can be made up to 1 day in advance and refrigerated until needed.)

5. To prepare the tarragon-macerated strawberries, bruise the tarragon sprigs with the side of a knife or by twisting them in your hands. Toss together the strawberries, sugar, and tarragon and let stand for 20 minutes. Remove the tarragon and discard.

6. Strain the tarragon syrup through a fine sieve, discarding the solids. Whip the cream with the confectioners' sugar until thickened. Add the tarragon syrup and whip until soft peaks form.

7. To serve, split 8 of the shortcake biscuits in half and place the bottoms on plates. Top with some of the strawberries and then with the cream. Cover with the top of the shortcakes and serve immediately.

SERVING SUGGESTION

- For a composed dessert, serve with scoops of Strawberry Sorbet (page 21).

CARAMELIZED BRIOCHE PUDDING WITH BLACKBERRY CREAM AND FRESH BLACKBERRIES

Although it falls somewhere between French toast and bread pudding, there is no mistaking that this luxurious dish is meant for dessert and not breakfast. In it, slices of brioche are soaked in a delicately spiced, cream-enriched custard before being panfried until golden brown. A sprinkling of cinnamon sugar on top is caramelized into a crunchy, sweet crust that seems as if it can barely contain its puddinglike interior. Although this brioche pudding makes a marvelous base for any fruit compote, I especially like it with blackberries, which provide a juicy-tart contrast to the satiny-sweet custard. Feel free to substitute another seasonal fruit, such as the Blueberry Topping (page 8), Lemon Thyme–Macerated Raspberry Compote (page 238), or even the Maple-Glazed Winter Squash and Apple Compote (page 125).

Yield: 6 servings

BLACKBERRY CREAM AND COMPOTE

- 2 half-pints blackberries
- 2 tablespoons granulated sugar
- ¾ cup crème fraîche
- 2 tablespoons confectioners' sugar, or to taste

CINNAMON SUGAR

- 1 cup sugar
- ¼ teaspoon ground cinnamon

BRIOCHE PUDDING

- ½ cup heavy cream
- ½ cup milk
- 1 large egg
- 1 large egg yolk
- 3 tablespoons sugar
- ¼ teaspoon vanilla extract
- ¼ teaspoon ground cinnamon
- ⅛ teaspoon ground nutmeg
- ⅛ teaspoon ground cardamom
- 6 slices brioche, sliced ¾ inch thick (see Note)
- 6 tablespoons unsalted butter

1. To make the blackberry cream and compote, in a small bowl, combine a half-pint of the blackberries and the granulated sugar. Let macerate for 10 minutes. Purée the mixture in a blender and strain through a fine sieve, discarding the solids. Toss the remaining blackberries with about half of the purée and set aside. (The blackberry purée can be prepared up to 1 day ahead; toss with the berries no more than 4 hours before serving.)

2. In the bowl of an electric mixer fitted with a whisk attachment, combine the remaining blackberry purée, the crème fraîche, and the confectioners' sugar; beat until the mixture is smooth and holds medium peaks. Refrigerate until needed, up to 2 hours.

3. To prepare the cinnamon sugar, in a small bowl, mix together the sugar and cinnamon.

4. To make the brioche pudding, preheat the oven to 200°F. In a large bowl, combine the cream, milk, egg, egg yolk, sugar, vanilla, cinnamon, nutmeg, and cardamom and whisk until smooth. Dip the brioche slices in the custard and let soak for 15 to 30 seconds on each side. Melt 2 tablespoons of the butter in a large nonstick skillet over medium-high heat. Sprinkle 2 of the brioche slices on one side with cinnamon sugar and add them to the pan, cinnamon sugar–side down. Fry until golden brown and caramelized on one side, 2 to 3 minutes, then sprinkle the top with more cinnamon sugar and flip the brioche. Fry until golden brown, about 2 minutes longer. Transfer to a platter and keep warm in the oven. Repeat with the remaining butter and brioche.

5. To serve, place 1 slice of brioche on each plate and top with a dollop of blackberry cream and a spoonful of compote; serve immediately.

· Serve with Ginger Ice Cream
  (page 178), Frozen
  Orange-Blossom Honey Mousse
(page 156), or Orange–Cardamom
Shakes (page 208).

Note: You can make your own brioche (page 266), but this recipe works nicely with a good-quality bakery-bought brioche as well.

BUTTERMILK PANNA COTTA WITH STRAWBERRY ROSÉ GELÉE

Buttermilk panna cotta is one of my most versatile recipes, and I like to dress it up in countless ways. Here, I pair the silky, barely firm cream with a strawberry-infused rosé wine gelée. The combination of strawberries and cream is a natural, while the rosé, with its strawberry undertones, contributes an elegant, sophisticated note that's still fresh and floral. Since this dessert is at its most beautiful when the gelée is crystal-clear and the color of an old-fashioned rose, take care to cook the berries and wine gently, so the fruit does not break down and cloud the mixture. Then, after simmering, let it drain slowly through cheesecloth for as long as it takes to extract the liquid without pressing on the berries.

Yield: 6 servings

BUTTERMILK PANNA COTTA

1 tablespoon cold water
1½ teaspoons unflavored powdered gelatin
1¼ cups heavy cream
7 tablespoons sugar
2-inch piece of vanilla bean, halved lengthwise, pulp scraped (see page 180)
1¾ cups buttermilk

STRAWBERRY ROSÉ GELÉE

1 pint plus ¼ cup strawberries, hulled
7 tablespoons sugar
1 bottle (750 ml) rosé wine
1 tablespoon plus ½ teaspoon unflavored powdered gelatin

1. To make the panna cotta, place the water in a small bowl and sprinkle with the gelatin. Let the gelatin soften for 5 minutes.

2. Meanwhile, in a saucepan over medium-high heat, warm the cream with the sugar and vanilla bean and pulp, stirring until the sugar dissolves. Turn off the heat and add the soft- ened gelatin. Stir until it dissolves, then whisk in the buttermilk. Strain the mixture through a fine sieve into a measuring cup with a spout, then pour it into six 8-ounce ramekins, bowls, or parfait glasses. Chill until firm, about 3 hours.

3. To prepare the gelée, in a medium bowl, combine the strawberries with the sugar and let macerate for 20 minutes. In a medium saucepan, combine the strawberries and rosé wine and bring to a simmer over medium heat. Reduce the heat to low and simmer until most of the al-cohol is cooked off, about 1 hour. Strain the liquid through a cheese-cloth-lined sieve. Do not press on the berries; allow the liquid to drain slowly (this may take up to 5 min-utes). Discard the solids.

4. Place 2 tablespoons water in a small bowl and sprinkle with the gel-atin. Let the gelatin soften for 5 min-utes. Add ½ cup of the rosé mixture to the softened gelatin and stir until the gelatin dissolves. Add the gelatin mixture to the remaining rosé mix- ture and stir gently. Strain through a cheesecloth-lined sieve into a clean heatproof glass measuring cup with a spout and let it come to room temperature. Check the gelée after 20 minutes. If you see gelatin crystals clinging to the sides of the measuring cup, place it in the microwave for 20 seconds, then stir well. (Alterna-tively, place the measuring cup in a pot filled halfway with simmering water and stir until the gelatin dis-solves.)

5. When the panna cottas are set, very gently pour a thin stream of the rosé gelée down the sides of the ramekins to coat the tops of the cus-tards (do this slowly; the creams are fragile). Chill until the rosé gelée is set, about 1 hour.

VARIATION

For a whimsical presentation, pour a thin layer of the rosé mixture into 8 champagne saucers or martini glasses. Allow to set in the refrigerator (about 1 hour), leaving the remaining rosé mixture out at room temperature. Loosen the panna cottas from the ramekins by dipping the bottoms in warm water. Carefully unmold them onto the set layer of rosé gelée. Pour a thin stream of the liquid rosé mixture around the panna cotta, coming halfway up the sides. Return to the refrigerator to set completely (about 2 hours).

SERVING SUGGESTIONS
· Serve with fresh strawberries.
· For something more complex, add scoops of Strawberry Sorbet (page 21).
· For a composed dessert, add Anise Shortbread (page 175).

BLACKBERRY COMPOTE

This sweet-tart compote is a terrific way to use plump, juicy blackberries as they come into season in July. Since I prefer not to cook berries, this recipe contains only fresh, ripe fruit, some left whole and some made into a vibrant purple purée to bind the compote. I find that it really captures the bright, fleeting taste of summer berries at their best. The amount of sugar listed below is only a guide. Taste your berries to determine how sweet they are, and use just enough sugar to counterbalance their acidity.

Yield: 4 servings

4   half-pints blackberries
2 to 4 tablespoons sugar, to taste

1. In a small bowl, combine 1 half-pint of the blackberries and the granulated sugar. Let macerate for 10 minutes. Purée the mixture in a blender and strain through a fine sieve, discarding the solids.

2. Toss the remaining 3 half-pints of blackberries with the purée. Use the compote the same day for the freshest flavor.

SERVING SUGGESTION
· Serve with Orange-Cornmeal Shortbread (page 88) and/or Ginger Ice Cream (page 178).

LEMON THYME—MACERATED RASPBERRY COMPOTE

I find that the fresh, summery essences of berries and herbs go hand in hand. In this recipe, the bright yet savory taste of lemon thyme (a citrus-scented variety available in farmer's and specialty markets) makes a brilliant counterpart to the vibrant, assertive flavor of raspberries. I like to serve this sophisticated compote on its own as a fruit salad, with a drizzle of cream, or use it to dress up ice cream, custards, or slices of pound cake. Its unusual flavor makes for a memorable dessert.

Yield: 4 servings

3   cups raspberries
¼   teaspoon fresh lemon thyme
    leaves
2   tablespoons sugar, or to taste

In a blender or food processor, purée
1 cup of the raspberries with the
lemon thyme leaves and sugar. Let
the mixture stand for 10 minutes.
Toss gently with the remaining raspberries. Serve immediately.

SERVING SUGGESTIONS
· Serve with whipped crème
  fraîche.

· For something more complex, add
  Vanilla Shortbread (page 191).
· For a composed dessert, add
  Honey–Lemon Thyme Sorbet
  (page 163).

RASPBERRY SORBET

There's only one reason to make this vermilion sorbet: fresh, local, peak-of-ripeness raspberries, and lots of them. Otherwise, you can buy good raspberry sorbet—a product that's much better than the homemade kind prepared with indifferent fruit. But if you do come into a windfall of berries, be sure to try this sorbet; you'll be rewarded with the deepest-flavored, richest, most intense dessert imaginable.

Yield: 1 quart

6 cups fresh raspberries
1 cup plus 2 tablespoons sugar, or to taste

1. In a large bowl, toss together the raspberries and six tablespoons of the sugar, or more to taste. Let the mixture rest for 1 hour.

2. Meanwhile, in a small saucepan, combine the remaining ¾ cup of sugar with ½ cup water and bring to a simmer over medium heat. Simmer the mixture, stirring, until the sugar dissolves, about 2 minutes. Remove from the heat and let cool.

3. Transfer the berries to a food processor or blender and purée until very smooth. Strain through a fine sieve, pressing hard on the solids; discard the solids.

4. In a large bowl, whisk together the raspberry purée and sugar syrup. Cover and chill until cold, at least 3 hours, or overnight. Freeze in an ice-cream maker according to the manufacturer's instructions.

SERVING SUGGESTIONS
- Serve with Vanilla Shortbread (see page 191).
- For a composed dessert, add Lemon Verbena Custards (page 154) and fresh raspberries.

STRAWBERRY SORBET

As with raspberry sorbet, you must have plenty of stellar berries to make preparing this sorbet worthwhile. But, unlike raspberry sorbet, which you can buy at a pretty high quality, one never sees good strawberry sorbet in the freezer case of even high-end grocery stores. This is probably because strawberries have an elusive flavor. If you're not using intense berries, you're not going to capture it. Look for flavorful strawberries in summer in farmer's markets, and don't settle for anything less than the very best!

Yield: 1 quart

1   quart fresh strawberries, hulled
    and quartered
¼   cup sugar
1¼ cups Simple Syrup (page 261)
1   teaspoon fresh lemon juice

1. In a large bowl, toss the strawberries with the sugar. Let the mixture rest for 2 hours.

2. Transfer the berries to a food processor or blender and purée with ¾ cup water until very smooth. Strain through a fine sieve, pressing on the solids to extract all their juice, then discard the solids.

3. In a large bowl, whisk together the strawberry purée, Simple Syrup, and lemon juice. Cover and chill until cold, at least 3 hours, or overnight. Freeze in an ice-cream maker according to the manufacturer's instructions.

SERVING SUGGESTIONS
• Serve with fresh strawberries.
• For something more complex, add Cornmeal-Nut Biscotti (page 140) or Mixed-Pepper Tuiles (page 174).
• For a composed dessert, serve the sorbet and berries floating in Papaya-Lime Soup (page 104); garnish with the cookies.

STONE FRUITS

Luscious, juicy, sweet, and versatile, stone fruits symbolize the height of summer. They have pits, rather than seeds, and conveniently, the pit is usually very easy to pull away from the fruit. These fruits include peaches, nectarines, plums, cherries, and apricots, and they are an essential ingredient in some of our most classic American desserts, like cherry pie and peach cobbler. The desserts in this chapter run the gamut from very simple, like the Sour Cherry Sorbet, to more involved, like the White Peach–Rosé Champagne Gelée with Champagne-Peach Sorbet. But all contain the fresh, luscious, ripe taste of summer so characteristic of these fruits.

Plums have a very long season, spanning the entire summer and into the fall. Italian prune plums and the larger Empress plums are well suited to cooking, since they are relatively dry yet packed with flavor. They also take on a beautiful, reddish-purple hue. As they cook, they release their juices and intensify in flavor, becoming soft and jamlike, with a hint of spiciness to their skins. The round, juicy varieties of plums are too watery for cooking and can best be appreciated fresh. Italian prune plums should feel firm all over except for a slight softening at the tip when you buy them. Juicy varieties of plums should have firm flesh and shiny skins.

Prunes are dried plums. Look for soft, juicy prunes that are not completely dried and leathery. Both of the recipes here call for plumping them up in Armagnac, which increases their flavor and makes them tender and lovely.

There are two varieties of peaches: cling and freestone. Yellow and white freestone varieties are the most flavorful. In general, yellow peaches have a tangy taste while white peaches are more gentle and subtle, with a slightly floral nuance. Apricots vary a lot, but they should all be plump, bright, and orange with velvety skin. Peaches, nectarines, and apricots are particularly superior when they are ripened on the tree. Since these fruits must be unripe for shipping, this is another incentive to buy them at local farmer's markets. This said, I also find that if peaches and apricots are not at their best fresh, they can transform when cooked. For example, a mealy peach with great flavor is no fun eaten out of hand, yet can still be wonderful baked into a Peach Tarte Tatin.

Stone fruits are fragrant when ripe (with the exception of cherries), so scent is really the best gauge of ripeness, or of its potential. Look for a peach that smells like a peach or an apricot that smells like an apricot, then let them ripen at home by placing them in a brown paper bag and leaving them out at room temperature for a few days.

Cherries have a very short season, from June to July, but they are reliable, and I think absolutely delicious. They have taut skins that pop when you bite into them, releasing their dark, sweet juice. Cherries come in white, red, and blush, and in two varieties, sweet and sour. Sour cherries are best when you are cooking the cherries or using their juice for sorbet. They are brighter red and almost translucent. Cherries seem to vary most in terms of size, and the bigger they get, the more expensive they get. Look for bright, shiny cherries with firm skin, and store them in the refrigerator.

WINE NOTES: STONE FRUITS

Cherries are well balanced in terms of sweetness and acidity, making them easy to pair with wines. I enjoy matching cherry desserts with a Californian muscat wine made by Quady of black muscat grapes. These grapes yield a portlike wine (though it is not fortified) with a slight orange-blossom note, a well-suited match with the cherry flavor.

Peach, plum, apricot, and nectarine desserts call for lighter, less assertive wines; a Chenin Blanc–based wine from the Loire Valley would be ideal. These white wines have an almost ethereal fruity quality with similar notes of peach, melon, and apricot. Their cleansing acidity is well suited to the more gently flavored stone fruits.

For the most delicate flavors in this chapter, like those of the White Peach–Rosé Champagne Gelée with Champagne Peach Sorbet, serve a champagne demi-sec to complement the subtlety of the dessert while creating the added textural element of the bubbles.

CHERRY CHEESECAKE TART WITH A RED WINE GLAZE

The cherry cheesecake gets a complete makeover in this recipe. Red and white cherries are glazed in red wine and flavored with star anise, which elevates this fruit topping to a new level of sophistication. The cheesecake itself, made without eggs, is particularly light and creamy. It's got a very satisfying cheese-and-sweet-cream flavor that marries perfectly with the slightly tart, spicy cherries. And unlike most deep, thick cheesecakes, this tart is only an inch and a half high, so there is a greater proportion of fruit to cheese.

I bake my own graham crackers for the crust, and they are rich with a caramel flavor and a snappy texture. If you want to make homemade graham crackers, use the dough for the graham cracker tart shell in Blueberry–Cream Cheese Tarts (page 8), but bake the dough in a big sheet or in squares. Then, crush the crackers with a rolling pin. If, however, the extra baking seems like too much of a commitment, store-bought graham crackers can be substituted.

Yield: 8 servings

GRAHAM CRACKER CRUST

- 1¾ cups graham cracker crumbs
- 2½ tablespoons sugar
- 6 tablespoons unsalted butter, melted

CHEESECAKE FILLING

- 1 teaspoon unflavored powdered gelatin
- 1½ cups heavy cream
- ½ cup (4 ounces) cream cheese, softened
- ½ cup sour cream
- 3 tablespoons sugar
- ½ teaspoon vanilla extract
- ¼ vanilla bean, split lengthwise, pulp scraped (see page 180)

CHERRY TOPPING

- 2 cups red wine, preferably a Pinot Noir
- 1 cup sugar
- 1 star anise
- ¼ teaspoon vanilla extract
- 1½ cups red cherries, pitted and halved
- 1½ cups white cherries, pitted and halved

1. To make the crust, preheat the oven to 350°F. In the bowl of a food processor or mixer fitted with a paddle attachment, combine the graham cracker crumbs and sugar. Process or mix until well combined, then slowly drizzle in the butter until the crust comes together. Press it into the bottom and up the sides of a 10-inch tart pan. Bake for 10 minutes, then transfer to a wire rack to cool completely.

2. To prepare the filling, in a medium bowl, sprinkle the gelatin over ¼ cup of the heavy cream. Allow the gelatin to soften for 5 minutes. Meanwhile, in a small saucepan over medium heat, bring ½ cup of the cream and the cream cheese to a simmer. Whisk until the mixture is smooth and the cream cheese melts. Add the mixture to the bowl with the softened gelatin and whisk until the gelatin dissolves. Strain through a fine sieve into a clean bowl and let cool to room temperature.

3. In the bowl of an electric mixer, whip the remaining ¾ cup of heavy cream, the sour cream, sugar, vanilla extract, and vanilla pulp until the mixture holds medium peaks. Fold a third of it into the cream cheese mixture, then fold in the remaining whipped cream mixture in two additions. Pour the filling into the cooled tart shell and refrigerate until set, about 4 hours. (The tart can be prepared up to 1 day ahead.)

4. To prepare the topping, in a small saucepan, bring the red wine, sugar, and star anise to a simmer. Reduce the heat to very low and simmer until the sauce is syrupy and sticky, about 1 hour and 15 minutes (don't allow the sauce to caramelize—it should stay bright red). Strain the mixture, discarding the solids, and stir in the vanilla extract. Refrigerate until cooled, at least 1 hour.

5. Just before serving, toss the cherries with ¼ cup of the red wine glaze. Spoon them over the tart,

mounding them in the center. Serve the tart with some of the remaining red wine syrup drizzled on the plates, if desired.

VARIATION

If cherries are out of season, make a fruit-topped cheesecake using Caramel Blood Oranges (page 89) instead.

SERVING SUGGESTIONS

• Serve with scoops of Sour Cherry Sorbet (page 39).
• For a composed dessert, add candied fennel (see page 124).

BING CHERRY AND WHITE CHERRY NAPOLEONS WITH BLACK MINT

As a kid, my favorite double-dip ice-cream cone at Friendly's was Cherry Orchard and Mint Chocolate Chip. This napoleon features those same flavors, though in a somewhat more elegant way. A toasted-almond pastry cream takes on the luscious role of the ice cream, and the classic pairing of almond and cherry is both subtle and pleasing. An accent of peppery black mint adds just the right note of brightness. Crisp squares of phyllo dough provide a crunchy foil for all the creamy, juicy fruitiness between the layers.

I use two kinds of cherries here, not only because they look gorgeous, but because white cherries are slightly tangy, and they create a nice contrast to the fleshy red Bings.

Yield: 8 servings

NAPOLEON LAYERS
4 tablespoons unsalted butter, melted
2 tablespoons confectioners' sugar
5 sheets phyllo dough, thawed

ALMOND PASTRY CREAM
½ cup sliced almonds
5 tablespoons sugar
1 cup milk
4 large egg yolks
2 tablespoons cornstarch
1 teaspoon vanilla extract
Pinch of salt
¼ cup heavy cream

CHERRY FILLING
1 large sprig of black mint (peppermint)
2 cups Bing cherries, pitted and quartered
2 cups white cherries, pitted and quartered
2 teaspoons sugar

1. To make the napoleon layers, preheat the oven to 400°F. Cut two pieces of parchment paper to fit a baking sheet. Place one of the pieces of parchment on a work surface and brush the top lightly with melted butter, then use a sifter to sprinkle the parchment with 1 tablespoon of the confectioners' sugar in an even layer. Butter one side of the other piece of parchment paper and set aside. Cover the buttered and sugared parchment with a sheet of phyllo dough and butter lightly. Repeat the process until all the phyllo sheets are stacked and buttered. Sprinkle the remaining tablespoon of confectioners' sugar over the top sheet of phyllo. Using a small, sharp knife, trim the edges of the phyllo to the same size as the parchment paper, then, without cutting through the paper on the bottom, cut the phyllo into 2 × 2-inch squares. There will be approximately 40. Transfer the phyllo to a baking sheet and cover with the remaining sheet of buttered parchment (buttered side down). Bake for 10 to 12 minutes, until golden brown. Transfer to a wire rack and let cool. (The phyllo squares can be prepared up to 3 days ahead; store airtight at room temperature.) Reduce the oven temperature to 350°F.

2. To make the almond pastry cream, spread the almonds in a single layer on a baking sheet. Toast them in the oven until almost dark brown (just this side of burnt), 9 to 10 minutes. Transfer to a wire rack to cool completely. Coarsely grind the nuts in a food processor with 3 tablespoons of the sugar.

3. In a medium, heavy saucepan, combine the ground almonds and milk. Bring to a boil over medium heat, stirring to dissolve the sugar. Turn off the heat and allow the mixture to steep until cooled. Strain through a fine sieve, discarding the solids.

4. Bring ¾ cup of the almond-infused milk to a simmer in a medium saucepan over medium heat. Meanwhile, in a large bowl, whisk together the remaining ¼ cup of almond milk, the egg yolks, cornstarch, and the remaining 2 tablespoons of sugar. Remove the almond milk from the heat and add a little to the egg yolk mixture to warm it, whisking constantly to keep the yolks

from cooking. Pour the egg yolk mixture back into the hot milk mixture, whisking constantly as you pour.

5. Return the custard to the stove and bring to a boil. Cook for 2 minutes over high heat, whisking constantly, until it is as thick as pudding; strain the custard through a sieve into a clean bowl, stir in the vanilla and salt, and let cool. Cover the surface with plastic wrap and refrigerate.

6. Once the custard is thoroughly chilled, whisk it until smooth. In a medium bowl, whip the cream until it holds stiff peaks. Whisk one fourth of it into the chilled pastry cream to lighten it, then fold in the remaining whipped cream in two additions.

7. To prepare the cherry filling, bruise the mint leaves with the side of a knife or by crushing them in your hands. In a medium bowl, stir together the cherries, sugar, and mint. Let them infuse for 15 minutes.

8. To assemble, place one phyllo square on a plate and top with 1 tablespoon pastry cream followed by 1 tablespoon cherries. Repeat layering, then top with a third phyllo square. Repeat with the remaining ingredients, then serve immediately.

SERVING SUGGESTIONS
· Serve with candied almonds (see page 261).
· For something more complex, add Almond-Milk Granité (page 145).
· For a composed dessert, add a drizzle of Red Wine–Cherry Sauce (page 264).

SPICED ITALIAN PRUNE PLUM CRISP

Served warm from the oven, this fragrant plum crisp makes a heavenly late-summer treat. The cinnamon and cardamom really bring out the inherent spicy flavors that develop inside cooked prune plums; and the nutty crisp topping is a delectable textural contrast to the soft, flavorful fruit that bubbles colorfully beneath it.

Yield: 8 to 10 servings

1¼ cups all-purpose flour

⅓ cup plus 1 tablespoon ground walnuts

½ cup granulated sugar

¼ cup firmly packed dark brown sugar

¼ teaspoon ground cinnamon

⅛ teaspoon ground cardamom

½ cup (1 stick) unsalted butter, melted and cooled to room temperature

2¼ pounds Italian prune plums, pitted and quartered (6 cups)

1. Preheat the oven to 375°F. In a large bowl, whisk together the flour, walnuts, ¼ cup of the granulated sugar, the brown sugar, cinnamon, and cardamom. Slowly drizzle in the butter and combine with a fork until the mixture is crumbly. Do not allow the mixture to come together in a ball. Break up any large crumbs with your fingers. The crumbs should be smaller than 1 inch in size (otherwise they won't cook all the way through).

2. In another large bowl, combine the plums and the remaining ¼ cup of granulated sugar and toss well. Spoon the fruit into a buttered 2-quart gratin or shallow casserole dish, mounding the fruit in the center. Evenly sprinkle the crumbs on top of the fruit.

3. Bake the crisp until the fruit is bubbling and the topping browned, 50 to 55 minutes. Serve hot or warm.

SERVING SUGGESTION
• Serve with whipped crème fraîche or scoops of Basil Ice Cream (page 158).

PRUNE–ARMAGNAC BREAD PUDDING

This is the ultimate winter comfort dessert. Gently baked in a water bath for a soft, puddinglike creaminess, it is bread pudding taken from dowdy to extravagant by the addition of Armagnac-soaked prunes. Soaking prunes in Armagnac both softens them and gives the fruit a sophisticated flavor boost. The custard then acts as a smooth base for pockets of that concentrated, sweet prune flavor. Coarse raw sugar, sprinkled on top, bakes into a crunchy, caramelized brûlée crust that gives the dish a crowning textural contrast. Use homemade Buttery Brioche (page 266) if you like.

Yield: 10 to 12 servings

1   cup coarsely chopped prunes
¼   cup Armagnac
10 ounces brioche (1 small loaf),
      crusts trimmed and cut into
      1- to 1¼-inch cubes
      (about 7 to 8 cups)
2   cups heavy cream
2   cups milk
1   cup granulated sugar
4   large eggs
4   large egg yolks
½   teaspoon vanilla extract
2   tablespoons turbinado (raw) sugar

1. Place the prunes in a small saucepan and add enough water to cover. Over medium heat, bring the mixture to a simmer, then turn off the heat. Let the prunes steep for 45 minutes, then drain them well. Stir in 2 tablespoons of the Armagnac, cover, and reserve. (The prunes can be prepared up to 1 week in advance and refrigerated until needed.)

2. Preheat the oven to 275°F. Spread the brioche cubes out on a baking sheet and toast for 20 minutes, or until lightly browned. Transfer to a wire rack to cool.

3. In a medium saucepan, over medium heat, bring the heavy cream, milk, and ½ cup of the granulated sugar to a simmer. Meanwhile, in a medium bowl, whisk together the whole eggs, egg yolks, and remaining ½ cup of sugar. Remove the milk mixture from the heat and add a little to the egg mixture to warm it, stirring constantly to keep the yolks from curdling. Pour the egg yolk mixture into the hot milk mixture, stirring the milk constantly as you pour. Stir in the remaining 2 tablespoons of Armagnac and the vanilla. Strain through a fine sieve into a clean bowl and allow to cool completely. (The custard can be prepared up to 3 days ahead and refrigerated.)

4. Add the toasted brioche cubes to the cooled custard and let soak for 1 hour. Preheat the oven to 325°F. Gently fold the reserved prunes into the custard. Pour the mixture into an 8 × 12-inch glass baking dish or shallow 2-quart gratin or baking dish. Place the baking dish into a larger pan and put it on the oven rack. Pour enough very hot water into the large baking pan to reach two thirds of the

way up the sides of the pudding. Cover the large baking pan with foil. Bake the pudding for about 30 minutes, then lift up a corner of the foil to allow the steam to escape. Re-cover the pan and bake for another 25 minutes. Remove the foil.

5. Sprinkle the turbinado sugar over the top of the pudding and continue to bake, uncovered, for another 10 to 15 minutes, until the center is set (it should not seep any liquid when pressed with the back of a spoon). Remove the pan from the oven and preheat the broiler. Broil the pudding for 1 to 2 minutes, watching carefully, until the top is lightly browned and the sugar is caramelized. Serve the pudding warm, or reheat before serving.

SERVING SUGGESTION
· Serve with candied walnuts (see page 261) and whipped crème fraîche.

NECTARINE-BLUEBERRY COBBLER

Cobblers are simple, homey desserts in which ripe, seasonal fruits are baked until thick and almost jammy under a tender biscuit crust. Here, I pair nectarines and blueberries, though this is a flexible combination. You could substitute peaches or apricots for the nectarines, or omit the berries and make this with all nectarines; the results will be just as rewarding.

Yield: 6 servings

COBBLER DOUGH

1⅔ cups all-purpose flour
3½ tablespoons granulated sugar
1½ tablespoons baking powder
⅛ teaspoon salt
6 tablespoons cold unsalted butter, cut into ½-inch cubes
⅔ cup plus 1 tablespoon heavy cream
1 tablespoon turbinado (raw) sugar

NECTARINE-BLUEBERRY FILLING

6 cups pitted and diced nectarines (about 3 pounds)
1½ cups blueberries
3 tablespoons granulated sugar
2 tablespoons tapioca

1. To prepare the cobbler dough, in the bowl of a food processor or an electric mixer fitted with the paddle attachment, combine the flour, granulated sugar, baking powder, and salt. Pulse or mix to combine. Add the butter and pulse or mix until the flour resembles coarse meal. Add ⅔ cup of the cream and mix or pulse until the dough starts to come together, scraping down the dough paddle and mixing bowl if necessary.

2. Turn the dough out onto a lightly floured surface and gently pat it together, incorporating any stray crumbs. Using a small ice-cream scoop or a large spoon, form the dough into 2-inch balls (you will have 8 to 10 balls), then flatten them slightly into ¾-inch-thick rounds. Wrap the dough rounds in plastic wrap and chill for 20 minutes (and up to 2 hours). Preheat the oven to 350°F.

3. Meanwhile, to make the filling, in a large bowl, toss together the nectarines, blueberries, granulated sugar, and tapioca. Let the mixture macerate for 20 minutes.

4. Spread the filling in a shallow 2½-quart casserole dish. Arrange the biscuits on top, leaving about an inch between them. Brush the biscuits with the remaining tablespoon of cream and sprinkle with the turbinado sugar. Bake the cobbler until the filling is bubbling and the nectarines are tender, about 1 hour. Serve warm.

SERVING SUGGESTION

- Serve with scoops of Sweet-Corn Ice Cream (page 127) or Yogurt Sorbet (page 213).

PEACH TARTES TATIN

Out of all the desserts in this book, this one was the most challenging to translate into a recipe that can be easily made at home. That's because peaches are so juicy they have a tendency to dilute the caramel and make it runny, which in turn makes the pastry soggy. At the restaurant, I bake the tartes Tatin in thin, disposable aluminum cups, which encourages the moisture in the fruit to condense, leaving the pastry crisp and buttery and the caramel rich, dark, and intense. But since these cups are not readily available to the home cook, I adapted the recipe to muffin tins.

After countless tries, I discovered that precooking the fruit before laying the pastry on top allows the juices to evaporate; the peaches emerge gloriously translucent, almost candied in the thick, deeply flavored sauce. Perfect!

Yield: 6 servings

1   teaspoon light corn syrup
¾   cup sugar
4   tablespoons unsalted butter, softened and cut into 1-inch pieces
3   large peaches, unpeeled, halved, and pitted
8   ounces puff pastry, preferably all-butter, thawed if necessary

1. Preheat the oven to 400°F. Place 3 tablespoons water and the corn syrup in a medium saucepan over low heat. Add the sugar and stir until the sugar resembles wet sand. Increase the heat to high and cook without stirring until the mixture is a dark amber caramel, 7 to 10 minutes. Remove the pan from the heat and whisk in the butter until smooth.

2. Divide the caramel among six 2½-inch muffin cups. Place one peach half, cut side down, on top of the caramel in each of the six cups. Cover the pan with foil and pierce all over with a knife. Bake the peaches for 15 minutes, then uncover and bake for 45 minutes longer.

3. Meanwhile, prepare the puff pastry. On a floured surface, roll out or unfold the pastry to ¼ inch thick and prick all over with a fork. Chill the pastry for 30 minutes.

4. Using a round cutter or a knife, cut out 6 puff pastry rounds slightly larger than the muffin cups. Place the rounds directly on top of the peaches and press the edges of the pastry to seal them against the muffin cups. Bake for about 20 minutes, until the puff pastry is golden brown and the peaches are fork-tender but not mushy.

5. Allow the tartes Tatin to cool for at least 1 hour before inverting onto a serving dish. Alternatively, bake the tartes up to 12 hours in advance, let them cool completely in the tins, then reheat them in a 300°F. oven for 5 to 7 minutes, or until hot.

SERVING SUGGESTIONS
· Serve with a drizzle of basil syrup (see page 262).
· For something more complex, add Black Pepper Ice Cream (page 179) or Ginger Ice Cream (page 178).
· For a composed dessert, add White Peach–Rosé Champagne Gelée with Champagne-Peach Sorbet (page 36).

APRICOT-MUSCAT SOUP

Muscat is a beautifully floral, honey-scented white wine. While it's sweet enough to sip with dessert, it also makes a lovely aperitif, since it's not too syrupy or cloying. Here, I combine muscat with apricots, which to me have similar honey-floral qualities. Simmered gently and then puréed, it makes an elegant cold fruit soup that is both light and concentrated. Although you can serve the soup by itself for a sophisticated dessert or intermezzo, it also pairs well with myriad garnishes. See the serving suggestions below for a few of my favorite ways to dress it up.

Yield: 6 servings

2¼ pounds apricots, unpeeled, quartered, and pitted (5¼ cups)

2¼ cups plus 3 teaspoons muscat wine, such as Beaumes-de-Venise

1 cup sugar

1. In a medium saucepan, combine 3½ cups water with the apricots, 2¼ cups of the muscat, and the sugar. Bring the mixture to a boil over high heat, then reduce the heat to low and simmer gently until the apricots are very tender and much of the alcohol has evaporated, 35 to 40 minutes.

2. Purée the mixture in a blender or food processor until smooth. Pass the soup through a fine sieve and discard the solids. Chill until thoroughly cold, at least 3 hours.

3. Serve the soup in bowls, each drizzled with an additional ½ teaspoon of the muscat just before serving.

SERVING SUGGESTIONS
- Serve with whipped crème fraîche and fresh berries or cherries.
- For something more complex, add Citrus Lace Tuiles (page 90) or candied almonds (see page 261).
- For a composed dessert, add scoops of Sour Cherry Sorbet (page 39).

ROASTED APRICOTS WITH CHAMOMILE

In my opinion, the sweet, tart, floral characteristics of apricots aren't fully unleashed until they are cooked. Here, I've roasted them with chamomile flowers and vanilla, which enhances their complex, luscious taste. Bunches of just-picked chamomile are available in farmer's markets at the same time as apricots, making them ideal partners in more ways than one. Not only do they both possess a similar summery freshness, but the acid in the apricots brightens and balances the gently perfumed flavor of the chamomile. Together, they make a simple and seasonal dessert that's exquisite on its own, and even better as an aromatic topping to plain cakes and ice creams.

Yield: 4 servings

1½   cups sugar
¼   cup fresh chamomile flowers
1   vanilla bean, split lengthwise,
     pulp scraped (see page 180)
8   apricots, unpeeled, halved and
     pitted

1. Preheat the oven to 375°F. In a medium saucepan, combine the sugar and 1 cup water; bring to a boil over high heat, stirring to dissolve the sugar. Add the chamomile and vanilla pod and pulp. Lower the heat to medium and simmer for 5 minutes. Strain through a fine sieve into an 8 × 8-inch baking dish.

2. Arrange the apricots, cut side down, in the syrup. Roast for 10 minutes, then turn so the cut sides are up and baste well with the pan juices. Roast for an additional 5 to 8 minutes, until the apricots are tender but still retain their shape. Serve the apricots warm, or cool to room temperature. (The apricots will keep for 3 days, refrigerated. Bring to room temperature before serving.)

VARIATION
If fresh chamomile is unavailable, replace it with 1 chamomile tea bag.

SERVING SUGGESTIONS
· Serve with whipped crème fraîche.
· For something more complex, add Cornmeal–Nut Biscotti (page 140).
· For a composed dessert, add small bowls of Apricot–Muscat Soup (page 33).

WHITE PEACH–ROSÉ CHAMPAGNE GELÉE WITH CHAMPAGNE-PEACH SORBET

This cool peach gelée is the most elegant "Jell-O mold" you'll ever make. The whole dessert is a rhapsody of peach: the transparent champagne-peach gel is topped with pale pink mini-scoops of sorbet and tender, blushing slices of white peach. Lemon verbena imparts its herbaceous characteristics to the mix, lending complexity and rounding out the lush, gentle flavors of the peaches and champagne. The result is an intriguing, multitextured dessert served at three different temperatures. On a hot summer day, nothing could be more refreshing or beautiful.

Yield: 8 servings

GELÉE

1 bottle (750 ml) brut rosé champagne
2 cups sugar
5 large sprigs of lemon verbena, plus additional for garnish
10 white peaches (about 5 pounds), unpeeled
5 teaspoons powdered unflavored gelatin

½ cup sugar
1 teaspoon fresh lemon juice, or to taste

1. To make the gelée, in a large saucepan over medium heat, bring the champagne, 3 cups of water, the sugar, and the lemon verbena to a boil. Reduce the heat and simmer gently for 10 minutes. Add the peaches and an additional cup of water. Cut a circle of parchment paper to fit into the saucepan and lay it on top of the mixture to keep the peaches submerged. Simmer the peaches for 20 minutes, or until they are very tender but not mushy. Discard the lemon verbena, and allow the peaches to cool in their poaching liquid.

2. Using a slotted spoon, transfer the peaches to a bowl and set aside. Strain the poaching liquid through a fine sieve and reserve. Pour ½ cup of the liquid into a medium saucepan and sprinkle the gelatin over the top. Let the gelatin soften for 5 minutes, then place the saucepan over low heat and stir constantly until the gelatin dissolves, 1 to 2 minutes. Measure 4 cups of the reserved poaching liquid into a bowl. Pour about ¼ cup of this liquid into the pan with the gelatin mixture and stir well, then stir the gelatin mixture into the bowl of liquid. (Reserve the poaching liquid that remains after 4 cups are measured out.)

3. Strain the gelatin mixture through a fine sieve into a clean heatproof glass measuring cup with a spout and let it come to room temperature. Check the mixture after 20 minutes. If you see gelatin crystals clinging to the sides of the measuring cup, place it in the microwave for 20 seconds, then stir well. (Alternatively, place the measuring cup in a pot filled halfway with simmering water and stir the mixture until the gelatin dissolves.) Pour the mixture into a 9-inch ring mold or round cake pan and refrigerate until firm, at least 4 hours.

4. Meanwhile, to make the sorbet, halve 7 of the peaches, remove their pits, and purée them in a blender or food processor until smooth. Push the purée through a strainer, discarding the solids.

5. In a small saucepan, bring the sugar, ½ cup water, and ¼ cup of the reserved peach poaching liquid to a simmer, stirring until the sugar dissolves. Mix the syrup into the peach purée along with the lemon juice. Cover and chill the mixture thoroughly, for at least 3 hours. Transfer to an ice-cream maker and freeze according to the manufacturer's directions.

6. To serve, peel, halve, and pit the remaining 3 peaches and slice them

into sixths. To unmold the gelée, dip the bottom of the mold briefly into hot water and slide a small knife around the edges. Invert it onto a platter and shake if necessary to release the gelée. If using a ring mold, fill the cavity with scoops of peach sorbet and the poached peach slices. Alternatively, place the sorbet and peaches around the gelée. Garnish with sprigs of lemon verbena and serve immediately.

SERVING SUGGESTION
- Serve with Gingersnaps (page 176), Citrus Lace Tuiles (page 90), or Lemon–Poppy Seed Shortbread (page 86).

PRUNE–ARMAGNAC ICE CREAM

Classically French, prune-Armagnac ice cream is one of the most graceful ways to serve a prune. Whereas most fruits become hard and icy when frozen, these prunes remain chewy, soft, Armagnac-imbued confections. This is because they have been dried, then plumped in alcohol, which resists freezing solid. The Armagnac also gives the ice cream an incredibly smooth texture, creating a dessert that is lusciously rich and frozen, yet warming.

Yield: 1½ quarts

2   cups roughly chopped pitted
    prunes
3   tablespoons Armagnac
3   cups milk
1   cup cream
1¼ cups sugar
12 large egg yolks
Pinch of salt

1. Place the prunes and enough water to cover in a saucepan. Bring the mixture to a simmer over medium heat, then turn off the heat. Let the prunes cool in the liquid, then drain them well. Stir in the Armagnac, cover, and refrigerate overnight.

2. In a large, heavy saucepan, bring the milk, cream, and 1 cup of the sugar to a simmer. Meanwhile, in a large bowl, whisk together the egg yolks and the remaining ¼ cup of sugar. Remove the milk mixture from the heat and add a little to the egg yolk mixture to warm it, whisking constantly to keep the yolks from cooking. Pour the egg yolk mixture into the hot milk mixture, whisking the milk constantly as you pour.

3. Return the custard to the stove and cook it over low heat, stirring constantly with a wooden spoon, until it thickens enough to coat the back of the spoon. Remove from the heat and strain it into a bowl. Stir in the salt and let cool completely.

4. Chill the custard until it's thoroughly cold, at least 4 hours. Freeze in an ice-cream maker according to the manufacturer's instructions. Fold the Armagnac-soaked prunes into the ice cream immediately after freezing while it's still soft. Transfer to a container and place in the freezer until frozen solid, at least 2 hours.

SERVING SUGGESTIONS
• Serve with Orange-Cornmeal Shortbread (page 88) or Pecan Sandies (page 144).
• For a composed dessert, add Maple Baked Apples with Dried Fruit and Nuts (page 70).

SOUR CHERRY SORBET

During their brief season, you can preserve the height-of-summer flavor and brilliant red color of sour cherries by juicing and freezing them. Since sour cherries are too tart to eat out of hand, they are traditionally baked into pie, but this refreshingly icy sorbet is an even more summery celebration of their vibrant fruit flavor.

Yield: 1 pint

3   cups sour cherries, pitted
2   tablespoons sugar
⅔   cup Simple Syrup (page 261)
⅛   teaspoon ascorbic acid (vitamin C powder; available at health food stores and pharmacies)

1. In a medium bowl, combine the cherries and sugar. Let them macerate for 30 minutes, then purée the mixture in a food processor or blender. Push the purée through a fine sieve and stir in the Simple Syrup, ⅓ cup water, and the ascorbic acid.

2. Chill the mixture until it's very cold, about 4 hours. Freeze in an ice-cream machine according to the manufacturer's directions.

SERVING SUGGESTIONS
· Serve with fresh cherries and whipped crème fraîche.
· For something more complex, add Chocolate Biscotti with Pistachios and Sour Cherries (page 227).
· For a composed dessert, add candied almonds (see page 261) and a drizzle of Red Wine–Cherry Sauce (page 264).

FIGS, MELONS, AND GRAPES

This chapter represents my favorite time of year, as summer ends and fall begins. During this transition season, some days are warm and summery, and some are cool and autumnal. In keeping with the season, these desserts range from crisp and refreshing, like the Watermelon Granité, to warming and spicy, like the Spiced Red Wine–Fig Compote. The flavors of figs, melons, and grapes are earthy and intense, yet simultaneously light and bright. This is one of the few chapters in which many of the serving suggestions call for other desserts within the same chapter, making it very self-contained. Figs, melons, and grapes really exemplify the saying "What grows together goes together": they are harvested at the same time, and they taste superb in combination.

Melons are sweet, spicy, and musky, but with their high water content, I find them best suited to soups, sorbets, granités, and of course eating fresh. There are few desserts more succulent than a chilled slice of perfectly ripe melon. Although countless types of melon are available in farmer's markets, you should be able to find all the ones I use here in the supermarket. Just make sure to choose a ripe one; look for a heavy fruit with a deeply perfumed scent.

Figs can be eaten fresh, but their elusive flavor is greatly intensified when they are cooked. Even a mediocre fig can be transformed into an extraordinary cooked dessert. Black and green figs are available all over the country, and I specify which to use depending on the recipe. Choose figs that are a little bit soft and very plump; they shouldn't be wrinkly or feel at all dried out. Just-picked black figs will have a bluish iridescence to them that will help indicate their freshness.

Although I love to eat all kinds of grapes out of hand as a snack, for dessert making, I definitely prefer Concord grapes. No other kind of grape will give you the same intensity of flavor. Along with cranberries and blueberries, Concord grapes are one of the few Native American fruits. They are spicy, sweet, and jammy, with a taste and scent so powerful it seems almost unreal. But they do have their disadvantages. They can be hard to find; farmer's markets and specialty food shops will be your best options. They are also tedious to seed, since each grape has to be done individually. I halve the grapes with a very sharp knife, then use the tip to scoop out the seeds.

Melons are not only sweet, they are also very refreshing because of their high volume of water. This suggests an equally refreshing dessert wine, such as the Piedmontese Moscato d'Asti, which has a lower level of alcohol and some effervescence, giving it a pop on the palate that allows the flavor of melon to shine.

Desserts featuring grapes or figs are a good occasion for the ports. There is a wide range of styles of port, from the fruit-forward intensity of a ruby to the almost dry, earthy, sublime notes of a tawny, and ultimately the majesty of a vintage port. Let the weight of the dessert be your guide: light with a lighter, tawny port; heavier with a more flamboyant late-bottled vintage (LBV) or vintage port.

FIG AND CONCORD GRAPE CLAFOUTI

A clafouti is a sweet baked "pancake" studded with cherries or other seasonal fruit. The French have many versions. In my interpretation, the combination of sliced red-fleshed figs and purple Concord grapes makes a gorgeous dessert with all the vibrancy of a stained-glass window—and it tastes as good as it looks. The custardy batter envelops the fruit, absorbing the juices and their spicy, musky flavors.

If you can't get Concord grapes, simply use more figs, or substitute red grapes.

Yield: 6 to 8 servings

4 large eggs
½ cup milk
½ cup heavy cream
¾ cup plus 2 tablespoons sugar
1 teaspoon vanilla extract
1-inch piece of vanilla bean, split
   lengthwise, pulp scraped
   (see page 180)
Pinch of salt
¼ cup all-purpose flour
1 tablespoon unsalted butter,
   melted
9 fresh figs, halved lengthwise
½ cup Concord grapes, seeded

1. In a blender, place the eggs, milk, cream, ¾ cup of the sugar, the vanilla extract, vanilla pulp, and salt. Blend the mixture until it is very smooth, about 30 seconds. Add the flour and pulse until well combined. Pass the batter through a fine sieve, then let it rest at room temperature for 30 minutes.

2. Preheat the oven to 425°F. Brush a 9-inch quiche or pie plate or a cast-iron skillet with the melted butter and sprinkle with the remaining 2 tablespoons of sugar. Arrange the figs in the pan, cut side up, and then top with the grapes. Pour the batter over the fruit. Bake the clafouti for 15 minutes, then lower the heat to 375°F. and bake until the center is just set, 10 to 12 minutes. Serve immediately.

SERVING SUGGESTION
• Serve with scoops of Ginger Ice Cream (page 178).

FIG–CORNMEAL TART

This dessert is reminiscent of a Fig Newton but with a major difference. Where the cookie is soft and full of chewy dried figs, this tart has a crispy shell layered with a fresh fig jam. The combination of figs nestled in a sweet, rich pastry is unbeatable. For this dessert, I use green figs, which have a bright, honeyed taste. Simmered with Armagnac, honey, and vanilla, they make a perfect, almost creamy foil for the juicy sliced figs that crown the top.

The cornmeal in the crust provides contrasting texture, one that for me echoes the gentle crunch of the fig seeds in the filling.

Yield: 8 servings

CORNMEAL CRUST
1¼ cups all-purpose flour
3   tablespoons fine yellow cornmeal
Pinch of salt
1   large egg yolk
1½ tablespoons heavy cream
½   teaspoon vanilla extract
6   tablespoons unsalted butter, softened
3   tablespoons sugar
1   teaspoon grated orange zest

FIG FILLING
3   pints green figs, trimmed
⅓   cup fresh orange juice
⅓   cup Armagnac
⅓   cup sugar
½   vanilla bean, split lengthwise, pulp scraped (see page 180)
½   teaspoon freshly grated nutmeg
½   teaspoon grated orange zest
2   tablespoons unsalted butter

1. To make the cornmeal crust, in a medium bowl, whisk together the flour, cornmeal, and salt. In a small bowl, whisk together the egg yolk, cream, and vanilla.

2. In the bowl of an electric mixer fitted with the paddle attachment, beat the butter, sugar, and orange zest until combined, about 1 minute. Add the egg yolk mixture and beat until just combined. Add the flour mixture in two batches, scraping down the sides of the bowl between additions. Mix until the dough is smooth. Scrape the dough onto a piece of plastic wrap and form it into a disk. Chill for at least 1 hour, until firm.

3. Preheat the oven to 325°F. On a lightly floured surface, roll the dough out to a 12-inch round. Fit the dough into a 10-inch tart pan with a removable bottom, trimming away any excess. Prick the crust all over with a fork. (The crust can be frozen for up to 3 months; see page xxv.) Bake the tart crust until it's evenly pale golden, 18 to 22 minutes. Transfer to a wire rack to cool.

4. To prepare the filling, quarter 1 pint of the figs and reserve. Cube the remaining figs and place them in a saucepan with the orange juice, Ar-magnac, sugar, vanilla bean and pulp, nutmeg, and orange zest. Simmer the mixture over medium-low heat until thick and jamlike, 1 to 1½ hours. Stir in the butter until melted. Let the fig mixture cool, then remove the vanilla pod. (You can make the filling a day ahead; keep it refrigerated, then bring it to room temperature before serving.)

5. Just before serving, spread the filling in the crust and decorate the top with the quartered figs.

SERVING SUGGESTIONS
- Serve with whipped crème fraîche and a drizzle of honey.
- For a composed dessert, serve with scoops of Concord Grape Sorbet (page 54) and Orange-Blossom Honey Mousse (page 156) or Brandied-Fig Ice Cream (page 53).

GRAPE FOCACCIA WITH ROSEMARY

I got the idea for this recipe from reading about the grape harvest in Italy. For a few weeks during autumn, ripe grapes are picked and pressed into juice to make wine. Some of the extra grapes (there are plenty left over) end up scattered on top of bread dough and baked into focaccia. When I saw the overflowing baskets of Concord grapes in my local farmer's market in the fall, I was inspired to bake them into an American version of this Italian tradition.

Since Concord grapes have so much pectin, they practically cook down to jam while in the oven, and this focaccia always reminds me of an adult version of bread and jelly. When served with good cheese, like Gorgonzola or ricotta salata, it makes a perfect cheese-and-fruit course. Or snack on a warm slice with espresso in the afternoon, a glass of wine in the evening. If you can't get Concord grapes, substitute red or black grapes.

Yield: 8 to 10 servings

¾ cup plus 2 tablespoons warm water (about 105° to 110°F.)

1½ teaspoons sugar

1¼ teaspoons active dry yeast

1¾ cups plus 2 tablespoons all-purpose flour

½ teaspoon salt

1 tablespoon plus 1 teaspoon dry milk powder

3½ tablespoons unsalted butter, softened and cut into bits

4 tablespoons unsalted butter, melted and cooled

1 cup halved Concord grapes, seeded

1 teaspoon fresh rosemary needles

2 tablespoons turbinado (raw) sugar

2 teaspoons coarse sea salt, such as fleur de sel (see page 269)

1. In the bowl of an electric mixer fitted with a paddle attachment, stir together the water, sugar, and yeast. Let the mixture sit until foamy, about 15 minutes.

2. Meanwhile, in another bowl, stir together the flour and salt. Add the milk powder and 1½ tablespoons of the softened butter to the yeast mixture and mix well. Add the flour mixture and set the mixer to the lowest setting. Mix for 2 minutes. Attach the bread hook to the mixer, raise the speed to medium-low, and knead for 8 minutes longer. The dough will seem very wet.

3. Brush a large bowl with a generous coating of the melted butter. Scrape the dough into the bowl and then turn to coat it with the butter. Brush more of the melted butter on top of the dough. Cover the bowl with plastic wrap and let it rise in a cool place (not warm, about 65°F.) until the dough doubles in bulk, 1½ to 2 hours.

4. Press the dough down with a floured hand. Turn the dough out onto a floured surface and form it into a ball. Place it on a large baking sheet brushed with melted butter and brush the top with more of the melted butter. Cover the ball with clean, damp dish towels and set aside to rise for 20 minutes.

5. Divide the dough in half and shape into 2 balls. Dip your fingers in the melted butter and press and stretch each ball out into a 9-inch circle. The dough should be slightly dimpled from pressing with your fingers. Brush the tops with more melted butter (the aim is to use it all up), and cover with the damp towels. Let the dough rise in a cool place for 1¼ hours.

6. Preheat the oven to 450°F. Top the dough evenly with the grapes, rosemary, and the remaining 2 tablespoons of softened butter bits. Sprinkle with the turbinado sugar and the salt. Bake the focaccia for about 15 minutes, until the crust is golden brown and puffed around the edges. Let cool for at least 10 minutes before serving. Serve warm or at room temperature.

- Serve with wedges of Roquefort or other cheese.

- For a composed dessert, serve with scoops of goat-yogurt sorbet (see Variation, page 213) and Roasted Figs with Roquefort, Hazelnuts, and Banyuls Glaze (page 48).

ROASTED FIGS WITH ROQUEFORT, HAZELNUTS, AND BANYULS GLAZE

There is something inherently gratifying about a classic cheese course, one that combines tangy, salty cheeses with sweet fruit and crunchy, toasted nuts. I love to end meals this way, so I decided to create a dish that would fulfill that urge. I crumble Roquefort over fleshy figs, then bake them until the cheese melts and the fruit warms through. To finish, I drizzle a thin, peppery Banyuls syrup on the top and garnish with either candied or toasted hazelnuts. To me, it's a wholly satisfying and truly unique dessert. But if you would rather serve it as a fruit-and-cheese course, follow it with something as simple as a plate of cookies or chocolate truffles.

The Banyuls, an unusual sweet wine with a sherrylike character, can be hard to find. If you can't get it, substitute half sweet-cream sherry and half good red table wine.

Yield: 4 or 5 servings

BANYULS GLAZE
¾ cup sweet Banyuls wine
2 tablespoons sugar
1 small bay leaf, preferably fresh
1 sprig of fresh thyme, preferably lemon thyme
¼ teaspoon cracked black peppercorns

ROASTED FIGS
1 pint fresh figs, halved
½ cup crumbled Roquefort cheese (about 2 ounces)
Freshly ground black pepper
2 tablespoons chopped candied hazelnuts (see page 261) or regular toasted hazelnuts

1. In a small saucepan, combine the Banyuls, sugar, bay leaf, thyme, and peppercorns. Bring the mixture to a simmer over high heat, then reduce the heat to low. Cook the mixture at a bare simmer for about 15 minutes, then remove the bay leaf and thyme with a slotted spoon. Continue simmering until the glaze is reduced by a third and becomes syrupy, about 20 minutes. Strain through a fine sieve and discard the peppercorns. (The Banyuls glaze can be made up to 3 days ahead and stored in the refrigerator; bring to room temperature before using.)

2. Just before serving, preheat the oven to 500°F. Lay the figs in one layer in a shallow gratin or baking dish. Sprinkle evenly with the cheese and pepper. Roast the figs until the cheese melts and turns lightly golden brown in parts, and the figs soften, about 5 minutes.

3. Sprinkle the hazelnuts evenly over the figs and drizzle with the glaze. Serve immediately.

SERVING SUGGESTION
• Serve with Cornmeal-Nut Biscotti (page 140) and/or Concord Grape Sorbet (page 54).

CONCORD GRAPE PARFAITS

These striking parfaits—alternating layers of jewel-like Concord grape gelée and creamy panna cotta—remind me of a very sophisticated cousin of the cream cheese and jelly sandwich.

A pinch of ascorbic acid (vitamin C powder) keeps the grapes from oxidizing and turning brown. It's sold with the vitamins in health food stores or pharmacies.

Yield: 8 servings

1¼ pounds Concord grapes, stemmed (about 4 cups)
2½ tablespoons granulated sugar
¼ teaspoon ascorbic acid
4 teaspoons unflavored powdered gelatin
1½ cups heavy cream
3 tablespoons confectioners' sugar

1. Place the grapes in the bowl of a watertight food processor and add the sugar and ascorbic acid. Pulse the mixture until it is a rough purée, about 10 times. (Or purée the grapes in batches in a blender, or use an immersion blender in a large bowl.) Let the mixture rest for 30 minutes.

2. Purée the grapes until the mixture is as smooth as possible, about 2 minutes. Strain through a fine sieve, pressing down on the solids; discard the solids. Measure out 2 cups of grape purée (save the rest for another purpose).

3. Place ¼ cup of water in a small saucepan. Sprinkle 2¼ teaspoons of the gelatin over the top and let the gelatin soften for 5 minutes. Place the pan over low heat and stir constantly until the gelatin dissolves, 1 to 2 min-

utes. Pour about ¼ cup of the grape mixture into the pan with the gelatin mixture and stir well. Then pour the gelatin mixture back into the remaining grape purée.

4. Pour 1 cup of the grape purée into a clean saucepan. Strain the remaining grape purée into a clean bowl, cover with plastic wrap, and reserve it at room temperature.

5. In a small bowl, sprinkle 1½ teaspoons of the gelatin over 2 tablespoons of water. Let soften for 5 minutes. Meanwhile, heat the grape purée in the saucepan to a simmer over medium heat. Add the softened gelatin to the hot grape purée and stir the mixture constantly until the gelatin dissolves, about 1 minute. Strain the mixture through a fine sieve and let cool completely (you can insert the bowl in an ice bath to speed this up if you wish).

6. Beat 1 cup of the cream with 2 tablespoons of the confectioners' sugar until it forms soft peaks. Fold the cream into the cooled 1 cup of grape purée (not the reserved grape purée in the covered bowl). Spoon

the mixture into 8 parfait glasses and chill until firm, at least 1 hour.

7. Carefully spoon the reserved grape purée (from the covered bowl) on top of the whipped cream–grape mixture, dividing it equally among the glasses. Chill the parfaits until the grape layer is firm, at least 1 hour.

8. Place the remaining ½ cup cream in a small saucepan. Sprinkle on the remaining ¼ teaspoon of gelatin and let soften for 5 minutes. Place the pan over the lowest heat and stir constantly until the gelatin dissolves, about 1 minute. Stir in the remaining tablespoon of confectioners' sugar. Strain the cream into a bowl and let it cool completely (or use an ice bath).

9. Divide the cream among the parfait glasses over the grape layer. Chill the parfaits until the cream is set, about 1 hour.

SERVING SUGGESTIONS
• Serve with Cornmeal-Nut Biscotti (page 140).
• For a composed dessert, add scoops of Concord Grape Sorbet (page 54).

HONEYDEW MELON SOUP WITH FIGS AND
ORANGE-FLOWER CRÈME FRAÎCHE

The beauty of this soup lies in its extraordinary simplicity. All you have to do is purée ripe honeydew melon in the blender, then dress it up with crème fraîche spiked with orange-flower water and some sliced fresh figs—no cooking required! It's a very easy and elegant way to serve ripe summer fruit.

Yield: 6 servings

1 ripe honeydew melon
   (5 pounds), peeled and
   cubed (about 8 cups)
½ cup sugar
6 fresh figs
1 cup crème fraîche
1 teaspoon orange-flower water

1. In a large bowl, combine all but ½ cup of the honeydew melon and the sugar. Toss well. Let the mixture sit for 15 minutes to dissolve the sugar.

2. Purée the melon using a food processor, immersion blender, or regular blender (if using a regular blender, purée the fruit in batches). Strain the purée through a fine sieve; discard the solids. Chill the soup until it's very cold, at least 3 hours.

3. Just before serving, trim the figs, halve them lengthwise, and slice them thin. Cut the remaining honeydew into ¼-inch cubes. Whip the crème fraîche with the orange-flower water just until the cream thickens very slightly (the beaters will leave faint marks in the cream).

4. To serve the soup, divide it among 6 soup plates. Garnish each portion with teaspoon-size dollops of the crème-fraîche, the figs, and the cubed melon.

SERVING SUGGESTIONS
• Serve with Orange-Cornmeal Shortbread (page 88) or Citrus Lace Tuiles (page 90).
• For a composed dessert, float scoops of Concord Grape Sorbet (page 54) in the soup.

SPICED RED WINE–FIG COMPOTE

As soon as fresh purple figs are available in late summer, I look forward to putting this fig compote on the menu. Although most people think of dried figs when you say the word "compote," I prefer using fresh, ripe figs at their peak. I like their bright flavor and soft, plump texture. But I also love the warm spiciness of a traditional dried fig compote. So for my version, I simmer the figs with all the ingredients found in the classic recipe, including red wine, cinnamon, star anise, and cloves. Then, at the end, I fold in even more fresh figs. The combination of the fresh and cooked fruit creates a deep, layered flavor. On its own, its intensity is best complemented with a little whipped cream, whipped crème fraîche, or vanilla ice cream.

Yield: 6 to 8 servings

2   pints fresh figs
1   whole clove
2   strips orange peel (each about
      1 × 3 inches)
1¾ cups port
1¼ cups dry red wine
1   cup sugar
½   cinnamon stick
1   star anise

1. Preheat the oven to 325°F. Trim the figs. Set aside 7 of the most ripe. Quarter the rest and put them in a large saucepan.

2. Stick the clove into 1 strip of the orange peel and add it to the saucepan along with the other strip of orange peel, the port, red wine, sugar, cinnamon stick, and star anise. Bring the mixture to a boil, stirring occasionally to dissolve the sugar.

3. Pour the fig mixture into a 9 × 13-inch baking pan and place it in the oven. Bake the figs, stirring occasionally, until the mixture is slightly syrupy and the figs take on a deep red color, about 2 hours and 15 minutes. Transfer the pan to a wire rack and let the fig mixture cool.

4. Meanwhile, quarter the remaining 7 figs. Stir the quartered fresh figs into the compote. Serve immediately, or refrigerate for up to 4 days. Bring to room temperature before serving.

SERVING SUGGESTIONS
- Serve with whipped crème fraîche.
- For a composed dessert, make a fig shortcake by replacing the tarragon-macerated strawberries (see page 12) with the compote, or make a napoleon by replacing the tamarind-glazed mangos (see page 97) with the figs, then garnish with scoops of goat-yogurt sorbet (see Variation, page 213).

BRANDIED-FIG ICE CREAM

This is an extravagant ice cream, not so much in terms of its ingredients (though best-quality figs can be expensive), but because of the time commitment necessary to make it. Each fig needs to be halved and hollowed, its dark, sticky, sweet pulp scraped out with a spoon or melon baller. Then the fig hearts are mixed with good brandy and stirred into a custard base. Dried figs, with their low moisture content, give this ice cream a resonant figgy flavor highlighted by the warm notes of the brandy. And, having removed any distracting hard bits of fig skin, the labor-intensive technique produces a rich, satiny ice cream punctuated by pleasantly crunchy fig seeds. Make it during the holiday season, and get the kids to help wield the melon baller. It's definitely worth the extra effort!

Yield: 1 quart

3   cups milk
1   cup cream
1¼ cups sugar
12 large egg yolks
3   pounds dried Calimyrna figs
    (about 78 figs)
2   tablespoons brandy
Pinch of salt

1. In a heavy saucepan, combine the milk, cream, and 1 cup of the sugar. Bring the mixture to a simmer. Meanwhile, in a medium bowl, whisk together the egg yolks and the remaining ¼ cup of sugar.

2. Remove the milk mixture from the heat and add a little to the egg yolk mixture to warm it, whisking constantly to keep the yolks from cooking. Pour the egg yolk mixture into the hot milk mixture, whisking the milk constantly as you pour.

3. Return the custard to the stove and cook it over low heat, stirring constantly with a wooden spoon, until it thickens enough to coat the back of the spoon. Remove from the heat and pour it into a bowl. Let cool completely.

4. Meanwhile, to prepare the figs, slice each fig in half lengthwise, and using a spoon or melon baller, scrape out the flesh, leaving the hard skins. You should have about 2 cups of packed fig flesh. Set aside.

5. Strain the custard into a blender or food processor and add the fig flesh, brandy, and salt. Blend or process until the figs are well dispersed into the custard. Chill the custard until it's thoroughly cold, at least 4 hours.

6. Freeze in an ice-cream maker according to the manufacturer's instructions.

SERVING SUGGESTIONS
• Serve with a sprinkling of candied walnuts (see page 261).
• For something more complex, add Caramel Blood Oranges (page 89).
• For a composed dessert, add Gingersnaps (page 176) or Pecan Sandies (page 144).

CONCORD GRAPE SORBET

Of all the sorbets in this book, this may be my favorite. Its concentrated spicy and fruity flavor is one of the reasons to look forward to fall. Fresh Concord grapes give the sorbet a distinctive purple hue and vibrant grape-juice-like flavor—without being overly sweet and cloying.

To get the fullest, deepest color, I let the grapes macerate overnight. Once you break their skins, grapes oxidize and start to turn brown, muddying the color. I use ascorbic acid (vitamin C powder) to maintain a beautiful shade. It's sold with the vitamins in health food stores or pharmacies.

At Gramercy Tavern we buy up case after case of these grapes, freezing the purée before it's churned so that we can have this sorbet long after the season is over. I suggest you do the same.

Yield: 2½ cups

1   pound Concord grapes, stemmed (about 3 cups)
2   tablespoons sugar
¼   teaspoon ascorbic acid
½   cup Simple Syrup (page 261)

1. Place the grapes in the bowl of a water-tight food processor and add the sugar and ascorbic acid. Pulse the mixture until it is a rough purée, about 10 times. (Or purée the grapes in batches in a blender, or use an immersion blender in a large bowl.) Let the mixture rest for at least 30 minutes at room temperature, or overnight in the refrigerator.

2. Purée the grapes until the mixture is very fine, about 2 minutes. Strain through a fine sieve, pressing down on the solids; discard the solids.

3. Stir the Simple Syrup and ¼ cup water into the grape mixture. Chill until the mixture is thoroughly cold, at least 3 hours. Freeze in an ice-cream maker according to the manufacturer's instructions.

SERVING SUGGESTIONS
- Serve with Cornmeal-Nut Biscotti (page 140) or Orange-Cornmeal Shortbread (page 88).
- For something more complex, add Roasted Figs with Roquefort, Hazelnuts, and Banyuls Glaze (page 48).

CANTALOUPE SORBET

Nothing could be better than a juicy, fragrant melon in the summertime—except possibly this sorbet, which has the same luscious sweetness of a ripe cantaloupe but is even more satisfying in its frozen state. Just be sure not to use a soft, overripe melon; if the melon is mushy, the sorbet can take on a funky flavor.

Yield: 3¼ cups

1   ripe cantaloupe (2½ pounds), peeled, seeded, and cubed (about 6 cups)
⅓   cup sugar
½   cup plus 2 tablespoons Simple Syrup (page 261)

1. In a large bowl, toss together the cantaloupe and sugar. Let the mixture sit for 15 minutes to dissolve the sugar.

2. Purée the cantaloupe using a food processor, immersion blender, or regular blender (if using a regular blender, purée the fruit in batches). Strain the purée through a fine sieve lined with cheesecloth, discarding the solids.

3. Stir ½ cup plus 2 tablespoons water and the Simple Syrup into the cantaloupe mixture. Chill until it's very cold, about 3 hours. Freeze in an ice-cream machine according to the manufacturer's directions.

SERVING SUGGESTIONS
• Serve with candied hazelnuts (see page 261) or Pecan Sandies (page 144).
• For something more complex, add fresh cantaloupe or Lemon Thyme–Macerated Raspberry Compote (page 19).
• For a composed dessert, add Crème Fraîche Panna Cotta (page 206).

WATERMELON GRANITÉ

There's not much you can do to improve upon nature when it comes to a chilled slice of ripe, sweet summer melon. But in the case of watermelon, you *can* remove the seeds. In this simple recipe, I pretty much do just that: find good, fresh watermelons, cut out the seeds, and freeze the pulp into a rough, icy granité. The flavors are about as pure and cool as can be, and the color is spectacular, especially if you can find red, yellow, orange, and even white watermelons (which are available at farmer's markets and specialty markets). Serve a few of the different-colored granités along with slices of their respective melons and you're guaranteed one of the most dazzling summer desserts there is.

Yield: 3 cups; 6 to 8 servings

4½ pounds watermelon, peeled, seeded, and cubed (about 6 cups)

⅓ cup sugar

1. In a large bowl, combine the watermelon and sugar. Toss well. Let the mixture sit for 15 minutes to dissolve the sugar.

2. Purée the watermelon using a food processor, immersion blender, or regular blender (if using a regular blender, purée the fruit in batches). Strain the purée through a fine sieve; discard the solids.

3. Pour the mixture into a shallow metal pan and place it in the freezer. Freeze the granité for 45 minutes, then use a fork to stir it up (the aim is to break down any ice crystals). Make sure to stir around the sides of the pan. Repeat the stirring every 30 minutes until the granité has a texture between an Italian ice and a snow cone. It will take 2½ to 4 hours, depending upon the size and depth of your pan and the temperature of your freezer.

SERVING SUGGESTIONS
- Serve with fresh watermelon.
- For something more complex, add Citrus Lace Tuiles (page 90).
- For a composed dessert, add goat-yogurt sorbet (see Variation, page 213).

APPLES, PEARS, AND QUINCES

Apples, pears, and quinces are at their peak in the fall, and nothing tastes more purely of autumn to me. Compatible with flavors like maple, honey, brandy, and spice, these combinations say fall is here and winter's on the way.

I can't stress enough the rewards of frequenting your local farmer's markets when shopping for these fruits. Each week of the year I buy fruits at their peak, and though they may not have the picture-perfect looks of the waxed fruits at a supermarket, they have an immeasurably superior flavor.

The variety of apples and pears can be astounding. Sometimes you'll find old-fashioned heirloom fruit with unique personalities, and it's fun to experiment with them. Some of my favorite apples are Cortlands, Mutsus, Macouns, and Pippins. McIntoshes that are crisp and unbruised are a treat, too. Unlike their namesakes at the supermarket, the aptly named Red Delicious apples at the Union Square Greenmarket in Manhattan are small, crunchy, sweet, and marvelously juicy. These are fruits the way they were supposed to be, before they were bred to be shipped around the globe. Always look for crisp, unwaxed apples.

When cooking with pears, choose small, firm varieties. Pears should be firm enough that they hold together when cooked, but not so rock-hard that they do not have any flavor or juice. Bartletts and Red Bartletts are full-flavored, delicately scented, and available almost anywhere. They are my favorite all-around pear for dessert recipes. Bosc is another common pear that is good, sweet and flavorful for eating out of hand. Seckel pears have a spiciness that is lovely uncooked. If you have very ripe, soft pears, the best use for them is to simply slice them up and eat them raw, dripping with sweet, juicy flavor.

Quinces can be hard to find, but they are worth seeking out for their exuberant floral taste. They are yellow, slightly furry, gnarled-looking fruits, but nonetheless they are beautiful in their asymmetry; and they have a lovely fragrance unlike that of any other fruit. Place a bowl of quinces on your kitchen table and it will impart a sweet perfume that will mildly scent your house for days. Quinces are always cooked, since their tart, hard flesh is too astringent to eat raw. When poached with spices and vanilla or made into jam, they take on a rosy hue and a wonderfully nuanced flavor.

WINE NOTES: APPLES, PEARS, AND QUINCES

When I think of apple, pear, and quince desserts, a buttery, baked richness comes to mind that is both aromatic and textural. A Tokaji Aszú or an older Sauternes from Bordeaux, France, can mimic this honeyed, vanilla richness. These wines are in keeping with the straightforward aspects of the desserts, and they also introduce an earthlike intensity that complements the fruit. Since the simpler, more fruit-forward desserts in this chapter tend to have more acidity and less sweetness, they require something light and fragrant, like a German Riesling in the Aüslese format.

APPLE TARTES TATIN

There is no room for improvement on this classic French upside-down apple tart. The combination of the tender baked fruit, rich caramel, and buttery, flaky puff pastry is both age-old and delicious. Since the apples need a lot of caramel to bake into something translucent and nearly candied, it's important to cook the caramel until it is very dark in color. This keeps the tarte Tatin from becoming cloying. Using a tart, crisp apple, such as a Granny Smith or Mutsu, also helps counterbalance the sweetness. While a traditional tarte Tatin is baked in a large skillet, I like to make mine in individual servings. Not only is it more elegant, it also seems to yield the most consistent results.

Yield: 6 servings

1 cup sugar

1 teaspoon light corn syrup

4 tablespoons unsalted butter, cut into 1-inch pieces

4 medium Granny Smith apples, peeled, halved, and cored

8 ounces puff pastry, preferably all-butter, thawed

1. Place ¼ cup water in a medium saucepan over low heat. Add the sugar and corn syrup, increase the heat to high, and cook, swirling the pan occasionally, until the mixture caramelizes into a deep amber brown, 7 to 10 minutes. Remove the pan from the heat and whisk in the butter until melted and smooth. Divide the caramel among six 4-ounce glass or ceramic ramekins.

2. Slice each apple half lengthwise into 4 wedges. To slice these wedges, hold them down on a cutting board with one hand and carefully cut through them so that each wedge is thinly sliced but retains its original shape. Holding the slices together, lay 2 of the wedges in the bottom of a ramekin. Fan out the slices so they lie flat and overlap to cover the bottom of the ramekin in an even layer. Place 2 more sliced wedges on top of the fanned slices. Repeat with all the ramekins, then continue to add apple slices in this manner until each ramekin is filled to the top.

3. On a floured surface, roll out or unfold the pastry to ¼ inch thick and prick all over with a fork. Preheat the oven to 400°F. Chill the pastry for 30 minutes.

4. Using a round cutter or a knife, cut out 6 pastry rounds slightly larger than the ramekins. Place the rounds directly on top of the apples and tuck them gently into the edges of the ramekins so they adhere to the sides. Place the ramekins on a baking sheet lined with a nonstick liner or parchment paper. Bake for 15 minutes, then lower the oven temperature to 375°F. and bake until the puff pastry is golden brown, the apples are fork-tender but not mushy, and the caramel is thick and bubbling, about another 10 minutes.

5. Allow the tarts to cool for at least 1 hour, so that the caramel sets, before inverting onto serving dishes. Alternatively, bake the tarts up to 12 hours in advance, let them cool completely, then reheat them in a 300°F. oven for 5 to 7 minutes, or until hot.

SERVING SUGGESTIONS
- Serve with Golden Raisin Verjus (page 265).
- For something more complex, add Green-Apple Sorbet (page 75).
- For a composed dessert, add Goat-Cheese Cheesecake (page 204).

PEAR CRISPS WITH DRIED SOUR CHERRIES

This is a terrific fall dessert. Soft, syrupy pears and tart sour cherries are nestled under a nutty, spiced topping, which is baked until crunchy and golden brown. At the restaurant, the topping crumbs that fall from the crisps onto the baking tray are one of my favorite snacks, and my staff and I can't resist nibbling on them whenever the crisps come out of the oven. Be sure to bake the crisps until the juices bubble up thickly; otherwise, not enough of the moisture will evaporate, and the fruit will be soggy.

Yield: 8 servings

1   cup dried sour cherries
Water or fruity red wine, such as a
        Zinfandel, to cover
8   ripe pears (about 2¼ pounds),
        peeled, cored, and sliced (5 cups)
½   cup granulated sugar
1¼   cups all-purpose flour
⅓   cup plus 1 tablespoon coarsely
        ground almonds, toasted
¼   cup firmly packed dark brown
        sugar
¼   teaspoon ground cinnamon
⅛   teaspoon ground nutmeg
½   cup (1 stick) unsalted butter,
        melted and cooled to room
        temperature

1. In a small saucepan, combine the cherries with enough water or wine (or a combination) to cover them by 2 inches. Bring the mixture to a simmer over medium heat, then turn off the heat and let cool. Let the cherries soak overnight in the refrigerator, or for at least 8 hours, until they are plump and soft. Drain the cherries, reserving the juices.

2. In a large bowl, combine the pears, drained cherries, and ¼ cup of the granulated sugar and toss well. Mix in ½ cup of the cherry soaking liquid, or whatever cherry soaking liquid is left plus enough water to make ½ cup. Let the mixture stand for 30 minutes.

3. Meanwhile, preheat the oven to 375°F. In a large bowl, whisk together the remaining ¼ cup of granulated sugar, the flour, almonds, brown sugar, cinnamon, and nutmeg. Slowly drizzle in the butter and stir with a fork until the mixture is crumbly and all the flour is incorporated. Do not allow the mixture to come together in a ball. Break up any large crumbs with your fingers. The crumbs should be smaller than 1 inch in size (otherwise they won't cook all the way through).

4. Spoon the fruit into eight 8-ounce ramekins and place them on a baking sheet. Evenly sprinkle the crumbs on top of the fruit. Bake the crisps until the filling is bubbling and the topping is browned, about 40 minutes. Serve hot or warm.

SERVING SUGGESTIONS
- Serve with scoops of Sour Cherry Sorbet (page 39) or Pear Sorbet (page 74).
- For something more complex, add whipped crème fraîche or Licorice Ice Cream (page 196).

APPLE-BUTTER CREPES

This cozy, autumnal dessert puts an American harvesttime spin on the typical French crepe. The crepes are spread with spicy, homemade apple butter, then warmed in a fragrant Calvados sauce. Although you could buy a good brand of jarred apple butter for the crepes, slowly simmering it yourself really makes all the difference. The recipe will yield leftover apple butter, which keeps in the refrigerator for at least a week. It is delicious on toast or stirred into yogurt. The crepes can also be made in advance. Prepare them up to one day ahead and refrigerate them, wrapped in plastic. Then reheat them in the sauce just before serving.

Yield: 6 servings

APPLE BUTTER

6   apples, peeled, cored, and sliced
    into eighths
2   cups apple cider
2   whole cloves
½   cinnamon stick
1   star anise

CREPES

1   cup all-purpose flour
⅔   cup milk
¼   cup heavy cream
⅓   cup plus 1 tablespoon sugar
2   large eggs
1   large egg yolk
½   vanilla bean, split lengthwise,
    pulp scraped (see page 180)
Pinch of salt
Melted butter for the pan,
    if necessary

CALVADOS SAUCE

6   tablespoons sugar
6   tablespoons unsalted butter
6   tablespoons Calvados, apple
    brandy, or apple cider
¾   teaspoon vanilla extract

1. To prepare the apple butter, in a medium saucepan, combine the ap-ples and cider. Tie the cloves, cinna-mon, and star anise in a piece of cheesecloth and add it to the pan. Bring the mixture to a simmer over medium heat, then reduce the heat to low and slowly cook until the ap-ples are reduced to a soft purée and all of the liquid has evaporated, about 4 hours. Discard the cheesecloth-wrapped spices. Set the apple butter aside to cool completely. Store the apple butter, covered, in the refriger-ator until needed.

2. To prepare the crepes, in a blender, combine the flour, milk, cream, sugar, eggs, egg yolk, vanilla pulp, and salt. Blend until smooth. Pass the mixture through a fine sieve; discard the solids. Cover and chill for at least 8 hours and up to 2 days.

3. Heat a heavy, preferably nonstick, 8-inch skillet over medium-high heat. Brush the pan with butter if it's not nonstick. Add about 3 table-spoons of the crepe batter to the pan and swirl to evenly distribute the bat-ter (it should just coat the bottom of the pan). Pour any excess batter back into the batter bowl. Cook the crepe until the bottom is browned and small bubbles appear on the top, about 45 seconds. Flip and cook until browned on the other side, about 10 seconds. Transfer to a plate and repeat with the remaining batter, buttering the pan occasionally if the crepes begin to stick. You should have about 15 crepes.

4. Choose 12 of the nicest crepes and reserve. Use the remaining crepes for another purpose. Spread one side of each crepe with 1 tablespoon of the apple butter. Set aside on baking sheets.

5. To prepare the sauce, combine the sugar with 6 tablespoons water in a large skillet over medium heat. Sim-mer, stirring occasionally, until the sugar dissolves, about 2 minutes. Add the butter, Calvados, and vanilla and bring the mixture to a simmer. Sim-mer, stirring, until the mixture re-duces slightly, about 2 minutes. Reduce the heat to low.

6. Place one of the crepes, apple-butter side up, into the sauce in the pan and let it heat through, about

30 seconds. Using tongs or a fork, fold the crepe into quarters, then transfer it to a serving platter; tent with foil to keep warm. Repeat with the remaining crepes. Serve at once, with some of the sauce.

SERVING SUGGESTIONS
· Serve with candied walnuts (see page 261) and whipped crème fraîche.
· For something more complex, add Maple-Glazed Winter Squash and Apple Compote (page 125).
· For a composed dessert, add Green-Apple Sorbet (page 75), or omit the whipped crème fraîche and substitute Crème Fraîche Panna Cotta (page 206) or Buttermilk Ice Cream (page 211).

SPICED-QUINCE BUTTER CAKE

Quinces are strange-looking fruit that have an astringent taste when eaten raw. But poached quinces are another matter entirely. Once cooked, the flesh takes on a lovely pink cast and a honeyed, floral taste. Here, quinces are simmered with spices, orange zest, and white wine, then baked on top of a delicate almond-butter cake. The cake has a brittle, sugary crust that provides crisp contrast to the tender crumb and the luscious, plump fruit. You can prepare both the quinces and cake batter up to one week in advance; store them in the refrigerator until needed.

Yield: 6 to 8 servings

QUINCE

- 1   large quince, peeled, cored, and cut into 16 slices
- 1½   cups sugar
- 1   cup dry white wine
- 1   whole clove stuck into a 2-inch strip of orange peel
- ½   cinnamon stick
- 1   star anise

CAKE

- ½   cup (1 stick) unsalted butter, cut into pieces
- 1⅓   cups confectioners' sugar
- ½   cup almond flour
- ⅓   cup cake flour
- ½   teaspoon ground cinnamon
- ¼   teaspoon ground nutmeg
- ⅛   teaspoon ground cloves
- ⅛   teaspoon ground cardamom
- 4   large egg whites (½ cup)
- ½   teaspoon grated orange zest

1. To prepare the quince, in a large saucepan, combine the quince, 3 cups water, the sugar, wine, orange peel with clove, cinnamon, and star anise. Cut a round of parchment paper slightly smaller than the pot and lay it on top of the quince (this will keep the fruit submerged; you can also use a sturdy, heatproof plate). Bring the mixture to a boil over high heat, then reduce the heat to medium-low and simmer until the quince is tender and spongy, about 1¼ hours. Let the quince cool in the poaching liquid. Drain the quince pieces on layers of paper towel. Discard the liquid.

2. To make the cake, preheat the oven to 400°F. In a large skillet over medium heat, melt the butter. Continue to let the butter cook until the white milk solids fall to the bottom of the skillet and turn a rich hazelnut brown. Strain the browned butter through a fine sieve into a clean bowl, discarding the solids.

3. Sift together the confectioners' sugar, almond flour, cake flour, cinnamon, nutmeg, cloves, and cardamom. Place the sifted ingredients in the bowl of an electric mixer fitted with the whisk attachment. On the lowest speed, add the egg whites and orange zest; mix until all the dry ingredients are moistened. Increase the speed to medium and beat until very smooth. Decrease the speed to low and stir in the browned butter, then increase the speed to medium and beat until smooth.

4. Butter a 10-inch tart pan with a removable bottom or a springform pan. Pour in the batter and smooth the top. Arrange the quince slices on the batter. Bake for 25 to 30 minutes, or until the cake is golden brown. Transfer to a wire rack and cool completely. Remove the sides of the pan before serving.

SERVING SUGGESTION

- Serve with candied walnuts (see page 261) and/or Brandied-Fig Ice Cream (page 53).

CARAMELIZED-APPLE BLINI

I love these little silver-dollar blini. They're especially soft and airy, with a lovely toasty flavor that comes from the yeast in the batter. It's a great all-purpose blini recipe for both savory and sweet preparations, one that is particularly convenient since they can be made ahead and warmed up at the last minute. Here, I serve them with crème fraîche and with apples that are cubed and caramelized until they turn a gorgeous glassy brown.

Yield: 6 servings, plus extra blini

BLINI
1¼ cups all-purpose flour
1¼ teaspoons active dry yeast
½ teaspoon salt
1 large egg, separated
3½ tablespoons vegetable oil
1 cup milk
Melted butter for the pan,
    if necessary
Crème fraîche, for serving

CARAMELIZED APPLES
1½ cups sugar
1 vanilla bean, split lengthwise,
    pulp scraped (see page 180)
2 to 3 Mutsu or Granny Smith
    apples, peeled, cored, and
    diced into ¼-inch cubes
    (to yield 2 cups)
⅓ cup apple juice
1 tablespoon unsalted butter

1. To make the blini, in a large bowl, mix together the flour, yeast, and salt. In another bowl, whisk the egg yolk. Slowly drizzle the oil into the yolk, whisking constantly so the mixture emulsifies like a mayonnaise. Make a well in the center of the flour mixture and pour in the egg mixture and milk; whisk well. Cover the bowl with plastic wrap and set it aside in a warm place to rise until doubled, about 1½ hours.

2. Meanwhile, prepare the caramelized apples. Place a 10-inch nonstick skillet over high heat and let it get very hot. Sprinkle in about ¼ cup of the sugar. Cook until it begins to melt, shaking and stirring from time to time. Sprinkle in another ¼ cup of the sugar and continue to add more sugar as it melts and caramelizes. When almost all the sugar has melted, add the pulp from the vanilla bean and stir to incorporate. When the sugar is completely melted and caramelized to a deep amber brown, cover with the apples in a single layer. Cook until the apples soften and release some of their juices, 2 to 3 minutes, basting often with a spoon. Turn off the heat and set the apples aside.

3. In a clean metal bowl, beat the egg white with a whisk or electric beaters until soft peaks form. Fold the egg white into the risen blini batter.

4. Heat a heavy, preferably nonstick, skillet over medium-high heat. Brush the pan with butter if it's not nonstick. Add about 2 tablespoons of the batter to the pan for each blini, forming little pancakes. Cook the blini until the bottoms are golden and small bubbles appear on the top, 2 to 3 minutes. Flip and cook until browned on the other side, about 1 minute. Transfer to a plate and tent with foil to keep warm. Continue making blini with the remaining batter, buttering the pan occasionally if the blini begin to stick. (The blini can be made up to 1 week ahead and frozen; wrap them in foil and reheat in a 300°F. oven before serving.)

5. Just before serving, finish preparing the apples. Add the apple juice to the pan and simmer until the caramel melts and thins, 1 to 2 minutes, basting the apples with the syrup. Add the butter, stirring gently so as not to break up the apples. To serve, place 3 blini on a plate and top with crème fraîche and some of the caramelized apples.

SERVING SUGGESTIONS
· Serve with candied walnuts or pecans (see page 261).
· For a composed dessert, add Green-Apple Sorbet (page 75).

QUINCE THUMBPRINT COOKIES

This recipe was inspired by my mother. Every year at Christmas, she made what seemed like a countless number of cookies in all different flavors. It was only when I was older that I realized her secret: she used the same basic dough for all the varieties, flavoring each one differently. Some were plain and cut out into shapes; some had ground nuts added and were formed into crescents, then sprinkled with confectioners' sugar; some were dipped in chocolate; and some were made into thumbprint cookies filled with jam. We all loved them, and every year we looked forward to Mom's cookies. In fact, we loved them so much that my mother always had to hide them from us kids, especially my brother and me. One year, just after my mother had put the finishing touches on trays and trays of cookies, she looked out the window and noticed my brother and me coming home from school. She quickly hid the cookies under her bed so we wouldn't gobble them up. But unbeknownst to her, the dog found them and polished them off. Poor Mom; in addition to losing her whole day's work, she also had to deal with the sick dog!

In this recipe, I shape my mother's basic dough into thumbprints and fill them with homemade quince jam. The more you cook quince, the more color it takes on. Here, it's reduced to a deep rose-colored preserve. The jam itself is nuanced and delicious and can keep for several weeks in the refrigerator. It's superb on toast and even better on toasted pound cake. But before you finish it off, be sure to make a batch of these cookies. They are buttery jewel-like mouthfuls that are sure to be the first ones grabbed from the cookie jar.

Yield: 2 cups jam; 5½ dozen cookies

QUINCE JAM

4	quinces, peeled, cored, and cut into eighths
1	cup dry white wine
1	cup sugar
1	vanilla bean, split lengthwise, pulp scraped (see page 180)

COOKIES

1½	cups (3 sticks) unsalted butter, softened
¾	cup confectioners' sugar
1	teaspoon vanilla extract
2	cups all-purpose flour
1	cup cornstarch
½	teaspoon salt
1	cup finely ground toasted walnuts

1. To prepare the quince jam, in a saucepan, combine the quinces, 3 cups water, the wine, sugar, and vanilla pod and pulp. Cut a round of parchment paper slightly smaller than the opening of the pot and lay it on top of the quince (this will keep the fruit submerged; you can also use a sturdy, heatproof plate). Bring the mixture to a boil over high heat, then reduce the heat to medium-low and simmer until the quince slices are extremely tender and spongy, about 2 hours. Remove the parchment and mash the quince using either the back of a spoon or a potato masher. Continue to simmer the quince mixture until it looks like jam, about 1½ to 2 hours longer, stirring occasionally. Let cool, discard the vanilla pod, then store in the refrigerator until needed.

2. To make the cookies, in the bowl of an electric mixer, cream the butter and sugar until smooth and light, about 2 minutes. Beat in the vanilla. Sift in the flour, cornstarch, and salt and beat until just incorporated. Fold in the walnuts. Cover the dough and chill for at least 4 hours.

3. Preheat the oven to 325°F. Form heaping teaspoonfuls of cookie dough into balls and place on ungreased cookie sheets about 1 inch apart. Using a moistened thumb, press a deep indentation into the center of each cookie.

4. Bake for 13 to 15 minutes, until very lightly golden. Meanwhile, place the quince jam in a pan and bring it to a simmer over low heat. Just after the cookies have baked, when they are still warm, spoon warm quince jam into each thumbprint. Let cool completely on racks before serving.

SERVING SUGGESTION
• Serve with Orange–Cardamom Shakes (page 208) or Bay Leaf Flan (page 152).

MAPLE BAKED APPLES WITH DRIED FRUIT AND NUTS

This is a simple, delicious dessert that also makes a warming and special brunch dish or breakfast. Although many baked-apple recipes are on the lean side (my mother always ate them when she was dieting), my version is luxurious yet still homey. I stuff the apples with a mix of brown sugar, dried fruit, and nuts, then bake them in a sauce of apple cider, maple syrup, and plenty of butter, which cooks down to a rich, thick glaze. I like to use Cortlands here because of their good squat shape and their complex fruity flavor, but any firm, tart baking apple will do.

Yield: 6 servings

⅓ cup firmly packed dark brown sugar

3 tablespoons roughly chopped dried cherries

3 tablespoons chopped dried figs

2 tablespoons roughly chopped sliced toasted almonds

2 tablespoons roughly chopped toasted pecans

6 large, firm baking apples, such as Cortlands, cored but not peeled

3 tablespoons unsalted butter, cut into 6 pieces

½ cup apple cider

2 tablespoons maple syrup

1. Preheat the oven to 400°F. In a small bowl, mix together the brown sugar, dried fruit, and nuts.

2. Place the apples in a baking pan or casserole dish and stuff their cavities with the fruit and nut mixture. Place a piece of butter on top of the stuffing.

3. Pour the apple cider and maple syrup into the bottom of the baking pan and bake the apples, basting every 5 to 7 minutes, until they are tender, 25 to 35 minutes.

4. When the apples are tender, transfer them to a serving platter and cover with foil to keep warm. Pour the pan juices into a small saucepan and bring to a boil over high heat. Simmer the mixture until it becomes syrupy and reduces to a sauce, about 10 minutes. Serve over the apples.

SERVING SUGGESTIONS

- Serve with yogurt, whipped crème fraîche, or Ginger Ice Cream (page 178).
- For a composed dessert, add Guinness Stout Ginger Cake (page 173).

ROASTED CHESTNUT-HONEY PEARS

The inspiration for this recipe came from watching Tom Colicchio, the chef at Gramercy Tavern, glaze root vegetables with chestnut honey and thyme. I thought the flavors would work beautifully with pears. I love the earthy, piney, autumnal nuances of chestnut honey and thyme, and I find that these two ingredients add an unusual complexity to the gentleness of the pears. This is a very easy recipe that can be pulled together in just a few minutes, whenever you have some pears that are ripening faster than you can keep up with. Once you transform your surplus fruits, you'll have an intense dessert that keeps well and is easy to reheat.

Yield: 6 servings

4 tablespoons chestnut honey
6 small firm, ripe pears, such as
   Comice, peeled, halved, and
   cored
5 sprigs of fresh thyme, preferably
   lemon thyme
2 tablespoons unsalted butter, cut
   into pieces
Pinch of salt

1. Preheat the oven to 350°F.

2. In a large ovenproof skillet over low heat, simmer 2 tablespoons of the honey until it begins to reduce and caramelize, about 10 minutes.

3. Add the pears, cut side down, and simmer over medium-low heat until they begin to turn golden brown around the edges, about 15 minutes. Turn the pears cut side up, scatter the tops with 3 sprigs of the thyme, and transfer the skillet to the oven. Roast the pears until they are tender, 20 to 30 minutes, depending upon their ripeness.

4. Meanwhile, in a small saucepan, simmer the remaining 2 tablespoons of honey with the remaining 2 sprigs of thyme for 2 minutes. Slowly whisk in the butter, then stir in the salt. Keep warm.

5. Drizzle the honey-butter mixture over the pears and serve hot or warm. (You can make the pears 1 day ahead and refrigerate them; reheat in a 300°F. oven for 10 to 15 minutes. Make the honey-butter mixture while reheating.)

SERVING SUGGESTIONS
• Serve with Frozen Ricotta–Chestnut-Honey Cream (page 210).
• For something more complex, add Chestnut Honey–Roasted Pine Nuts (page 262).
• For a composed dessert, add Citrus Lace Tuiles (page 90) or Chestnut-Honey Madeleines (page 184).

This remarkable recipe is really three creations in one preparation. Pears are poached in a combination of port, verjus, and spices until they take on a luminous ruby color. Then the fruit is removed from the liquid, some of which is frozen into granité while the last bit reduces to a syrup in which to candy the ginger. Served altogether, it's a stunning dessert with a seductive, deeply spiced flavor.

Be sure to find firm but not hard pears for poaching. Bosc is a good variety, but any small, firm pear will do.

Yield: 8 servings

8   small pears, peeled
1   bottle (750 ml) ruby port
2   cups white verjus (see page 269)
2   cups sugar
8   cardamom pods
½   cinnamon stick
3   whole cloves
½   ounce fresh gingerroot, peeled and sliced thin
1   ounce fresh gingerroot, peeled and cut into matchsticks

1. In a large saucepan, combine the pears, port, verjus, sugar, cardamom, cinnamon, cloves, and sliced (not matchstick) ginger. Cut a round of parchment paper slightly smaller than the pot and lay it on top of the pears (this will keep the fruit submerged; you can also use a sturdy, heatproof plate). Bring the mixture to a boil over high heat, then reduce the heat to low and simmer until the pears are just tender, about 25 minutes. Let the pears cool in the poaching liquid, then refrigerate the mixture overnight (keep the parchment paper on the pears so that they stay submerged)—this will give the pears their intense ruby color.

2. Transfer the pears to a plate lined with a paper towel and blot them dry. Strain the poaching liquid, then measure out 3 cups and place it in a saucepan; reserve the remaining liquid. Add the gingerroot matchsticks. Bring the mixture to a bare simmer over low heat and continue to simmer until it reduces and turns syrupy, 1½ to 2½ hours (the time will vary depending upon the depth of your saucepan). Strain the gingerroot matchsticks out of the poaching liquid and set them aside; reserve the reduced poaching liquid.

3. Meanwhile, pour the remaining liquid into a shallow metal pan, add ¼ cup water, and place it in the freezer. Freeze the granité for 45 minutes, then use a fork to stir it up (the aim is to break down any ice crystals). Make sure to stir around the sides of the pan. Repeat the stirring every 30 minutes until the granité has a texture somewhere between that of an Italian ice and a snow cone. It will take 2½ to 4 hours, depending upon the size and depth of your pan and the temperature of your freezer.

4. Cut the pears in half lengthwise, core them, and serve with the granité, reduced poaching syrup, and gingerroot matchsticks.

SERVING SUGGESTION
• Serve with whipped crème fraîche and/or Gingersnaps (page 176).

PEAR SORBET WITH POACHED PEAR COMPOTE

This elegant dessert showcases two dimensions of pear flavor and texture. You start by poaching ripe pears, then churning some of the poaching liquid into a pale sorbet along with uncooked pears. The poached pears are then simmered into a compote with vanilla and ginger, to be served with the sorbet. The sorbet, made from fresh pears, has a particularly delicate, pure flavor, whereas the compote has more character and depth. If you are deciding between pear recipes, bear in mind that these pears are more subtly spiced compared to the intense flavor of the Ginger-Port Poached Pears.

Yield: 6 to 8 servings

1½ cups dry white wine

1½ cups sugar

13 small ripe pears, peeled, halved, and cored

½ ounce fresh gingerroot, peeled and cut into 4 pieces

1 vanilla bean, split lengthwise, pulp scraped (see page 180)

⅛ teaspoon ascorbic acid (vitamin C powder; available at health food stores and pharmacies)

½ cup Simple Syrup (page 261)

1. In a large saucepan, combine 3 cups of water, the wine, sugar, and 8 of the pears. Cut a round of parchment paper slightly smaller than the opening of the pot and lay it on top of the pears (this will keep the fruit submerged; you can also use a sturdy, heatproof plate). Bring the mixture to a boil over high heat, then reduce the heat to low and simmer until the pears are very tender, 30 to 35 minutes. Let the pears cool in the poaching liquid.

2. Strain the mixture, setting aside the pears and 2 cups of the poaching liquid. Reserve the remaining poaching liquid for another purpose (for example, reduce the sauce to create a pear syrup). Coarsely chop the pears, then return them to the saucepan along with the ginger and vanilla pod and pulp. Cook over medium heat, stirring and mashing the fruit with the back of a spoon, until the mixture is a relatively dry, very rough purée, about 15 minutes. Remove the vanilla pod and ginger. Let the compote cool, then refrigerate it until needed.

3. To make the sorbet, roughly chop the remaining 5 pears. Place them in a blender or food processor with the

2 cups of reserved poaching liquid and the ascorbic acid and purée until very smooth. Strain the mixture through a fine sieve, discarding the solids. Stir in the Simple Syrup and ½ cup of water. Chill the sorbet mixture until it is very cold, at least 4 hours.

4. Freeze the sorbet in an ice-cream maker according to the manufacturer's instructions.

SERVING SUGGESTIONS

· Serve with Macerated Dried Sour Cherries (page 265).

· For something more complex, add Gingersnaps (page 176).

· For a composed dessert, add Crème Fraîche Panna Cotta (page 206).

GREEN-APPLE SORBET

This sorbet owes its citrusy, fresh taste to sparkling apple cider. The cider brightens, refreshes, and intensifies the apple flavor, adding a new dimension and a sweetness that goes nicely with the tartness of the green apples. The result is a vibrant sorbet with a pleasing note of effervescence.

Although this recipe calls for a juicer, if you don't have one, you can always ask your local health food store or juice bar to make green apple juice in their juicer. Just be sure to add a pinch of ascorbic acid right away, before the juice has time to oxidize and turn brown! Then rush home and strain the juice through cheesecloth before continuing with the recipe.

Yield: 1 quart

4 green apples (such as Granny Smith)
½ teaspoon ascorbic acid (vitamin C powder; available at health food stores and pharmacies)
1½ cups sparkling cider
1½ cups Simple Syrup (page 261)

1. In a juicer, juice the apples to yield 1½ cups juice. Immediately mix in the ascorbic acid to prevent discoloration.

2. In a large bowl, stir together the apple juice, cider, and Simple Syrup. Chill until the mixture is thoroughly cold, at least 3 hours. Freeze in an ice-cream maker according to the manufacturer's instructions.

SERVING SUGGESTIONS
· Pour a splash of Calvados or sparkling apple cider over the sorbet, and serve with whipped crème fraîche.
· For something more complex, add Quince Thumbprint Cookies (page 68) or Pecan Sandies (page 144).

PEELING CITRUS

In many of the recipes in this section, I call for peeling the citrus and removing the white membranes around each segment. The best way to do this is as follows:

1. Cut the top and bottom off the fruit and stand it up on a cutting board on one of the flat sides.
2. Using a small knife, cut away the peel and white pith, following the natural curve of the fruit. Now the flesh should be completely exposed.
3. Working over a bowl to catch the juices, cut the segments of fruit away from the membranes that connect them. The segments will fall into the bowl. Use both the fruit and juice in recipes.

CITRUS FRUITS

In the doldrums of winter, there are few things nicer than a bright, fresh citrus fruit. As fall fruits go out of season, sweet and juicy blood oranges, clementines, and kumquats begin to appear in markets; and while oranges and grapefruits can be found year-round, they are really at their best in the winter.

Citrus fruits are refreshing and light, and very versatile. I use the entire fruit, treating the pulp as I would other fruits and flavoring desserts with the oil found in the fruit's skin. The zest of citrus fruits contains all of the fruit flavor, while the juice contains a tartness and sweetness not found in the zest. For example, to flavor a custard with orange without causing it to curdle in reaction to the fruit's acidity, I infuse the custard with orange zest. For a citrus parfait or curd, I use both juice and zest. I make caramel blood oranges by stirring peeled sections of fruit into a freshly made caramel, and I serve a semolina pudding flavored with orange zest beside a minted salad of citrus segments.

In all their forms, the strong, clear tastes of citrus fruits make them perfect for cutting through the heaviness of creamy winter desserts, or for refreshing the palate after a big cold-weather meal. Their flavor also marries perfectly with wintry spices like cinnamon, ginger, and anise, or assertive ingredients like chocolate and coffee. For example, in the Lime-Gingersnap Parfait, a bright-tasting frozen lime mousse is layered on top of a spicy gingersnap crust for the perfect pairing.

To choose sweet, juicy citrus, look for fruits that are plump all over, without soft spots. They should feel heavy with juice. Their color need not be vibrant as long as the skin has shine, indicating that it has retained its oil. They keep wonderfully in the refrigerator, so buy nice-looking fruit whenever you see it and don't worry about using it all up quickly.

Citrus desserts can be well balanced in terms of sweetness and acidity, allowing for a wine that is equally balanced but slightly sweeter than the dessert itself. Muscat de Beaumes-de-Venise, either natural or fortified, is an excellent choice. The overwhelming floral tones of the wine combined with its relatively high levels of acidity are a perfect match with citrus flavors. For the Lime-Gingersnap Parfait and the Semolina Pudding with Minted Citrus Salad, you can enjoy a sweet wine that adds an additional flavor element, like the spice tones of the dried Malvasia grape wine from southern Italy called Malvasia delle Lipari. Prosecco Sabayon with Clementines and Blood Oranges is in keeping with the light, bubbly characteristics of a demi-sec champagne, which is not too sweet and provides a lovely flavor complement to the clementines and kumquats in the dish.

LEMON-LIME SOUFFLÉ TART

If you want to impress with a citrus dessert, take the time to make this spectacular tart—the uptown cousin of the lemon meringue pie. The filling, which is made by folding a potent lemon-lime pastry cream into sweet, billowy meringue, is spooned into an almond cookie crust and baked. Like a soufflé, it puffs and browns in the oven, but unlike a soufflé, it can sit out for up to 30 minutes before serving, so it doesn't need to be timed perfectly. And if you want to make this ahead, you can simply freeze the whole assembled tart unbaked, then let it thaw in the refrigerator for 4 hours before baking.

Although this tart is terrific as is, at Gramercy Tavern, I embellish it even further by spooning some Lemon Curd (page 263) into the crust before adding the filling. It makes a creamy counterpart to the ethereal souffléd top.

Yield: 6 to 8 servings

ALMOND CRUST
½ cup (1 stick) unsalted butter, softened
⅓ cup confectioners' sugar
1 large egg, lightly beaten
Grated zest of ½ lemon
1½ cups all-purpose flour
½ cup plus 2 tablespoons almond flour
Pinch of salt

LEMON-LIME SOUFFLÉ FILLING
2 cups plus 2 tablespoons sugar
4 large eggs, separated
3 tablespoons all-purpose flour
3 tablespoons fresh lemon juice
3 tablespoons fresh lime juice

Confectioners' sugar, for dusting

1. To make the crust, in the bowl of an electric mixer set with the paddle attachment, beat the butter and confectioners' sugar until combined, about 1 minute. Beat in the egg and zest.

2. In a medium bowl, whisk together the all-purpose flour, almond flour, and salt. Add the flour mixture to the butter mixture in two batches, scraping down the sides of the bowl between additions. Mix until the dough is well combined. Scrape the dough onto a piece of plastic wrap and form it into a disk. Chill for at least 1 hour, and up to 3 days.

3. On a lightly floured surface, roll the dough out to a 14-inch round about ⅛ inch thick. Fit the dough into a 10-inch tart pan with a removable bottom. Trim away any excess dough and use a fork to prick the crust all over. Chill the dough for 30 minutes.

4. Preheat the oven to 325°F. Bake the tart crust until it's pale golden, 20 to 25 minutes. Transfer to a wire rack to cool. (The tart shell can be made 8 hours ahead.)

5. Preheat the oven to 375°F. To prepare the filling, in a stainless-steel bowl, whisk together 5 tablespoons of the sugar, the egg yolks, flour, lemon juice, and lime juice. Place the bowl over a pot of gently simmering water and whisk the mixture constantly to avoid curdling the eggs. Continue whisking until the mixture gets quite thick, about 8 minutes. Strain through a fine sieve into the bowl of an electric mixer.

6. Beat the lemon-lime cream on high speed until thick, cool, and light, about 5 minutes.

7. In a clean bowl of an electric mixer, beat the egg whites until they hold soft peaks. Slowly add the remaining 5 tablespoons of sugar and beat until stiff peaks form, taking care not to overbeat the whites.

8. Fold a third of the meringue into the lemon-lime cream to lighten it, then fold in the remaining meringue in two batches. Spoon the soufflé topping into the tart crust, mounding it attractively.

9. Bake the tart until the soufflé is golden brown and spongy, 20 to 25 minutes. Dust the top with confectioners' sugar and serve warm.

SERVING SUGGESTIONS
• Serve with Lemon Curd (page 263) and/or Lemon-Ginger Sauce (page 262).
• For something more complex, add Lemon Confit (page 261).
• For a composed dessert, add Lemon Verbena Ice Cream (page 161).

LIME-GINGERSNAP PARFAIT

This vibrant dessert combines the soft, melt-in-the-mouth qualities of a frozen mousse with the plucky, tart tastes of lime and ginger. Since I have them on hand, I crush my homemade gingersnaps (see page 176) into crumbs for the crust. If you have the time, you can do the same. Otherwise, purchase good-quality gingersnaps and crush them in a food processor, or use a rolling pin.

A perfect make-ahead dessert, this parfait can be prepared and frozen for up to 1 week.

Yield: 10 to 12 servings

1   cup gingersnap crumbs
    (about 4 ounces)
6   large eggs
1¼ cups sugar
½   cup fresh lime juice
    (about 4 limes)
Grated zest of 2 limes
1   tablespoon grated peeled fresh
    gingerroot (see page 165)
4   tablespoons unsalted butter,
    softened, cut into pieces
Pinch of salt
1½ tablespoons light corn syrup

1. Press the gingerbread crumbs in an even layer into the bottom of an 8-inch springform pan and set aside.

2. Break 3 of the eggs into a stainless-steel mixing bowl. Separate the remaining 3 eggs and add the yolks to the bowl with the whole eggs. Set the whites aside.

3. Add ½ cup of the sugar to the bowl with the whole eggs and yolks. Whisk in the lime juice, zest, and gingerroot. Place the bowl over a pot of gently simmering water and whisk the mixture constantly to avoid scrambling. Continue whisking until the curd thickens enough to hold its shape, about 10 minutes. Remove the bowl from the heat and whisk in the butter and salt. Strain the mixture through a fine sieve and reserve.

4. Place ¼ cup water in a small saucepan. Add the remaining ¾ cup of sugar and the corn syrup and bring to a boil. Cook without stirring until the sugar dissolves. Continue to cook the mixture until it reaches 248°F. (firm ball stage) on a candy thermometer. This will take about 10 minutes.

5. When the sugar reaches 230°F, begin to beat the egg whites in an electric mixer until they hold soft peaks. With the mixer on low speed, drizzle the hot syrup into the whites in a slow and steady stream, taking care not to let any of the syrup fall directly onto the beaters. Once the syrup is fully incorporated, increase the speed and whip until the mixture is cool, about 7 minutes.

6. Whisk about a quarter of the egg whites into the lime-ginger curd mixture to lighten it, then fold the remaining whites into the curd in two additions.

7. Spoon the lime mixture into the prepared crust and smooth the top. Wrap the pan in plastic, then freeze for at least 8 hours and up to 1 week.

8. To serve, unmold the parfait by wiping the sides of the pan with a hot, wet cloth. Dip a small knife in hot water and run it around the inside of the pan to loosen the parfait. Release the sides of the pan and either serve immediately or refreeze.

SERVING SUGGESTIONS
- Serve with fresh raspberries or strawberries.
- For something more complex, add Lemon-Ginger Sauce (page 262).

SEMOLINA PUDDING WITH MINTED CITRUS SALAD

This fragrant pudding takes its inspiration from the spiced, minted flavors of the Middle East. In it, a thick semolina cream is infused with orange zest, cinnamon, and cardamom and enriched with egg yolks. The whites are beaten separately, then folded in just before baking. The result is a light and fluffy pudding that's neither syrupy nor heavy—as many Middle Eastern desserts tend to be. Although you could serve the pudding on its own, I find it's at its brightest when accompanied by a cool, minty citrus salad. It makes a complex last course that showcases many diverse citrus flavors.

Yield: 7 servings

SEMOLINA PUDDING

½   cup (1 stick) unsalted butter, plus extra for the ramekins
4   cups milk
1   cup sugar
3   cardamom pods, cracked
1   cinnamon stick
1   star anise
½   vanilla bean, split lengthwise, pulp scraped (see page 180)
¾   cup semolina (Cream of Wheat)
2   teaspoons grated orange zest
5   large eggs, separated
2   large egg whites

CITRUS SALAD

½   cup sugar
½   cup loosely packed fresh mint sprigs, plus 1 tablespoon chopped fresh mint
6   blood oranges
2   navel oranges
2   clementines

1. Preheat the oven to 350°F. and generously butter seven 4-ounce glass or ceramic ramekins.

2. To prepare the pudding, in a medium saucepan, combine the milk, sugar, cardamom, cinnamon, star anise, and vanilla pod and pulp. Heat the mixture slowly over medium heat, stirring to dissolve the sugar. When the milk is hot but not boiling, gradually pour in the semolina, stirring continuously. Cook the cereal, continuing to stir, until it has thickened, about 10 minutes. Turn off the heat, spoon out the vanilla pod and spices, and stir in the butter and orange zest.

3. In a small bowl, beat the yolks with a little of the warm semolina to temper them. Then stir them into the pot of cooked semolina.

4. In the bowl of an electric mixer, beat the egg whites until they hold stiff peaks. Fold a third of the whites into the semolina to lighten it, then gently fold in the rest in two additions.

5. Pour the mixture into the ramekins and place them in the center of a larger baking pan. Pour enough very hot water into the baking pan to reach two thirds of the way up the sides of the ramekins. Cover the baking pan with foil and pierce all over with a knife. Bake for 20 minutes, then lift up a corner of the foil to let the steam escape. Re-cover the pan and bake for an additional 25 to 30 minutes, until the centers are firm. Transfer the puddings to a wire rack to cool slightly. (The puddings may be made up to 3 days ahead and refrigerated.)

6. To prepare the citrus salad, in a small saucepan, bring ¼ cup water to a boil. Add the sugar and the ½ cup of mint sprigs and reduce the heat to a simmer, stirring until the sugar dissolves. Continue to simmer the syrup gently until it thickens, about 7 minutes longer. Let the syrup cool completely, then strain it into a large, clean bowl, discarding the solids. (The syrup may be made up to 3 days in advance; store it in the refrigerator in a covered container.)

7. Peel the citrus fruits, removing the white membranes around the segments. (See page 76 for tips.) Add the citrus segments to the mint syrup and toss to combine.

8. When the puddings are cool enough to handle, run a small knife around the sides of the ramekins and invert onto a plate. (Or let the pud- dings cool, then reheat for about 5 minutes in a 300°F. oven before unmolding.) Serve the puddings with some of the citrus salad on the side, garnished with the chopped mint.

SERVING SUGGESTIONS
· Serve with mint syrup (see page 262) and/or Candied Kumquats (page 261).

· For something more complex, add Blood-Orange Sorbet (page 93).
· For a composed dessert, add Orange-Cornmeal Shortbread (page 88).

PROSECCO SABAYON WITH CLEMENTINES AND BLOOD ORANGES

Prosecco is a sparkling wine from Italy with a refreshing grapefruitlike flavor that makes it a natural with citrus fruits. Here, the wine, egg yolks, and sugar are whipped into an elegant sabayon, which makes a cloudlike and luxurious alternative to custard sauce.

The sabayon can be made right before your dinner party, and it will hold in the fridge for a few hours. It takes just a few minutes to make, but you must watch it carefully; if it starts to get the least bit curdled, pull the bowl away from the heat. Do not stop whisking for even a moment or the eggs will scramble.

Yield: 6 servings

6   clementines
3   blood oranges
4   large egg yolks
¼   cup sugar
⅓   cup Prosecco or other sparkling
       wine
¼   cup heavy cream, whipped to
       soft peaks

1. Peel the clementines and oranges, removing the white membranes around the segments. (See page 76 for tips.)

2. In the top of a double boiler, or in a large metal bowl, whisk together the egg yolks and sugar. Add the Prosecco and whisk well.

3. Set the double boiler top or bowl over simmering water and whisk constantly until the mixture is very thick and glossy, about 4 minutes. It should hold its shape when spooned onto a plate. Transfer the mixture to a clean bowl set in a larger bowl of water and ice and whisk until the mixture feels cold. Fold in the whipped heavy cream.

4. To serve, arrange the fruit in 6 bowls. Spoon the sabayon on top and serve immediately. Or cover and chill the sabayon for up to 4 hours before serving.

SERVING SUGGESTION
· Serve with Citrus Lace Tuiles (page 90) or Earl Grey Chocolate Truffles (page 230).

LEMON MACAROONS

Light, crisp, and slightly chewy in the center, these delectable little macaroons have a potent lemon flavor that belies their delicacy. Although these are terrific served as is, I also like to make sandwiches out of them, with Lemon Curd (page 263), raspberry jam, or buttercream in the center. These freeze well (unfilled) and will defrost in minutes, so if you have any leftovers, save them for a last-minute treat.

Yield: 10 dozen macaroons

2¼ cups confectioners' sugar
2 cups almond flour
2 tablespoons granulated sugar
¼ vanilla bean, split lengthwise, pulp scraped (see page 180)
5 large egg whites
Grated zest of 1 lemon

1. Preheat the oven to 200°F. In a medium bowl, combine the confectioners' sugar and almond flour. Place the granulated sugar in a small bowl, add the vanilla pulp, and rub the sugar and vanilla together with your fingers until the vanilla is fully incorporated into the sugar.

2. In the bowl of an electric mixer, beat the egg whites until they hold soft peaks. Slowly add the vanilla sugar and beat until stiff peaks form.

3. Sift a third of the almond flour mixture into the egg whites and fold gently to combine. Add the zest and sift in the remaining almond flour in two batches, folding gently to incorporate. Be careful not to overfold this mixture.

4. Spoon the mixture into a pastry bag fitted with a plain half-inch tip, or a Ziploc bag with a corner snipped off, and squeeze quarter-size mounds of batter onto nonstick baking sheets or baking sheets lined with nonstick liners.

5. Bake the macaroons for 5 minutes to dry them out, then remove the pans from the oven and raise the temperature to 375°F. Bake the macaroons for an additional 7 to 8 minutes, or until they are light brown. Cool on a rack before serving.

SERVING SUGGESTION
• Serve with Coconut Ice Cream (page 106).

LEMON–POPPY SEED SHORTBREAD

This extra-special shortbread is like a lemon–poppy seed pound cake made delicate, flat, and crisp. Poppy seeds add a great little crunch to the crumbly, buttery texture of shortbread, and their distinct musky, nutty flavor is wonderfully balanced by the brightness of lemon.

Make sure to use fresh poppy seeds. If you're not sure, taste them before adding them to the dough. Since they are high in oil, poppy seeds can turn rancid as quickly as nuts.

Yield: 20 cookies

1 cup (2 sticks) unsalted butter, softened
¾ cup confectioners' sugar
1½ teaspoons fresh lemon juice
1½ teaspoons grated lemon zest
½ teaspoon vanilla extract
2 cups all-purpose flour, sifted
1½ tablespoons poppy seeds
½ teaspoon salt

1. Using an electric mixer, beat the butter and sugar until creamy and smooth, about 2 minutes. Add the lemon juice, zest, and vanilla and beat well.

2. In a bowl, combine the flour, poppy seeds, and salt. Add the dry ingredients to the butter mixture and mix until well combined. Form the dough into a disk, wrap in plastic wrap, and chill for at least 3 hours and up to 3 days or freeze for up to 2 months.

3. Preheat the oven to 300°F. Roll the dough between two sheets of wax paper to a ¼-inch-thick rectangle (about 10 × 12 inches). If the dough seems soft, return it to the refrigerator to chill for an additional 30 minutes. Cut the shortbread into shapes with a 2-inch cookie cutter, or into 3 × 2-inch bars using a knife, and place them 1 inch apart on ungreased baking sheets (do not reroll the scraps). Prick the shortbread with a fork and bake until pale golden all over, 23 to 25 minutes. Cool on a wire rack.

SERVING SUGGESTIONS
- Serve with whipped crème fraîche and Lemon Thyme–Macerated Raspberry Compote (page 19).
- For a composed dessert, add Raspberry Sorbet (page 20).

ORANGE-CORNMEAL SHORTBREAD

These delicious, buttery, nubby shortbread cookies contain coarsely ground cornmeal, which lends them a crisp yet tender texture. The bright flavor of orange tempers the cookie's richness and balances the sweet, fresh flavor of corn. The cornmeal that you might have on hand for muffins is usually finely ground, and in these shortbread cookies it would have a sawdustlike effect on the texture. Look for coarse cornmeal in the Spanish section of supermarkets (Goya is one brand), or substitute the similarly coarse polenta in its place. Be sure to use fresh cornmeal, since it does not keep for a very long time.

Yield: 12 cookies

1   cup (2 sticks) unsalted butter, softened
¾   cup confectioners' sugar
2   teaspoons grated orange zest
1   teaspoon vanilla extract
1¾ cups all-purpose flour
6   tablespoons coarse cornmeal
½   teaspoon salt

1. Preheat the oven to 300°F. Butter two 6-inch cake pans and line them with parchment paper. Using an electric mixer fitted with the paddle attachment, beat the butter and sugar until creamy and smooth, about 2 minutes. Add the orange zest and vanilla and beat well. Beat in the flour, cornmeal, and salt until well combined.

2. Divide the dough in half and press it into the pans in an even layer. With a knife, score the dough in each pan into 6 wedges. Prick the shortbread with a fork and bake until pale golden all over, about 25 minutes. (Alternatively, press the dough into one 10-inch pan that has been buttered and lined with parchment paper. Score the shortbread into 12 wedges, and bake for about 30 minutes.) Let the shortbread cool in the pans for 20 minutes, then cut along the score lines and transfer the wedges to a wire rack to cool completely.

SERVING SUGGESTION

- Serve with Blackberry Compote (page 18) or Spiced Red Wine–Fig Compote (page 52) and Gingersnap Ice Cream (page 176).

CARAMEL BLOOD ORANGES

Cooking fruit brings out its flavor and juices, taking it from produce to dessert. Here, simply warming a combination of sweet and blood-orange sections in freshly made caramel turns them into an impressive dish. The juice from the oranges releases into the caramel, tempering its sweetness and creating a thick, rich sauce with a citrus tang. As a variation, you can also use a combination of oranges, blood oranges, and clementines.

Yield: 6 servings

8   small oranges, preferably a
    mixture of sweet and blood
    oranges
1   cup sugar
1   teaspoon light corn syrup
Pinch of salt

1. Peel the oranges, removing the white membranes around the segments. (See page 76 for tips.)

2. Place ½ cup water in a small, heavy saucepan. Add the sugar and corn syrup and cook over medium heat until the sugar dissolves. Raise the heat to high and cook the caramel, swirling the pan occasionally, until it turns deep amber brown, about 7 minutes. Immediately turn off the heat.

3. Very carefully add ¼ cup water to the pan (stand back, the caramel may splatter or bubble over). Set the saucepan over low heat and cook, stirring, until the caramel dissolves and is smooth, about 5 minutes. Turn off the heat. Add the orange segments and salt to the pan and gently stir to combine.

SERVING SUGGESTIONS
· Serve with Orange-Cornmeal Shortbread (page 88) or Citrus Lace Tuiles (page 90).
· For something more complex, add Brandied-Fig Ice Cream (page 53) or Earl Grey Ice Cream (page 195).

CITRUS LACE TUILES

It is surprising how much citrus flavor you'll discover when you bite into one of these crisp, lacy cookies. They have a distinct taste of orange, lemon, and caramelized sugar, and their delicate, brittle texture makes them a peerless garnish for creamy or frozen desserts. They will also shine on a cookie plate, served simply with coffee or tea.

Yield: 2½ to 3 dozen cookies

1⅔ cups sugar

1 cup all-purpose flour

¾ cup fresh orange juice

2 tablespoons fresh lemon juice

14 tablespoons (1¾ sticks) unsalted butter, melted and cooled to room temperature

¾ teaspoon grated lemon zest

¾ teaspoon grated orange zest

1. Using an electric mixer fitted with the whisk attachment, mix together the sugar and flour. With the mixer on low speed, drizzle in the orange juice and lemon juice and mix until smooth. Drizzle in the melted butter and add the zests. Increase the speed to medium and mix until the batter is completely smooth. Refrigerate for at least 2 hours.

2. Preheat the oven to 350°F. Use nonstick baking sheets, or line regular baking sheets with nonstick liners or parchment paper. For each tuile, drop a heaping teaspoon of batter onto the baking sheet, leaving 3 inches in between. Using a small offset spatula or the back of a spoon dipped in cold milk or water to prevent sticking, gently pat each mound of batter into a very thin, very even 4-inch round. Bake the tuiles until they are golden brown all over, 9 to 11 minutes.

3. Transfer the tuiles to a wire rack to cool for 1 minute. Using a plastic dough scraper or a spatula, carefully remove them from the pans and loosely drape the tuiles over a rolling pin until cool.

4. Cool the baking sheets between batches and then continue making tuiles until all the batter is used up.

SERVING SUGGESTION
- Serve with Ginger-Port Poached Pears with Granité and Candied Ginger (page 72), Semolina Pudding with Minted Citrus Salad (page 82), or Concord Grape Parfaits (page 49).

PINK GRAPEFRUIT–ROSEMARY SORBET

Orange and rosemary are a classic Italian combination, and here, I have extended this pairing to grapefruits. In my mind, it makes sense for the same reasons that the herbal bitterness of Campari goes so well with grapefruit juice. Rosemary is very strong and piney, while grapefruits are refreshing, light, and subtle. The result is an incredibly elegant pale pink dessert with clean, crisp flavors. It's an ideal refresher in the winter, perfect after a rich dinner, and it can also be served between courses as a palate cleanser.

Yield: About 1½ pints

1   cup Simple Syrup (page 261)
2   sprigs of fresh rosemary
2   cups strained pink grapefruit
    juice (from 3 to 4 grapefruits)

1. In a small saucepan, bring the Simple Syrup and rosemary to a simmer. Cook for 30 seconds, then strain the syrup into a medium bowl.

2. Stir the grapefruit juice into the rosemary syrup. Chill the mixture until it's very cold, about 3 hours. Freeze in an ice-cream machine according to the manufacturer's directions.

SERVING SUGGESTION
· Serve with grapefruit sections drizzled with honey and Cornmeal-Nut Biscotti (page 140).

BLOOD-ORANGE SORBET

When making this sorbet, keep in mind that you never know how sweet the oranges are going to be until you taste them. In general, Italian varieties are more tart, while Californian blood oranges can be as sweet as regular oranges. Taste the juice and simple syrup mixture while you're adding the lemon juice and stop when it tastes right to you.

Yield: About 1¼ pints

1½ cups strained blood-orange juice
    (from about 6 blood oranges)
¾ cup Simple Syrup (page 261)
1 to 2 tablespoons fresh lemon juice,
    strained (or to taste)

1. In a bowl, stir together the blood-orange juice and Simple Syrup. Add lemon juice to taste. Chill the mixture until it's very cold, about 3 hours.

2. Freeze in an ice-cream machine according to the manufacturer's directions.

VARIATION
To make orange sorbet, substitute an equal amount of freshly squeezed regular orange juice for the blood-orange juice.

SERVING SUGGESTIONS
- Serve with candied pistachios (see page 261) and/or Candied Kumquats (page 261).
- For something more complex, add Caramel Blood Oranges (page 89).
- For a composed dessert, add Frozen Orange-Blossom Honey Mousse (page 156) and Citrus Lace Tuiles (page 90), Espresso Shortbread (page 192), or Chestnut-Honey Madeleines (page 184).

TROPICAL FRUITS

In the depths of winter, the weather is warm and lush in tropical places. So this is when I use tropical fruits, rather than limiting myself to local fresh fruits, of which there are very few during the coldest months. I do make a point, however, of using fruits indigenous to the places where they are grown, so I will use bananas from Hawaii, but I won't use raspberries from Chile.

Using tropical fruits in the winter seems natural because their flavors work so well with cold-weather meals. Intense, sweet, and a little spicy, tropical fruits are warming and lush, yet refreshing and clean-tasting after a heavy meal. These fruits combine well with winter flavors like nuts and spices, and I play on this affinity in recipes like Banana-Pecan Strudels and Roasted Pineapple with Pink Peppercorns.

Perhaps because they are grown in consistent climates, I find that tropical fruits are reliably in good condition—it's hard to find a bad banana—so choosing them is a simple matter of recognizing their point of ripeness. For me, it's when they really smell like what they are. Bananas should be speckled brown, with no green anywhere. Passion fruits should feel heavy and be a little wrinkly, rather than shiny and hard like an eight ball. There are many tricks to deciding whether a pineapple is ripe. Some people swear by the ability to easily pull out the green waxy leaves on top of the fruit, while others go by the golden color of the skin. But as with other fruits, I rely on the scent. I determine ripeness by looking for fragrant pineapples that are heavy and yield slightly to the touch. Color is not always a clear indicator of ripeness, but in the case of mangos and papayas, avoid fruit that has brown spots. A ripe mango should be soft all over, and the smaller papaya should be soft and yellow. Tropical fruits do not store well, so they should be used soon after purchase.

WINE NOTES: TROPICAL FRUITS

These exotic desserts have a complex range of strong flavors and textures, so I would serve them with an ice wine (*Eiswein*) from Canada or Germany. They can be made with either Riesling or Vidal grapes that are pressed while frozen.

For the inherent freshness and delicacy of some tropical fruit sorbets, a fruit-based beer is a playful and well-matched partner. Choose a Belgian lambic infused with a mash of cherries or peaches, or pair the Banana Sorbet with an unfla- vored lambic, which has a twist of banana notes on its own. Tropical fruit ice creams allow for something not so light on its feet, such as an aged rum from the Caribbean Islands brimming with molasses and spice tones. Other than visiting, there is no better way to get into a tropical frame of mind than to close one's eyes and inhale the transporting nuances that this spirit can possess.

TAMARIND-GLAZED MANGO NAPOLEONS

Plump and luscious, mangos have a sweet, floral taste that I often turn to in winter. In this recipe, I glaze half the mango with tart tamarind and lime, then roast half of it until the pieces turn translucent and absorb the flavor. The fresh mango, in turn, gets tossed with a hint of basil and mint, two bright, sweet herbs that balance the lushness of the fruit. Just before serving, both mango mixtures are spooned between crisp phyllo pastry layers. It makes a juicy, tropical-toned napoleon that really shows off mangos to their best advantage.

Yield: 6 servings

4	tablespoons unsalted butter
2	tablespoons confectioners' sugar
5	sheets phyllo dough, thawed
5	tablespoons firmly packed dark brown sugar
2	tablespoons fresh lime juice
½	tablespoon tamarind concentrate (see page 269)
2	large ripe but firm mangos (about 2 pounds), peeled
2	fresh basil leaves, julienned
2	fresh mint leaves, julienned

1. Preheat the oven to 400°F. Melt 2 tablespoons of the butter in a small saucepan. Dice the remaining 2 tablespoons of butter and set aside.

2. Cut two pieces of parchment paper to fit an 11 × 17-inch baking sheet. Place one piece of parchment on a work surface and brush the top lightly with some of the melted butter, then sprinkle with 1 tablespoon of the confectioners' sugar. Butter one side of the other piece of parchment paper and set aside. Cover the buttered and sugared parchment with a sheet of phyllo dough and butter lightly. Repeat the process until all 5 phyllo sheets are stacked and buttered. Sprinkle the remaining tablespoon of confectioners' sugar over the top sheet of phyllo. Using a small, sharp knife, trim the edges of the phyllo to the same size as the parchment paper, then cut out twenty-one 3½ × 2-inch rectangles. Transfer to the baking sheet and cover with the remaining sheet of buttered parchment (buttered side down). Bake the phyllo stacks for 10 to 12 minutes, until golden brown. Transfer to a wire rack and let cool. (The phyllo layers can be prepared up to 3 days ahead; store airtight at room temperature.)

3. Preheat the oven to 425°F. To prepare the tamarind glaze, in a small saucepan over medium heat, combine the brown sugar, lime juice, and tamarind concentrate and stir until the sugar is dissolved and the syrup is smooth, about 3 minutes.

4. With a sharp knife, slice down the length of each mango on either side of the pit, which is approximately ½ inch thick. You will be left with four mango halves. Cut away any remaining flesh from the pit and cut it into ½-inch cubes or slices. Place two mango halves on a cutting board, flesh side up. Working with one half at a time, score the half into ½-inch slices, being careful not to cut through the skin on the underside. To remove the skin, run a sharp paring knife as close as possible to the skin, from one end of the half to the other, cutting away from yourself. The skin should fall away and fruit should remain intact. Repeat with the second half. Discard the skin and set the slices aside. Place the two remaining mango halves on a cutting board, flesh side up. Working with one half at a time, score the half into ½-inch cubes, being careful not to cut through the skin on the underside. Remove the skin as directed above. Set the cubes aside. Arrange the mango slices in one layer in the bottom of a baking pan and drizzle with 2 tablespoons of the tamarind glaze. Dot with the diced butter. Bake until the sliced mango is tender and translucent, about 20 minutes.

5. To assemble, place one phyllo rectangle on a plate and top with some

of the roasted mango. Top with a second phyllo rectangle and some of the diced mango. Top with a third phyllo rectangle. Repeat the process to make additional napoleons.

SERVING SUGGESTIONS
- Serve with a drizzle of basil syrup (see page 262).
- For something more complex, add scoops of Yogurt Sorbet (page 213).
- For a composed dessert, add scoops of Basil Ice Cream (page 158).

MAPLE-GLAZED BANANAS WITH WAFFLES

We Americans eat some unusually dessertlike breakfasts. For example, while we have waffles in the morning, smothered in maple syrup, in Europe they are considered dessert fare and are topped with strawberries and whipped cream. This recipe unites both traditions. I serve the waffles for dessert, but I combine them with the very American tastes of maple syrup and bananas. Few things taste better, no matter when you serve them.

The texture of this dessert will depend upon your waffle iron. I have one with very deep Belgian-waffle-like indentations, which yields light, crunchy waffles. If you are using a waffle iron with shallow indentations, be sure to cook the waffles until they are dark to get a deep, crisp crust that contrasts with the soft bananas. This waffle batter depends on yeast for its lightness, and it spends 8 hours in the refrigerator while the flavor slowly develops. It gives the waffles a depth and complexity that would be missing if you let it rise quickly at room temperature. So make the batter in the morning, giving it a chance to reach its most delicious potential just in time for dessert.

Yield: 10 to 12 servings

WAFFLES
4 tablespoons unsalted butter, plus additional for the waffle iron if necessary
2 cups milk
½ teaspoon active dry yeast
½ cup warm water
2 cups all-purpose flour
1 teaspoon sugar
½ teaspoon salt
2 large eggs
¼ teaspoon baking soda

MAPLE-GLAZED BANANAS
¾ cup maple syrup
6 firm bananas, peeled
2 tablespoons unsalted butter

1. In a small saucepan, melt the butter, then stir in the milk and turn off the heat. In a small bowl, dissolve the yeast in the warm water.

2. In a large bowl, combine the flour, sugar, and salt. Pour in the milk mixture and the dissolved yeast and mix well. Cover and refrigerate for 8 hours. Just before making the waffles, whisk in the eggs and baking soda until well combined.

3. Heat a waffle iron and brush with melted butter if it's not nonstick. Add ½ cup of batter at a time, brushing with more melted butter if the waffles begin to stick. Prepare the bananas while the waffles are cooking.

4. To prepare the bananas, in a large skillet or saucepan, bring the maple syrup to a simmer over medium-high heat. Allow to reduce by half, 3 to 5 minutes. Meanwhile, slice the bananas on the diagonal into ¾-inch slices.

5. Once the maple syrup is reduced, add the butter and stir until melted. Add the bananas and cook for 1 to 2 minutes to warm them through. Spoon the bananas over the waffles and serve immediately.

SERVING SUGGESTIONS
· Serve with candied pecans (see page 261).
· For a composed dessert, add Buttermilk Ice Cream (page 211) and/or Banana Sorbet (page 110).

BANANA-PECAN STRUDELS

Although they're not at all traditional, bananas are a perfect fruit to make into strudel since they aren't juicy and therefore won't make the crisp strudel pastry soggy. Adding toasted pecans lends both a crunchy element and a warm, nutty flavor.

This recipe makes individual strudels, each its own slim package. They can be served hot from the oven, or you can bake the strudels earlier in the day, then reheat them for a few minutes just before serving. They can even be assembled and frozen up to 2 weeks in advance, then baked straight from the freezer, with a few minutes added to the baking time.

Use a firm banana that is just beginning to speckle.

Yield: 4 servings

- 2   sheets phyllo dough, thawed
- 2   tablespoons unsalted butter, melted
- 4   tablespoons confectioners' sugar
- 4   tablespoons chopped toasted pecans
- 1   medium-ripe banana, sliced lengthwise in quarters
- 1   tablespoon honey

1. Preheat the oven to 400°F. Brush 1 phyllo sheet with some of the melted butter. Sift 2 tablespoons of the confectioners' sugar evenly on top. Sprinkle evenly with 2 tablespoons of the nuts. Cut the phyllo sheet in half lengthwise. Place one quarter of the banana along a short edge of each phyllo half. Starting with the short end, tightly roll up the banana in the phyllo. When you get almost to the end, dab a little bit of honey along the edge to help seal the package. Repeat with the remaining ingredients.

2. Just before baking, brush the tops of the strudels with more of the melted butter and place them seam-side down on a baking sheet (preferably lined with parchment paper or a nonstick liner). Bake until the strudels are golden brown, 13 to 15 minutes. Serve immediately.

SERVING SUGGESTION
- Serve with whipped crème fraîche, Caramel Ice Cream (page 193), or Maple Flan made without the walnut crust (page 189).

ROASTED DATES WITH SHERRY AND SPICES

In the depths of winter, when there are few fresh fruits around, dried fruits become of great importance in the pastry chef's pantry. Since dates tend to be more plump and moist than other dried fruits, I roast them with sherry, spices, and butter until they seem like a juicy fresh fruit that's been cooked, instead of a dried fruit. Dates have a wonderfully rich flavor that works extremely well with sherry—after all, sherry is a classic after-dinner accompaniment to dried fruit and nuts. Since dates are native to the Middle East, I spice them accordingly, with cinnamon, cardamom, and orange peel. The warmth of the sherry and spices makes this a delicious winter fruit dessert that goes wonderfully with citrus fruits.

The success of this dessert is dependent on using good, fat dates. Look for those that are smooth, glossy, and not too shriveled. The best dates usually need to be pitted by hand, but it takes only a few minutes and the results are worth it.

Yield: 6 servings

24 dates, pitted
1   cup dry or off-dry sherry (such as Fino or Amontillado)
¼   cup firmly packed dark brown sugar
4   cardamom pods, crushed
1   cinnamon stick
1   strip orange peel (about 1 inch × 3 inches)
4   tablespoons unsalted butter, cut into small pieces

1. Preheat the oven to 350°F. In a medium saucepan, combine the dates, sherry, brown sugar, cardamom, cinnamon, and orange peel with 1 cup of water. Bring the mixture to a simmer, then pour it into a shallow baking dish (reserve the saucepan). Bake the dates for 15 minutes, basting with the syrup every 5 minutes.

2. Remove the dates from the syrup. When the dates are cool enough to handle, slip them from their skins. Discard the skins and set the dates aside.

3. Strain the syrup back into the saucepan; discard the solids. Bring the syrup to a simmer. Let the syrup simmer until it is reduced by a third, about 7 minutes, then whisk the butter in bit by bit.

4. To serve, arrange 4 dates on each plate. Spoon some sauce over the tops and serve immediately.

SERVING SUGGESTIONS
• Serve with Cornmeal-Nut Biscotti (page 140).
• For something more complex, add Coconut Sorbet (page 107) or Frozen Orange-Blossom Honey Mousse (page 156).

ROASTED PINEAPPLE WITH PINK PEPPERCORNS

Pineapple is probably my favorite tropical fruit. Served fresh, it's cool and juicy. But when caramelized and roasted with vanilla and rum, it turns succulent, taking on buttery, toasty, candied characteristics that make this dish seem almost like a crustless tarte Tatin. Pink peppercorns lend intrigue, with a spicy, slightly floral scent. Make sure to use a fragrant ripe pineapple for this recipe.

Yield: 4 servings

1   cup sugar
1   teaspoon light corn syrup
1   pineapple, peeled, cored, and cut
    into 8 rings
1   vanilla bean, split lengthwise,
    pulp scraped (see page 180)
1   bay leaf
4   tablespoons unsalted butter
2   tablespoons dark rum (preferably
    Myers's)
1   tablespoon pink peppercorns
Pinch of salt

1. Preheat the oven to 375°F. Place ¼ cup water in a 10-inch ovenproof skillet over low heat. Add the sugar and corn syrup and increase the heat to high. Cook, swirling the pan occasionally, until the mixture is a deep amber-brown caramel, about 7 minutes. Add the pineapple, vanilla pod and pulp, and bay leaf, then bake, basting every 10 minutes, until the pineapple is tender and translucent, about 40 minutes.

2. Using a slotted spoon, transfer the pineapple to a serving platter and either place in a low oven or tent with foil to keep warm. (Alternatively, let the pineapple cool in the pan, then reheat for a few minutes before making the sauce.)

3. To prepare the sauce, whisk the butter, rum, pink peppercorns, and salt into the hot pan juices until smooth. Serve the sauce spooned over the roasted pineapple.

SERVING SUGGESTIONS
· Serve with Passion Fruit–Pineapple Sorbet (page 111).
· For something more complex, add fresh pineapple slices and Black Pepper Ice Cream (page 179).
· For a composed dessert, add macadamia-nut brittle (see Variation, page 142).

PAPAYA-LIME SOUP WITH STRAWBERRIES

Papaya is at its best uncooked, so it typically makes its way into recipes like fruit salad and sorbet. But this soup is a more elegant venue for the sweet, earthy fruit, and it's especially perfect for papayas too ripe for salad. I find the sweetness of papaya somewhat flat, so I add a little lime juice to round out and spark the flavor. The result is a refreshing, velvety, vivid orange soup that is entirely welcome after a rich meal. Serve it as is, or have fun dressing it up with other fruit like cubed melon, or with scoops of sorbet or ice cream.

Yield: 6 servings

2 large papayas, peeled, seeded, and cubed

¾ cups Simple Syrup (page 261)

¼ cup fresh lime juice, or to taste (from 2 to 3 limes)

1 pint strawberries, hulled and sliced in quarters

1. Purée the papaya in a food processor or blender. Put it in a bowl and stir in 1½ cups water, the Simple Syrup, and the lime juice, adding more lime juice to taste if necessary. Chill the mixture until very cold, at least 2 hours.

2. Serve the soup garnished with the strawberries.

SERVING SUGGESTIONS
• Serve with Strawberry Sorbet (page 21) and/or Coconut Sorbet (page 107).
• For something more complex, add Candied Coconut (page 266).
• For a composed dessert, add Crème Fraîche Panna Cotta (page 206).

COCONUT TUILES

I owe thanks to Nancy Silverton of the LaBrea Bakery in Los Angeles for providing the inspiration behind these thin, brittle wafers. Made from a sugary egg-white batter, these tuiles are caramelized and almost candylike. They can be spread out on baking sheets free-form or spooned into stencils to make perfect rectangles, squares, or stars. Either way, these crisp cookies make such a superb accompaniment to custards, dessert soups, sorbets, and ice creams that they have become an indispensable part of my repertoire.

Yield: 3½ dozen cookies

1¼ cups sugar

2½ tablespoons unsalted butter, at room temperature

7 large egg whites, at room temperature

2 cups shredded unsweetened coconut

¼ cup all-purpose flour

1. In the bowl of an electric mixer set on medium speed, beat the sugar and butter until the mixture resembles wet sand, about 2 minutes. Gradually add the egg whites and continue to beat until well mixed, scraping down the sides of the bowl and the beaters with a spatula as necessary.

2. In a small bowl, stir together the coconut and flour. Add to the egg white mixture and mix well. Transfer the mixture to a bowl, cover, and chill for at least 8 hours or overnight.

3. Preheat the oven to 325°F. Use nonstick baking sheets or line regular baking sheets with nonstick liners or parchment paper. For each tuile, drop a heaping teaspoon of batter onto the baking sheet, leaving 3 inches in between. Using a small offset spatula or the back of a spoon dipped in cold milk or water to prevent sticking, gently pat each mound of batter into a very thin, even 4-inch round. Alternatively, spoon the tuile batter into stencils and smooth the top. Bake the tuiles until they are golden brown all over, about 15 minutes. To achieve a uniform color, move the baking sheets around in the oven after 8 minutes.

4. As soon as the tuiles are finished baking, using a plastic dough scraper or a spatula, remove them from the pans and place on a wire rack to cool. If they stick to the pans, they may

have cooled too much; return them to the oven for 1 minute to loosen.

5. Cool the baking sheets between batches and continue making tuiles until all the batter is used up.

SERVING SUGGESTION

- Serve with fruit such as Caramel Blood Oranges (page 89), Roasted Dates with Sherry and Spices (page 101), Roasted Pineapple with Pink Peppercorns (page 103), or a berry compote (see pages 18 and 19).

Note: Stencils are available in kitchen specialty shops. Or you can make your own stencils by tracing shapes onto the lids of plastic containers. Use a matte knife (or any sharp knife) to cut out the shape.

COCONUT ICE CREAM

Coconut ranks among my favorite ice-cream flavors. But this recipe is a little bit different than most. Rather than being made into a custard, the egg yolks here are beaten until fluffy, then folded into a fragrant coconut cream. It makes a decidedly light and creamy ice cream, with a soft texture that's as smooth as whipped cream, but with the added indulgence of coconut.

Yield: 1½ pints

2   cups milk
2   cups heavy cream
1½ cups shredded unsweetened
    coconut
¾ cup plus 2 tablespoons sugar
8   large egg yolks
1   teaspoon vanilla extract
Pinch of salt

1. In a saucepan, bring the milk, cream, coconut, and ½ cup of the sugar to a simmer over medium heat, stirring occasionally. Turn off the heat and let the mixture cool at room temperature for at least 3 hours.

2. Strain the mixture into a bowl and discard the coconut.

3. Using an electric mixer, whip the egg yolks with the remaining 6 tablespoons of sugar until the mixture is thick and holds a ribbon when the beaters are lifted, about 3 minutes. Add the coconut-cream mixture, vanilla, and salt and mix well. Chill until the mixture is thoroughly cold, at least 3 hours, or overnight.

4. Strain again and freeze in an ice-cream maker according to the manufacturer's instructions.

SERVING SUGGESTIONS
· Serve with Coconut Tuiles (page 105).
· For something more complex, add Passion Fruit–Pineapple Sorbet (page 111).
· For a composed dessert, add Passion Fruit Caramel (page 263), macadamia-nut brittle (see Variation, page 142), and/or Candied Coconut (page 266).

COCONUT SORBET

For this recipe, I infuse shredded unsweetened coconut in regular whole milk. I find this has more intensity than canned coconut milk. As an added bonus, the whole milk makes for a particularly creamy sorbet. I also add a few drops of fresh lime juice to the mix. It's not a strongly pronounced flavor, but that little touch of acid really helps counterbalance the richness of the coconut.

Yield: 1 pint

2　cups whole milk
1　cup shredded unsweetened
　　coconut
¾　cup sugar
½　teaspoon fresh lime juice

1. In a medium saucepan, combine the milk, coconut, and sugar. Bring the mixture to a simmer over medium heat, stirring occasionally. Simmer the mixture until the sugar dissolves, about 2 minutes. Turn off the heat and let the mixture cool for 1 hour.

2. Strain the mixture into a bowl and discard the coconut. Stir in the lime juice, cover, and chill until thoroughly cold, at least 3 hours, or overnight. Strain again and freeze in an ice-cream maker according to the manufacturer's instructions.

SERVING SUGGESTIONS
- Serve with Tarragon-Macerated Strawberries (page 12) or Blackberry Compote (page 18).
- For something more complex, add Gingersnaps (page 176) or Lemon–Poppy Seed Shortbread (page 86).

COCONUT TAPIOCA SOUP

At Gramercy Tavern, the servers get two reactions when they mention this tapioca dessert. Customers either say, "Tapioca? Yuck, my mother made tapioca!" Or they say, "Tapioca? Yum, my mother made tapioca!" But whichever way they go, the servers always assure them this is *not* their mom's tapioca. Instead of using granulated minute tapioca and making a pudding with eggs, I use a combination of large and small pearl tapioca and simmer them with coconut milk and regular milk. The liquid cooks down to a luscious, creamy sauce, and the pearls transform from something simple and homey to an elegant dessert that looks like a plate of translucent, nearly opalescent bubbles.

While this coconut tapioca is delicious and satisfying on its own, I like to serve it with several Thai-inspired garnishes. Passion fruit–pineapple sorbet, passion fruit caramel, cilantro syrup, crisp coconut tuiles, and coconut sorbet combine with the pearls to create a textural bonanza in your mouth. One taste and you'll see why many people call this "dessert caviar," and why I consider it one of my signature desserts.

Yield: 6 servings

5   cups whole milk
½   cup sugar
¼   cup small pearl tapioca
    (not instant tapioca)
¼   cup large pearl tapioca
1   can (13.5 ounces) coconut milk
    (not cream of coconut)

1. Place 2½ cups of the milk and ¼ cup of the sugar in a saucepan. Place the remaining 2½ cups milk and ¼ cup sugar in another saucepan. Bring both mixtures to a simmer over high heat, stirring occasionally to dissolve the sugar. Add the small pearl tapioca to one saucepan and the large pearl tapioca to the other saucepan. Reduce the heat to low and simmer the mixtures, stirring occasionally, until the tapioca pearls are soft. This will take approximately 35 to 45 minutes for the small pearls and 55 to 65 minutes for the large.

2. When both tapioca mixtures are finished cooking, combine them in a large pot. Stir in the coconut milk, bring the mixture to a simmer, and cook for 2 minutes. Let the mixture cool completely, then cover and chill for at least 10 hours, or preferably overnight.

SERVING SUGGESTIONS
· Serve with Tarragon-Macerated Strawberries (page 12).
· For something more complex, add Coconut Tuiles (page 105).
· For a composed dessert, float scoops of Strawberry Sorbet (page 21) on the soup.

BANANA SORBET

This sorbet is so luscious it feels like it must contain cream or eggs. But all it has is banana flavor at its best, rounded out with a little lemon juice and sweetened with a light sugar syrup. Don't use regular simple syrup for this recipe; it's too thick to work well with the dense banana purée. To get the most intense banana taste, make sure to use really ripe, dark, speckled fruit. Unripe bananas not only lend a tannic quality, they also just don't have enough flavor to make this delectable sorbet worthwhile.

Yield: About 1 quart

1½   cups sugar
5   ripe bananas
2   teaspoons fresh lemon juice

1. In a small saucepan, bring 2 cups water and the sugar to a simmer over medium heat. Stir the syrup frequently to dissolve the sugar. Let the mixture simmer slowly for about 4 minutes. Pour the syrup into a bowl and let cool. (The syrup can be made several weeks in advance and stored covered in the refrigerator.)

2. In the bowl of a food processor or blender, purée the bananas. Pass the banana purée through a fine sieve and measure out 2 cups. Refrigerate or freeze the rest of the purée to use for another purpose.

3. Place the banana purée, sugar syrup, and lemon juice in a food processor or blender and purée until very smooth.

4. Cover the mixture and chill until thoroughly cold, at least 3 hours, or overnight. Freeze in an ice-cream maker according to the manufacturer's instructions.

SERVING SUGGESTIONS
• Serve with Pecan Sandies (page 144) or candied pecans (see page 261).
• For something more complex, add Caramel Blood Oranges (page 89).
• For a composed dessert, add Extra-Bittersweet Chocolate Sorbet (page 233) and/or Milk Chocolate Malted Ice Cream (page 232).

PASSION FRUIT—PINEAPPLE SORBET

This is an exceptionally refreshing sorbet. Pineapple softens the puckery tartness of passion fruit and rounds out its flavors without making it overly sweet. You should be able to find unsweetened pure passion fruit juice in health food stores, but you can also juice your own. You'll need a lot of fruit since passion fruits aren't particularly juicy. Cut the fruits open, pull out their pulp, and push it through a strainer. This is labor-intensive, but you will be left with the black seeds, which make a crunchy garnish that is fun to eat.

Yield: 1 quart

1   cup peeled, cubed pineapple
1   cup sugar
1⅓ cups unsweetened passion fruit
     juice or purée

1. Place the pineapple and ¼ cup of the sugar in a food processor or blender and purée until very smooth. Let the mixture rest for 1 hour.

2. Meanwhile, in a small saucepan, combine the remaining ¾ cup of sugar and 1 cup water and bring to a simmer over medium heat. Simmer the mixture, stirring, until the sugar dissolves, about 3 minutes. Remove from the heat and let cool.

3. Strain the pineapple mixture through a medium sieve (not a fine sieve). Measure out ⅔ cup of pineapple purée. Refrigerate or freeze the rest of the purée to use for another purpose.

4. In a large bowl, whisk together the pineapple purée, passion fruit juice, and sugar syrup. Cover and chill until cold, at least 3 hours, or overnight. Freeze in an ice-cream maker according to the manufacturer's instructions.

SERVING SUGGESTIONS
· Serve with Gingersnaps (page 176) or Candied Coconut (page 266).
· For something more complex, add Passion Fruit Caramel (page 263) and/or Vanilla Ice Cream (page 266).

VEGETABLES

The use of fruit is often accepted in savory preparations as a matter of course, especially with meat and duck, and foie gras is frequently served with lightly candied or stewed fruits. But use a vegetable in dessert and people think you're nuts! This is silly in my opinion, since so many vegetables are compatible with desserts. Some have natural sweetness that can be played up, as is the case with pumpkins, squash, tomatoes, and corn. Others have strong flavors that take well to sweetening, as is true for rhubarb and fennel. Sweetened and enhanced, these vegetables form the base for interesting desserts that will get people thinking. The classic carrot cake and zucchini bread are the forerunners in garnering acceptance for this use of vegetables, and in this chapter I present some less obvious but equally successful vegetable desserts.

Although some vegetables are terrific to use on their own, like corn, which I churn into a rich, subtle ice cream, others benefit from being mixed with fruit. In springtime, pairing rhubarb and strawberries is a classic way to celebrate the season. Autumnal winter squash is a natural with the crisp juicy apples that are harvested at the same time (Maple-Glazed Winter Squash and Apple Compote is a perfect example). And tomatoes are brilliant when combined with plums, which possess a similar juicy, fleshy texture.

Use vegetables, as you would fruits, in season, when their flavor is at its best. Frequent your farmer's market to find heirloom tomatoes in the summer and interesting varieties of winter squash that have thick, firm flesh and unparalleled flavor in autumn. Fresh corn sliced off the cob is as sweet as summer gets, and it can be candied for a wonderful, glistening garnish on corn and cornmeal desserts.

Whether you want to take advantage of the season's bounty or to surprise guests who have become jaded by too many fruit tarts and chocolate cookies, these vegetable desserts are unexpected, fun, and impressive.

Vegetable desserts can vary a lot depending upon how the vegetable is cooked, and the wines to serve with them vary accordingly. Rhubarb desserts are ideal partners for a late-harvest Zinfandel. The wine has a spicy portlike quality and a slight vegetal, briary, minty note that complements the tart, juicy rhubarb.

The exotic, orange, buttery, vanilla flavors of Sauternes are wonderful with desserts using corn, cornmeal, or winter squash. The Sauté of Tomatoes and Plums is balanced on its own, since the acid of the tomatoes and plums is offset by a light caramelized note, and an equally well-balanced, off-dry, sparkling red wine from the Piedmont region of Italy, called Brachetto d'Acqui, is a perfect pairing here.

Truffled Rice Pudding requires an earth-driven dessert wine, and a late-harvest Primitivo (the Italian equivalent of Zinfandel), with its portlike yet drier and earthier tones, has enough tannic acid to cut through the richness of the rice pudding. Much like the truffle, the wine begins with a touch of apparent sweetness, then finishes with a drier, more bitter tone.

CORNMEAL POUND CAKE

Simple, traditional, always delicious, pound cake is one of the most versatile desserts. I've added cornmeal to this one, which lends a nice toothsome crunch and toasty corn flavor that I find both contrasts with and enhances the butteriness of the cake.

Yield: 8 to 10 servings

1½ cups plus 2 tablespoons (3 sticks plus 2 tablespoons) unsalted butter, softened
1 cup plus 2 tablespoons sugar
6 large eggs
2 tablespoons milk
1½ teaspoons vanilla extract
2½ cups cake flour
½ cup coarse cornmeal
1¼ teaspoons baking powder
¼ teaspoon salt

1. Preheat the oven to 350°F. Butter and flour a 9 × 5-inch loaf pan. Using an electric mixer fitted with the paddle attachment, cream the butter and sugar until well combined, about 2 minutes.

2. In a bowl, whisk together the eggs, milk, and vanilla. Gradually add the egg mixture to the butter mixture, beating well to combine.

3. In another bowl, sift together the flour, cornmeal, baking powder, and salt. Add half of the dry mixture to the batter and beat to combine. Add the remaining dry mixture and gently fold in with a spatula.

4. Scrape the batter into the prepared pan and smooth the top with a spatula. Place the pan on a baking sheet and bake for 15 minutes. Lower the oven temperature to 325°F. and bake the cake for about 1 hour and 15 minutes longer, until a tester inserted into the middle of the cake comes out clean. If the top of the cake seems to be getting overly browned but the cake is not done, cover with foil and continue baking. Let the cake cool slightly on a rack before inverting.

SERVING SUGGESTIONS
- Serve with Sauté of Tomatoes and Plums (page 121) or Lemon Thyme–Macerated Raspberry Compote (page 19).
- For something more complex, add Sweet-Corn Ice Cream (page 127).
- For a composed dessert, add Candied Corn (page 264).

CORNMEAL CREPES WITH ORANGE-BUTTER SAUCE

In this dish, an American twist on crepes Suzette, thin, lacy crepes take on a pleasing nubbiness from a little bit of cornmeal mixed into the batter. Served with a zesty pan sauce made from orange juice, rum, butter, and nutmeg, it's an excellent combination that's both timeless and fresh. It's also extremely convenient, since you can prepare the crepes one day ahead, then simply reheat them in the sauce.

Yield: 8 servings

1½   cups milk
¾   cup plus 2 tablespoons
     all-purpose flour
½   cup heavy cream
6   tablespoons sugar
3   large eggs
½   vanilla bean, split lengthwise,
     pulp scraped (see page 180)
Pinch of salt
5   tablespoons coarse yellow
     cornmeal
1   cup (2 sticks) unsalted butter,
     plus additional melted butter for
     the pan, if necessary
2   cups freshly squeezed orange
     juice
1⅓ cups sugar
2½ tablespoons dark rum (preferably
     Myers's)
1   tablespoon grated orange zest
1½ teaspoons freshly grated nutmeg

1. In a blender, combine the milk, flour, cream, sugar, eggs, vanilla pulp, and salt. Blend until smooth.

2. Pass the mixture through a fine sieve and stir in the cornmeal. Cover and chill for at least 8 hours (and up to 2 days).

3. Heat a large, heavy, preferably nonstick skillet over medium-high heat. Brush the pan with butter if it's not nonstick. Add about ¼ cup of the crepe batter to the pan and swirl to evenly distribute the batter (it should just coat the bottom of the pan). Pour any excess batter back into the batter bowl. Cook the crepe until the bottom is browned and small bubbles appear on the top, about 45 seconds. Flip and cook until browned on the other side, about 30 seconds. Remove to a plate and repeat with the remaining batter, buttering the pan occasionally if the crepes begin to stick. (The crepes can be prepared 1 day ahead and stored well wrapped in the refrigerator.)

4. To prepare the sauce, combine the orange juice and sugar in a large skillet over medium heat. Simmer, stirring occasionally, until the sugar dissolves, about 2 minutes. Add the butter, rum, orange zest, and nutmeg and bring the mixture to a simmer. Simmer, stirring, until the mixture reduces slightly, 2 to 3 minutes. Reduce the heat to low.

5. Place one of the crepes into the sauce in the pan and let it heat through, about 30 seconds. Using tongs or a fork, fold the crepe into quarters, then transfer it to a serving platter; tent with foil to keep warm. Repeat with the remaining crepes. Serve at once, placing 2 crepes on each plate with some of the sauce.

SERVING SUGGESTIONS
· Serve with whipped crème fraîche and candied walnuts (see page 261) or Citrus Lace Tuiles (page 90).
· For something more complex, add Caramel Blood Oranges (page 89) and/or Blood-Orange Sorbet (page 93).
· For a composed dessert, omit the crème fraîche and add Ginger Ice Cream (page 178).

RHUBARB-ROSE COBBLER WITH ROSE CREAM

This dessert was inspired by a rhubarb-rose jam recipe that I saw in an English cookbook. Since roses and rhubarb are in season at the same time, and since our motto at Gramercy Tavern is "What grows together goes together," I decided to try combining the two in a homey cobbler. It worked like a charm. The acidity of the rhubarb tames the intense floral qualities of the rose water, and together they bake into a rich, jammy filling that peeks out between the tender biscuits on top. Sprinkling turbinado sugar on top of the biscuits gives them a gorgeous glaze and a lovely crunch. The rose-scented cream is purely optional, but I love the way it contrasts with the tart fruit. Although this cobbler is best served within an hour of coming out of the oven, it can be baked ahead and reheated in a 300°F. oven until hot, about 15 minutes.

Yield: 6 servings

COBBLER DOUGH

- 1⅔ cups all-purpose flour
- 3½ tablespoons sugar
- 1½ tablespoons baking powder
- ⅛ teaspoon salt
- 6 tablespoons cold unsalted butter, cut into ½-inch cubes
- ⅔ cup plus 1 tablespoon heavy cream
- 1 teaspoon turbinado (raw) sugar

RHUBARB FILLING

- 2 pounds rhubarb, trimmed and cut into ½-inch pieces (about 6 cups)
- 1 cup sugar
- 2½ tablespoons cornstarch
- ½ teaspoon rose water
- 1-inch piece of vanilla bean, split lengthwise, pulp scraped (see page 180)

ROSE CREAM

- 1 cup crème fraîche
- ¼ cup rose preserves

1. To make the cobbler dough, in the bowl of a food processor or an electric mixer fitted with the paddle attachment, combine the flour, sugar, baking powder, and salt. Pulse or mix to combine. Add the butter and pulse or mix until the flour resembles coarse meal. Add ⅔ cup of the cream and mix or pulse until the dough starts to come together, scraping down the dough paddle and mixing bowl if necessary.

2. Turn the dough onto a lightly floured surface and gently pat it together, incorporating any stray crumbs. Using a small ice-cream scoop or a large spoon, form the dough into eight to ten 2-inch balls, then flatten them slightly into thick rounds. (You will have 8 to 10 rounds.) Chill for 20 minutes (and up to 2 hours). Preheat the oven to 350°F.

3. Meanwhile, make the filling. In a large bowl, toss together the rhubarb, sugar, and cornstarch. In a small bowl, stir together the rose water and vanilla pulp, then toss with the rhubarb. Let the rhubarb macerate for 20 minutes.

4. Put the rhubarb in a shallow 2½-quart casserole dish in an even layer. Arrange the biscuit rounds on top, leaving about 1 inch between them. Brush the biscuits with the remaining tablespoon of cream and sprinkle with the turbinado sugar. Bake the cobbler until the rhubarb is bubbling and the biscuits are golden brown, 40 to 45 minutes.

5. While the cobbler is baking, prepare the rose cream. Beat the crème fraîche with an electric mixer set on medium-high speed until it thickens somewhat. Add the preserves and continue to beat until stiff peaks form. (The cream can be prepared ahead and refrigerated for up to 8 hours.)

6. Serve the cobbler warm, with the rose cream.

SERVING SUGGESTIONS
- Serve with scoops of Strawberry Sorbet (page 21).
- For something more complex, add Goat Yogurt–Rose Mousse (page 207) or Ginger Ice Cream (page 178).

TRUFFLED RICE PUDDING

I would not have tried turning a luxurious savory dish like black truffle risotto into dessert if Gramercy Tavern's chef, Tom Colicchio, had not been doing a truffle-tasting menu at the restaurant, which needed a truffled dessert course. But I'm really glad I did, because truffles were fun to experiment with and the results were extraordinary. This rice pudding has all the appeal of a truffled risotto, with the truffles adding their unique, compelling, earthy quality to the bland rice; but as a pudding it's seductively sweet, creamy, and incredibly special.

Yield: 6 to 8 servings

5   cups whole milk
½   cup plus 2 tablespoons sugar
¼   vanilla bean, split in half
     lengthwise, pulp scraped
     (see page 180)
¾   cup Arborio rice
½ to 1 ounce fresh or jarred black
     winter truffles
1   cup crème fraîche

1. In a large saucepan, bring the milk, sugar, and vanilla pod and pulp to a boil. Add the rice and allow to boil for 1 minute, then reduce to a low simmer. Stir occasionally, just to ensure that the rice is not sticking to the bottom, and cook until the rice is tender, 45 to 50 minutes.

2. Fill a large bowl with ice water. Scrape the pudding into a medium metal bowl and submerge it halfway into the water bath. Stir the pudding gently with a spatula until it cools. Remove the vanilla pod.

3. If using fresh truffles, use a stiff brush to clean all of the dirt and soil from their surface and crevices. If using jarred truffles, rinse them well. Finely chop the truffles.

4. Using a whisk or an electric mixer, whip the crème fraîche until it holds soft peaks. Gently fold it into the rice mixture. Fold in the truffles. Serve immediately, or chill for up to 4 hours.

SERVING SUGGESTION
None; this dessert is best enjoyed on its own.

SAUTÉ OF TOMATOES AND PLUMS

This is another dessert inspired by a tasting menu at the restaurant, this time tomatoes. But unlike the truffles in the previous recipe, tomatoes seemed like a natural ingredient to use in a dessert. They are, after all, botanically a fruit. I decided to combine them with plums for several reasons. The first is that they are both in season at the same time. They also have a similar succulent-firm flesh and tart sweetness. Sautéed in a dark, nutty caramel, their juices thicken into a luscious sauce that contrasts with the tartness of the fruit.

Although you have to serve this dessert straight from the pan, you can make the caramel ahead, then just toss in the fruit a few minutes before serving. Make sure to use sweet, ripe tomatoes, preferably a mix of heirloom varieties for the most gorgeous array of textures and colors.

Yield: 4 to 6 servings

½   pound mixed heirloom tomatoes
1   cup sugar
1   teaspoon light corn syrup
½   pound plums, pitted and sliced

1. Core and slice large tomatoes; halve the small cherry tomatoes. Set aside.

2. Place ¼ cup water in a large skillet. Add the sugar and corn syrup and cook over high heat, swirling the pan occasionally, until the mixture is deep amber brown and caramelized, about 7 minutes. (The caramel can be made up to 4 hours ahead; cover and leave in a warm place until serving, then reheat before adding the fruit.)

3. Add the tomatoes and plums and remove the skillet from the heat. Toss the fruit in the caramel, letting any hard bits of caramel dissolve in the juice of the fruit. Serve immediately.

SERVING SUGGESTIONS
· Serve with cheese, such as fresh goat cheese, wedges of aged cheddar, or fresh ricotta.
· For a composed dessert, serve the sauté with Basil Ice Cream (page 158) and Cornmeal Pound Cake (page 115) or Mixed-Pepper Tuiles (page 174).

PUMPKIN CLAFOUTI

A clafouti is a sweet baked "pancake," made popular in France, that is usually filled with cherries or other seasonal fruits. In most versions, while the clafouti bakes, the batter puffs up around the fruit and browns, becoming slightly crusty on top of the soft custardy center. In this recipe, however, I use puréed pumpkin mixed into the batter instead of adding chunks of fruit at the end. It makes for a particularly creamy, silken clafouti to which I add some chopped hazelnuts for crunch. This dessert could take the place of a pumpkin pie at Thanksgiving; since it's much lighter, your guests will be grateful to see it after the huge turkey dinner. The batter can be mixed ahead and then baked while you eat, or during the football interlude before dessert.

I call for a cheese pumpkin in this recipe. It's a thick, fleshy, rather squat pumpkin with a very dense flesh. If you can't find one, don't substitute regular pumpkin, which is much too watery. Instead, substitute butternut or Hubbard squash. In a pinch, you can also substitute canned unsweetened pumpkin purée instead of making your own.

Yield: 8 servings

- 1 4- to 5-pound cheese pumpkin or butternut or Hubbard squash
- 5 large eggs
- ¾ cup plus 2 tablespoons sugar
- ½ cup milk
- ½ cup heavy cream
- 1 teaspoon vanilla extract
- 1-inch piece of vanilla bean, split lengthwise, pulp scraped (see page 180)
- Pinch of salt
- ¼ cup all-purpose flour
- 1 tablespoon unsalted butter, melted
- ⅓ cup chopped toasted hazelnuts

1. Preheat the oven to 350°F. Cut the pumpkin or squash in half and scrape out the seeds. Place the halves, cut side up, on a baking sheet and bake for 1½ hours.

2. When cool enough to handle, scrape the flesh into a food processor and blend to a smooth purée. Line a sieve with a double layer of cheese-cloth or a clean kitchen towel and place over a bowl. Spoon the purée into the lined sieve and let it drain in the refrigerator overnight. The next day, pass the drained purée through a fine sieve to yield ⅔ cup (use any remaining purée for another purpose).

3. Place the eggs, ¾ cup of the sugar, the milk, cream, vanilla extract, vanilla pulp, and salt in a blender or food processor. Blend or pulse the mixture until very smooth, about 30 seconds. Add the pumpkin purée and blend well. Add the flour and pulse until well combined.

4. Pass the batter through a fine sieve, then let it rest at room temperature for 30 minutes.

5. Preheat the oven to 425°F. Brush a 9-inch quiche or pie plate with the melted butter and sprinkle with the remaining 2 tablespoons of sugar. Sprinkle the hazelnuts in the pan. Pour the batter over the nuts. Bake the clafouti for 15 minutes, then lower the heat to 375°F. and bake until the center is just set, about 12 minutes. Serve immediately.

SERVING SUGGESTIONS
- Serve with Concord Grape Sorbet (page 54).
- For a composed dessert, add candied hazelnuts (see page 261) and Cream-Cheese Ice Cream (page 212).

CANDIED FENNEL WITH PERNOD-ORANGE SORBET AND PERNOD WHIPPED CREAM

Fennel to me is synonymous with licorice, one of my all-time favorite flavors. Candying fennel bulbs, which brings out their natural sweetness, turns them into a confection with a compelling licorice taste that's heightened by Pernod-spiked whipped cream. For a bracing counterpoint, I like to serve the fennel with icy Pernod-orange sorbet. I have always loved to eat orange-fennel salads in the winter, so why not make those same flavors into a dessert? The result is deeply harmonious and refreshing.

Yield: 4 servings

PERNOD-ORANGE SORBET
1½ cups strained fresh orange juice
    (from about 6 oranges)
¾   cup Simple Syrup (page 261)
1 to 2 tablespoons freshly squeezed
    lemon juice, strained (or to taste)
1   tablespoon Pernod

CANDIED FENNEL
1   bulb of fennel, very thinly sliced
1¼ cups Simple Syrup (page 261)

PERNOD WHIPPED CREAM
⅔   cup heavy cream
1   tablespoon Pernod
Pinch of salt
1   tablespoon plus 1 teaspoon
    confectioners' sugar
⅛   teaspoon vanilla extract

1. To prepare the sorbet, in a bowl, stir together the orange juice and Simple Syrup. Add lemon juice to taste. Stir in the Pernod. Chill the mixture until it's very cold, about 3 hours. Freeze in an ice-cream machine according to the manufacturer's directions.

2. To prepare the fennel, preheat the oven to 300°F. Fill a large bowl with ice water. Boil water in a medium saucepan; blanch the fennel for 2 minutes. Drain and immediately plunge into the ice water to stop the cooking.

3. Drain the fennel and overlap the slices in a 9 × 12-inch baking pan. Cover with the Simple Syrup. Place a sheet of parchment paper on top of the fennel, then cover the pan with foil; prick the foil all over with a fork. Bake the slices until they are translucent, about 1 hour. Remove the foil and continue to bake the fennel until the juices are thick and syrupy, 30 to 55 minutes longer. Cool completely before serving.

4. Meanwhile, prepare the Pernod whipped cream. Using an electric mixer, beat all the ingredients until the cream holds firm peaks. Use immediately, or cover and refrigerate for up to 2 hours.

SERVING SUGGESTIONS
· Serve with Orange-Cornmeal Shortbread (page 88).
· For a composed dessert, add Caramel Blood Oranges (page 89).

MAPLE-GLAZED WINTER SQUASH AND APPLE COMPOTE

Although pumpkins are commonly used in autumn dessert recipes, other members of the winter squash family usually aren't. But for desserts, I find regular pumpkins too watery, with a tendency to fall apart. So when I thought about making a dessert combining apples and pumpkin, which have an affinity for each other, I decided to substitute butternut squash. Unlike pumpkin, butternut squash retains its color and shape when it is braised, as it is here in an intense, spicy maple sauce. The apples and squash are cut into cubes of the same size, and they both absorb the rich flavors of maple and spice while remaining very different in taste and texture. The squash becomes melting and pumpkin pie–flavored, while the apples keep their tart juiciness.

Yield: 4 servings

¾ cup maple syrup
1½ cinnamon sticks
2 whole cloves
1 medium butternut squash, peeled, seeded, and cut into ¾-inch cubes (about 2 cups)
¾ cup sugar
2 Granny Smith apples, peeled, cored, and cut into ½-inch cubes (to yield 1 cup)

1. In a large saucepan, combine the maple syrup, ¾ cup water, the cinnamon, and the cloves. Bring to a boil, then allow the mixture to reduce for 7 minutes over medium heat, until it is somewhat thickened. Once the syrup is reduced, add the squash and simmer until it is tender and partly translucent, 10 to 12 minutes. Transfer the squash with a slotted spoon to a plate, and simmer the remaining maple sauce until reduced by half, about 7 minutes longer. Strain the sauce into a clean sauté pan and discard the solids.

2. Meanwhile, prepare the caramelized apples. Place an 8-inch nonstick skillet over high heat and let it get very hot. Sprinkle in about ¼ cup of the sugar. Heat until it begins to melt, shaking and stirring from time to time. Sprinkle in another ¼ cup of the sugar and continue to add the remaining ¼ cup of sugar as it melts and caramelizes. When the sugar caramelizes to a deep amber brown, add the apples in a single layer and turn off the heat. Do not stir the apples; allow them to cool in the hot caramel, basting occasionally as they release their juice. If the caramel is still hard or contains candied lumps, add some of the reserved maple sauce to the pan and simmer for another 2 minutes to dissolve the lumps.

3. Add the apple and squash mixture to the remaining maple sauce in the pan and stir gently to combine. Simmer for 1 minute, then turn off the heat and serve warm or at room temperature.

SERVING SUGGESTIONS
• Serve with Cornmeal Pound Cake (page 115) or Gingersnaps (page 176).
• For something more complex, add scoops of Ginger Ice Cream (page 178) or Yogurt Sorbet (page 213).
• For a composed dessert, add Green-Apple Sorbet (page 75).

CHILLED RHUBARB SOUP

An old-fashioned name for rhubarb is "pie plant," since you'll usually find this red, celerylike vegetable baked under a crust. But here, I make it into a sophisticated soup that shows off its vibrant color, which can vary from an exquisite magenta to a delicate pink. It's a powerfully flavored dessert that gains a touch of spice from gingerroot, yet is incredibly easy to make. You can serve it on its own, in small, well-chilled portions, or dress it up in countless ways. No matter how you serve it, your guests are sure to be won over by its stunning color and lively taste.

Yield: 6 to 8 servings

6½ cups sliced, trimmed rhubarb (about 2½ pounds untrimmed)
1½ ounces fresh gingerroot, peeled and sliced into 12 quarter-size slices
1½ cups Simple Syrup (page 261)

1. Combine all the ingredients in a large saucepan; bring to a simmer over medium heat. Simmer for 10 to 15 minutes, stirring occasionally with a wooden spoon to break down the rhubarb. Force the soup through a medium (not fine) sieve, discarding the solids.

2. Pour the soup into a bowl and let cool completely. Chill the soup until thoroughly cold, at least 3 hours, and up to 2 days. Serve cold.

SERVING SUGGESTIONS
- Serve sliced strawberries or raspberries in the soup.
- For something more complex, float scoops of Strawberry Sorbet (page 21) and/or Ginger Ice Cream (page 178) in the soup.
- For a composed dessert, add Pistachio-Nut Brittle (page 142).

SWEET-CORN ICE CREAM

There are times when I am inspired to create a new dessert after eating something I've loved. But there are also times when my inspiration comes from eating something I didn't even like. In that case, the impetus shifts from "How can I do something as wonderful as this?" to "How can I make this better?"

This sweet-corn ice cream came from the latter impulse. The original dessert, sampled in a small Mexican restaurant, sounded unusual and intriguing but turned out to be riddled with distracting icy bits of corn kernels. Still, I love corn, and I was taken with the idea of doing my own perfectly smooth and silky corn ice cream.

The result has become a much anticipated early-fall classic at Gramercy Tavern. It is creamy-textured and luscious, with a subtle corn taste. Since the flavor of the ice cream is wholly dependent on the sweetness of the corn, make this ice cream only at the height of the season in August and September, with the freshest corn you can find.

Yield: About 1 quart

4	ears fresh corn, shucked
2	cups milk
2	cups heavy cream
¾	cup sugar
9	large egg yolks

1. Using a large knife, slice the kernels off the corncobs and place in a large saucepan. Break the cobs into thirds and add them to the pan along with the milk, cream, and ½ cup of the sugar. Bring the mixture to a boil, stirring, then turn off the heat. Using an immersion mixer or a blender, purée the corn kernels (not the cobs). Let the mixture infuse for 1 hour.

2. Bring the mixture back to a simmer, then turn off the heat. In a small bowl, whisk the egg yolks and remaining ¼ cup of sugar. Add a cup of the hot corn mixture to the yolks, whisking constantly so they do not curdle. Add the yolk mixture to the saucepan, whisking. Cook over medium-low heat, whisking constantly, until the custard thickens enough to coat the spoon, about 7 minutes.

3. Pass the custard through a coarse sieve, then through a fine sieve, pressing down hard on the solids; discard the solids. Let the custard cool, then cover and chill for at least 4 hours.

Freeze in an ice-cream maker according to the manufacturer's directions.

SERVING SUGGESTIONS
- Serve with Blackberry Compote (page 18).
- For something more complex, add Candied Corn (page 264).
- For a composed dessert, add Cornmeal Crepes with Orange-Butter Sauce (page 116), Orange-Cornmeal Shortbread (page 88), or Cornmeal-Nut Biscotti (page 140).

NUTS

Nuts are a staple of pastry making, and there are few desserts that would not be enhanced by their addition. They add indispensable richness and texture, with characteristics ranging from sweet and buttery, like almonds and chestnuts, to spicy and toasty, like hazelnuts and walnuts. Nuts can be used whole or chopped, in pastes such as almond, hazelnut, or chestnut, or in infusions like almond milk. When using nuts, feel free to substitute nuts of similar texture as your taste dictates. For example, if you are a walnut lover, use walnuts in place of pecans in the Pecan Sandies, or if you feel like experimenting, try making pine-nut granité in place of the Almond-Milk Granité.

As you will probably notice by the end of this chapter, I absolutely insist on toasting nuts before using them. I dislike the astringent, raw flavor of untoasted nuts. Once toasted, they become sweeter, nuttier, and more intense. While almonds taste bland and marzipanlike when raw, they become full-flavored and caramelized when toasted. Toasting pecans brings out an almost mapley flavor in them. While you can buy some nuts already toasted, they usually aren't toasted to the degree that I prefer. In that case, I simply toast them again. Cashews are a good example of this. For the Cashew–Chocolate Chip Crisps, I recommend buying toasted nuts, then toasting them again to bring out all of their wonderful buttery, rich, and complex nuances.

Buy nuts from a store that sells a lot of them, and taste them first to make sure that they're fresh. Keep fresh nuts in the freezer. They can be toasted in advance and stored, but I think it's best to toast them as needed. Nuts can be toasted in a skillet, but you have to really watch and stir them a lot, so I usually toast them in the oven. To do so, spread a single layer of nuts on a rimmed baking sheet and toast them at 350°F. until fragrant and golden in color, usually 5 to 12 minutes depending upon the nut. Stir the nuts a few times so they toast evenly. I include directions for toasting nuts in each recipe as well.

Nut desserts can have salt, crunch, warmth, sweetness, and even earthiness, and they are well suited to a vast range of beverages. The lightness of a Tuscan Vin Santo makes it perfect for dunking a nut-studded biscotti, while a Portuguese Madeira can have toasted, nutty tones of its own. Very sweet Spanish sherries made with Pedro Ximénez or Moscatel grapes contribute an unctuous feel that works well with deep nut flavors. You can also simply opt for a beer. For the Cashew–Chocolate Chip Crisps and the Macadamia-Nut Tart, a rich, warm chocolate stout from Rogue Brewery is a terrific match.

HAZELNUT TORTE

If I had to choose one nut to call my favorite, it would be the hazelnut. So when I find a nut recipe that I love and want to make my own, I adapt it to the hazelnut. This soft, flavorful cake began as Lindsay Shere's almond torte from Chez Panisse restaurant in Berkeley, California. After some experimentation I discovered that by substituting hazelnut paste for the almond paste in Lindsay's pound-cake-like recipe, I had an absolutely delicious, hazelnutty cross between a coffee cake and a genoise. It's a different sort of cake, moist yet light, and I think truly magnificent.

Yield: 8 servings

1   cup (2 sticks) unsalted butter
1   cup plus 2 tablespoons sugar
8   ounces unsweetened hazelnut
    paste or hazelnut butter
    (see page 269)
6   large eggs
1   teaspoon vanilla extract
1   cup cake flour
1   teaspoon baking powder

1. Preheat the oven to 325°F. Butter a 9-inch cake pan. Line the bottom with a circle of parchment paper, then butter the paper and flour the entire pan. In the bowl of an electric mixer fitted with the paddle attachment, cream the butter and sugar until light and smooth, about 2 minutes. Add the hazelnut paste and beat until just incorporated. Add the eggs one at a time, beating well after each addition. Beat in the vanilla.

2. In a small bowl, combine the flour and baking powder, then sift a third of it into the wet ingredients and gently fold to combine. Sift in the remaining dry ingredients in two additions, folding gently after each.

3. Pour the batter into the pan and smooth the top. Bake for 55 to 60 minutes, or until a cake tester comes out clean when inserted in the center. The torte should be puffy in the center and should spring back when lightly pressed.

4. Transfer to a wire rack to cool completely before serving.

SERVING SUGGESTIONS
· Serve with Pear Sorbet with Poached Pear Compote (page 74).
· For a composed dessert, add Caramel Ice Cream (page 193).

ALMOND BROWN-BUTTER CAKES

Made with almond flour, these simple yet rich cakes are the classic French after-school treats called *financiers*. They are scrumptious little mouthfuls, deliciously buttery and marzipanlike on the inside, with a golden-brown sugary crust on the outside. The browned butter enhances their nuttiness, and baking them in mini muffin tins makes them the perfect size for snacking. These are delightful plain and perfect for tea, but they also can be dressed up a bit. See the serving suggestions below for some ideas.

Yield: 15 small cakes

½ cup (1 stick) unsalted butter
1⅓ cups confectioners' sugar
½ cup almond flour
⅓ cup cake flour
4 large egg whites (about ½ cup)
2 to 3 tablespoons blanched
   sliced almonds

1. Preheat the oven to 400°F. In a large skillet over medium heat, melt the butter. Continue to let the butter cook until some of the white milk solids fall to the bottom of the skillet and turn a rich hazelnut brown. Strain the browned butter through a fine sieve into a clean bowl.

2. Sift together the confectioners' sugar, almond flour, and cake flour. Place the sifted ingredients in the bowl of an electric mixer fitted with a whip attachment. On the lowest speed, add the egg whites and mix until all the dry ingredients are moistened. Increase the speed to low and mix in the browned butter. Increase the speed to medium and beat until smooth. (The batter can be made up to 3 days in advance and refrigerated until needed.)

3. Butter and flour 15 mini muffin tins. Spoon the batter into the tins and place 2 or 3 almond slices on top of each. Bake the cakes for about 15 minutes, until they are golden brown around the edges. Transfer to a wire rack to cool completely.

SERVING SUGGESTION
- Serve with Strawberry Sorbet (page 21) and sliced fresh strawberries, or with Spiced Red Wine–Fig Compote (page 52).

MACADAMIA-NUT TART

Macadamia nuts and a delicate custard filling turn this tart into a luxurious and less sweet alternative to pecan pie. Macadamias are a little more expensive than other nuts, but I love their unique, soft flavor. Make sure to toast them well; otherwise their gentle taste will all but disappear against the brown sugar and vanilla in the filling.

Yield: 8 servings

TART DOUGH
1¼   cups all-purpose flour
1   teaspoon sugar
¼   teaspoon salt
7   tablespoons cold unsalted butter,
    cut into ½-inch pieces
1   large egg yolk
2 to 3 tablespoons milk

MACADAMIA TART FILLING
1¼   cups macadamia nuts
3   tablespoons unsalted butter
2   whole eggs
1   large egg yolk
¾   cup light corn syrup
¾   cup firmly packed light brown
    sugar
½   teaspoon dark rum
¾   teaspoon vanilla extract
¼   teaspoon salt

1. To prepare the tart dough, place the flour, sugar, and salt in the bowl of a food processor or mixer and pulse or mix to combine. Add the butter and pulse or mix until the mixture resembles coarse meal. Add the egg yolk and 2 tablespoons of the milk and pulse or mix until the dough comes together and begins to leave the sides of the bowl. If the mixture is too dry, add more milk to the dough, ½ tablespoon at a time.

Scrape the dough onto a sheet of plastic wrap, form it into a disk, and wrap well. Refrigerate until firm, at least 1 hour, and up to 3 days.

2. Preheat the oven to 350°F. On a lightly floured surface, roll the dough into an 11-inch disk. Press it into a 9-inch tart pan, trimming away any excess dough. Prick the dough all over with a fork. Chill for 10 minutes. Line the tart shell with foil and fill with dried beans, rice, or pie weights. Place on a baking sheet and bake for 20 minutes. Remove the beans and foil and bake for 12 to 15 minutes more, until set. Let the tart shell cool on a rack. (The tart shell can be made up to 8 hours in advance or frozen for up to 3 months; see page xxv.) Leave the oven on.

3. To prepare the filling, spread the macadamia nuts out on a baking sheet and toast in the oven until golden brown, 10 to 12 minutes. When the nuts are cool, chop them very roughly.

4. Meanwhile, in a small skillet over medium heat, melt the butter. Continue to let the butter cook until some of the white milk solids fall to the bottom of the skillet and turn a rich hazelnut brown. Strain the browned butter through a fine sieve into the bowl of an electric mixer. Let the butter cool for a few minutes, then add the eggs, yolk, corn syrup, brown sugar, rum, vanilla, and salt. Using the whip attachment, beat the mixture at medium speed until the ingredients are blended, then strain through a fine sieve. (The filling can be made up to 3 days in advance and stored in the refrigerator.)

5. Preheat the oven to 325°F. Spread the nuts in the bottom of the tart shell, then pour the filling over them. Place the tart pan on a foil-lined baking sheet and bake until the filling is set and golden brown on top, 35 to 40 minutes. Cool completely on a wire rack before serving.

SERVING SUGGESTIONS
· Serve with Coconut Sorbet (page 107).
· For a composed dessert, add fresh tropical fruit or Roasted Pineapple with Pink Peppercorns (page 103) and coconut cream (from Butterscotch Custards, page 183).

PINE-NUT TART WITH ROSEMARY

I love the subtle taste of pine nuts, especially here, where they are suspended in a buttery caramel and poured into an almond cookie crust. The caramel is infused with rosemary, which lends it an Italian flavor. A hint of honey gently underscores the pine nuance of the herb, and also makes the caramel especially soft and smooth. The result is a particularly sophisticated nut tart with a lovely, crunchy, slightly chewy texture.

Yield: 8 servings

ALMOND CRUST
½ cup (1 stick) unsalted butter, softened
⅓ cup confectioners' sugar
1 large egg, lightly beaten
1½ cups all-purpose flour
½ cup plus 2 tablespoons almond flour
Pinch of salt

PINE NUT–ROSEMARY FILLING
1 cup pine nuts
7 tablespoons unsalted butter
¾ cup sugar
3 tablespoons honey
3 tablespoons light corn syrup
1 cup heavy cream
½ teaspoon vanilla extract
2 large sprigs of fresh rosemary
Pinch of salt

1. To make the crust, in the bowl of an electric mixer fitted with the paddle attachment, beat the butter and confectioners' sugar until combined, about 1 minute. Beat in the egg. In a medium bowl, whisk together the flour, almond flour, and salt. Add the flour mixture to the butter mixture in two batches, scraping down the sides of the bowl between additions.

Mix until the dough just holds together. Scrape the dough onto a piece of plastic wrap, form it into a disk, and wrap well. Chill until firm, for at least 1 hour, or up to 3 days.

2. Preheat the oven to 325°F. On a floured surface, roll the dough out to a 12-inch round. Fit it into a 10-inch tart pan with a removable bottom. Trim away any excess dough, then use a fork to prick the crust all over. Chill for 10 minutes. Bake the tart crust until it's pale golden, 20 to 25 minutes. Transfer to a wire rack to cool. (The tart shell can be made 8 hours ahead or frozen for up to 3 months; see page xxv.)

3. To make the filling, preheat the oven to 350°F. Spread the nuts out in one layer on a baking sheet and toast them until fragrant and golden brown around the edges, about 5 minutes. Transfer the pan to a wire rack to cool, but keep the oven on.

4. In a heavy saucepan, melt the butter. Add the sugar, honey, and corn syrup. Stir the mixture occasionally over low heat until the sugar is dissolved. Raise the heat to high

and boil the mixture, stirring occasionally to keep the caramel from burning, until it turns a deep amber color, 12 to 14 minutes. Remove the saucepan from the heat and whisk in the cream (stand back, the caramel may splatter). Place over low heat and whisk until the caramel is smooth. Turn off the heat and stir in the toasted pine nuts, vanilla, rosemary, and salt. Let the mixture infuse for 15 minutes.

5. Wrap the outside of the cooled tart shell (still in the pan) with aluminum foil. Remove the rosemary sprigs and pour the pine-nut mixture into the shell. Place on a baking sheet and bake until golden russet brown, about 30 minutes. Transfer to a wire rack to cool completely before serving.

SERVING SUGGESTIONS
- Serve with scoops of Pink Grapefruit–Rosemary Sorbet (page 92).
- For a composed dessert, serve with Lemon Thyme–Macerated Raspberry Compote (page 19) and Crème Fraîche Panna Cotta (page 206).

CHESTNUT SOUFFLÉS WITH ARMAGNAC-NUTMEG CUSTARD SAUCE

This is an exquisite two-in-one dessert featuring the classic combination of chestnuts and Armagnac. It's particularly good to serve during the holidays since it manages to be cloudlike, full-flavored, and festive all at the same time.

Soufflés are actually not as last-minute as you might think: you can prepare them up to 2 hours in advance, refrigerate them, then bake them moments before serving. For optimal lightness, hold off on whipping the egg whites until right before you pop them in the oven. Ten minutes later, you'll have something truly impressive to serve your guests.

Yield: 6 servings

1½ cups milk
½ cup plus 2 tablespoons sugar, plus additional for the ramekins
5   large eggs, separated
3   large egg yolks
½   cup heavy cream
2   tablespoons Armagnac
¾   teaspoon vanilla extract
2   pinches of freshly grated nutmeg
2   tablespoons all-purpose flour
2   tablespoons cornstarch
6   tablespoons unsweetened chestnut paste (see page 269)
Unsalted butter for the ramekins

1. In a saucepan, bring 1 cup of the milk and ¼ cup of the sugar to a simmer, stirring to dissolve the sugar. Meanwhile, whisk together the egg yolks and another ¼ cup of the sugar. Remove the milk mixture from the heat and add a little to the egg yolk mixture to warm it, whisking constantly to keep the yolks from cooking. Pour the egg yolk mixture into the hot milk mixture, whisking the milk constantly as you pour.

2. Return the custard to the stove and cook it over low heat, stirring constantly with a wooden spoon, until it thickens enough to coat the back of the spoon. Strain the custard through a sieve into a clean bowl. Transfer half (about ⅔ cup) of the mixture to a clean saucepan.

3. Add the cream, 1 tablespoon of the Armagnac, ¼ teaspoon of the vanilla, and a pinch of nutmeg to the remaining custard in the bowl and whisk to combine. Chill this custard sauce until serving time (or up to 2 days).

4. In a small bowl, whisk together the remaining ½ cup of milk, the flour, and the cornstarch until smooth. Whisk the milk mixture into the custard in the saucepan and place over medium heat. Cook the custard, whisking, until it thickens and becomes puddinglike, about 3 minutes. Whisk in the chestnut paste and the remaining tablespoon of Armagnac, ½ teaspoon of vanilla, and pinch of nutmeg.

5. Preheat the oven to 400°F. Liberally butter and sugar six 4-ounce ramekins.

6. In the bowl of an electric mixer fitted with the whip attachment, beat the 5 egg whites until they form soft peaks. Gradually beat in the remaining 2 tablespoons of sugar, and continue beating to form stiff peaks. Whisk a third of the egg whites into the chestnut mixture to lighten it, then gently fold in the remaining whites in two additions.

7. Spoon the batter into the ramekins. Place the soufflés on a baking sheet and bake for 8 to 9 minutes, until well risen and spongy-firm. Using the back of a spoon, push in the center of each soufflé to create a cavity, then fill with the custard sauce. Serve immediately.

VARIATION

For one large soufflé, spoon the mixture into a buttered and sugared 1-quart soufflé dish and bake for 35 to 45 minutes. Serve with the sauce on the side.

SERVING SUGGESTION

· Serve the soufflés with scoops of Prune-Armagnac Ice Cream (page 38) instead of the custard sauce.

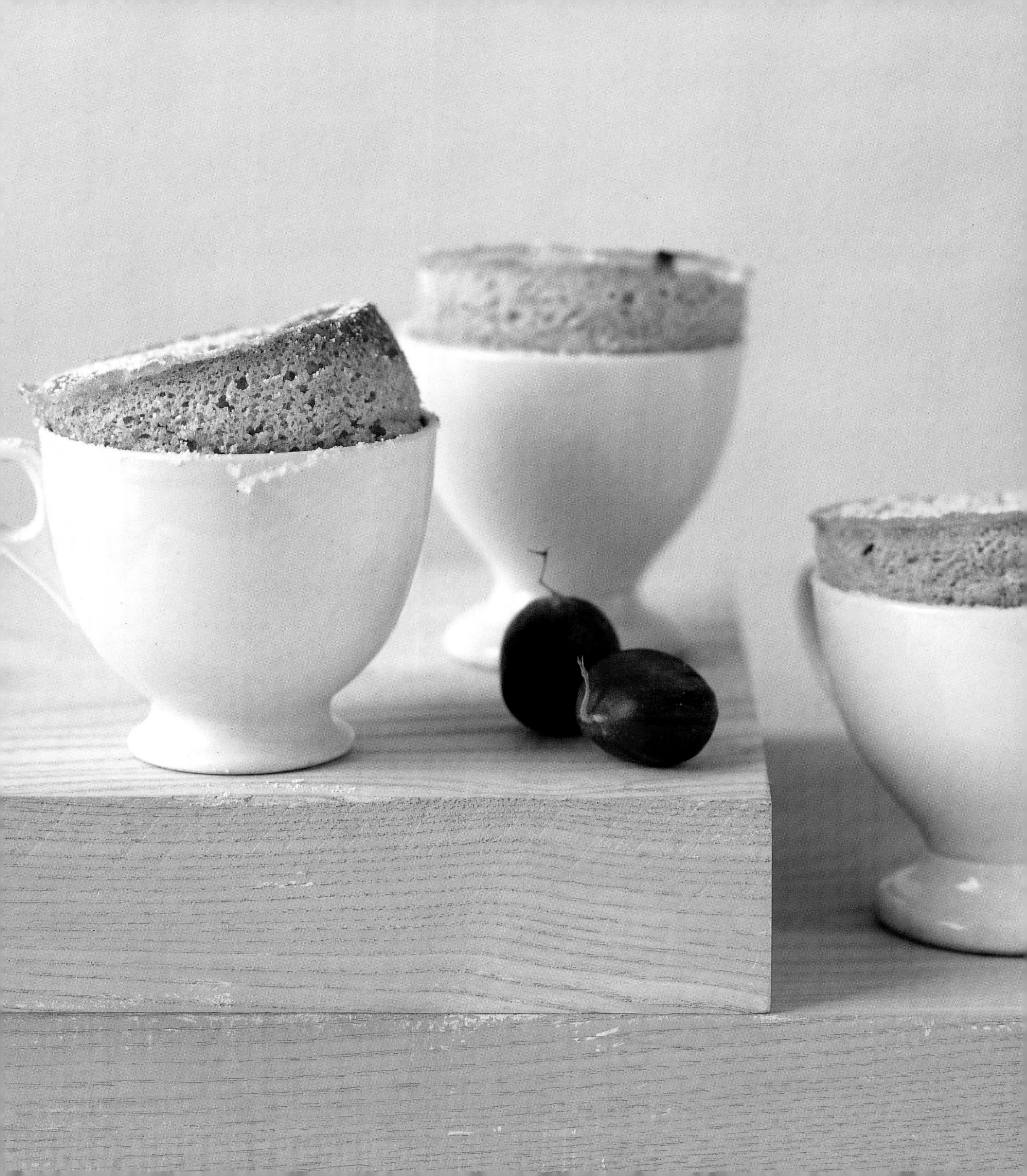

HAZELNUT PARFAITS

This is a parfait in the French sense of the word. In France, parfaits are rich, creamy mousses that usually focus on one ingredient, such as a nut, fruit, or liqueur. American-style parfaits are any kind of frozen or chilled dessert that is layered into a parfait glass or a coupe. In this recipe, intense hazelnut paste gives the parfait a luscious texture and a marvelously nutty flavor. It makes a wonderful autumn dessert that pairs perfectly with seasonal fruit.

Yield: 8 servings

1	cup plus 2 tablespoons heavy cream
½	cup plus 2 tablespoons sugar
1	teaspoon light corn syrup
6	large egg yolks
¼	cup unsweetened hazelnut paste or hazelnut butter (see page 269)
¼	teaspoon salt

1. Using an electric mixer, whip the heavy cream until it holds soft peaks; reserve in the refrigerator until needed.

2. Place 2 tablespoons water in a small, heavy saucepan. Add ½ cup of the sugar and the corn syrup and cook over medium-high heat until the syrup reaches 248°F. (firm ball stage) on a candy thermometer, about 10 minutes.

3. Meanwhile, when the syrup reaches 238°F., in the bowl of an electric mixer, whip the egg yolks and remaining 2 tablespoons sugar until they are light and fluffy and hold a ribbon when the beater is raised, about 5 minutes. When the syrup is ready, while mixing on low speed, drizzle the syrup into the yolks in a slow and steady stream. Be careful not to pour the syrup onto the beaters. Once the syrup is fully incorporated, increase the mixer speed and whip until the yolks are cool, about 5 minutes. Add the hazelnut paste and salt and mix until well combined.

4. Fold the reserved whipped cream into the hazelnut mixture in thirds. Gently spoon the parfait mixture into eight 4-ounce molds or parfait glasses. Cover with plastic wrap and freeze for at least 6 hours.

SERVING SUGGESTIONS
· Serve sprinkled with candied hazelnuts (see page 261).
· For something more complex, add Concord Grape Sorbet (page 54).
· For a composed dessert, add Pear Sorbet with Poached Pear Compote (page 74) or Spiced Red Wine–Fig Compote (page 52).

CORNMEAL–NUT BISCOTTI

These are one of my signature cookies, a recipe that was inspired by many of the wonderful ingredients I associate with Italy. Made with cornmeal, hazelnuts, almonds, orange, rosemary, and anise, these toothsome biscotti have a haunting, complex flavor that is nonetheless balanced and subtle. I really worked hard on this recipe. In my mind, I knew I wanted to fuse the flavors of the orange-rosemary buns that Andrew Chase, a former cook at Union Square Cafe, once made for breakfast, and the rosemary-cornmeal scones that Nancy Silverton makes at Campanile in Los Angeles. But getting the cookies just right took a lot of jiggling. Many tries later, I'm finally happy. These are unusually crumbly and buttery biscotti, with a great crunch thanks to the cornmeal and nuts. And they're excellent dipped in a glass of dessert wine, since they won't fall apart when you dunk them.

Yield: About 2½ dozen biscotti

½ cup coarsely chopped blanched almonds
¼ cup coarsely chopped skinned hazelnuts
4 tablespoons unsalted butter
1½ tablespoons finely grated orange zest
1 tablespoon minced fresh rosemary
1 cup all-purpose flour
½ cup coarse yellow cornmeal
½ cup sugar
1 teaspoon baking soda
1 teaspoon anise seeds
2 large eggs
Egg wash made with 1 egg and 1 tablespoon water

1. Preheat the oven to 350°F. Spread the nuts out on a baking sheet and toast them in the oven, stirring occasionally, until they are lightly golden around the edges, 8 to 10 minutes. Let cool on a wire rack (keep the oven on).

2. In a small saucepan, melt the butter over medium-high heat. Turn off the heat and add the orange zest and rosemary. Let cool.

3. In the bowl of an electric mixer set on low speed, mix together the flour, cornmeal, sugar, baking soda, and anise. Add the eggs one at a time, mixing well after each addition. Add the cooled, melted butter mixture and mix to combine. Stir in the nuts. Let the dough rest for 5 minutes.

4. With wet hands, form the dough into a log 2 inches wide and place it on a parchment-lined baking sheet. Brush the log with egg wash and bake until it is a deep golden brown, about 30 minutes. Let it cool on a wire rack. Reduce the oven temperature to 200°F.

5. Using a serrated knife, slice the log on a diagonal into ¼-inch-thick pieces. Arrange the biscotti on 2 parchment-lined baking sheets and dry them in the oven until crisp, about 1 hour. Let cool on a wire rack.

SERVING SUGGESTION
• Serve with Blood-Orange Sorbet (page 93), Roasted Apricots with Chamomile (page 35), or Roasted Chestnut-Honey Pears (page 71).

CASHEW–CHOCOLATE CHIP CRISPS

These cookies are a variation on the classic Toll House cookie. But where the typical chocolate chip cookie is fat and soft, these are brittle and crisp, since they contain less flour and a touch more sugar. I've also added cashews and a bit of orange zest, which make them quite elegant—as chocolate chip cookies go.

If hazelnuts are my favorite nuts, then cashews are a close second. Their delicate flavor puts them on the same level of flavor intensity as milk chocolate, so the combination here is pleasingly well balanced. While toasting all nuts is key, raw cashews in particular have a very astringent flavor, which mellows out to a rich buttery taste when toasted. Double-toasting the nuts as I do here brings out even more of their roasted, caramel nuances.

Yield: About 10 dozen small cookies

2½ cups toasted cashew nuts
2½ cups all-purpose flour
1   teaspoon salt
1   cup (2 sticks) unsalted butter
1¼ cups firmly packed light brown
    sugar
1¼ cups granulated sugar
1   teaspoon vanilla extract
Grated zest of 1 orange
2   large eggs
1¾ teaspoons baking soda
1   cup milk chocolate chips
1   cup semisweet chocolate chips

1. Preheat the oven to 350°F. Spread the nuts out in one layer on a baking sheet and bake them until they are golden brown, 7 to 10 minutes, stirring occasionally. Transfer the pan to a wire rack to cool. Reduce the oven temperature to 325°F.

2. In a food processor or nut grinder, finely grind ½ cup of the nuts with 1 tablespoon of the flour. Add the ground nut mixture to the remaining flour and mix in the salt. Coarsely chop the remaining 2 cups of nuts.

3. In the bowl of an electric mixer fitted with the paddle attachment, beat the butter, brown sugar, and granulated sugar until creamy, about 2 minutes. Add the vanilla and orange zest and beat well to combine. Add the eggs one at a time, scraping down the sides of the bowl after each addition.

4. In a small bowl, dissolve the baking soda in 1 teaspoon water. Add the mixture to the butter mixture and beat to combine. Add the flour mixture in two batches, scraping down

the sides of the bowl as necessary. Add the chocolate chips and remaining cashews and mix well.

5. Form heaping teaspoons of the dough into balls and place them 2 inches apart on baking sheets lined with parchment or wax paper. Bake the cookies until they are golden brown all over, about 15 minutes. For really evenly colored cookies, rotate the baking sheets after 5 minutes.

SERVING SUGGESTIONS
· Serve with scoops of Caramel Ice Cream (page 193) or Earl Grey Ice Cream (page 195).
· For a composed dessert, serve with Espresso-Orange Panna Cotta Parfaits with Coffee Gelée (page 186) and scoops of Blood-Orange Sorbet (page 93).

PISTACHIO-NUT BRITTLE

I adore all nut brittles. They combine two of my favorite treats: nuts and crunchy caramel candy. But this nut brittle is special. Made with pistachios, it looks absolutely gorgeous, like emeralds embedded in amber, and it's a stunning homemade gift that anyone would be thrilled to receive. You can eat this brittle on its own as a candy, or break it up and serve it over ice cream, custard, or soft fruit for a textural contrast. Any way you serve it, it's a terrific thing to have on hand. It will keep indefinitely in an airtight container.

Yield: 1 pound

1½ cups shelled pistachio nuts
1⅓ cups sugar
¼ cup light corn syrup
2½ tablespoons unsalted butter
¼ teaspoon plus ⅛ teaspoon baking soda
¼ teaspoon salt

1. Preheat the oven to 350°F. Spread the nuts out in one layer on a baking sheet and bake them until they are golden brown, about 10 minutes, stirring occasionally. Transfer the pan to a wire rack to cool.

2. Butter a baking sheet or line it with a nonstick liner. Set the pan on a cooling rack or trivet. Grease a spatula and set aside.

3. In a large, heavy saucepan, combine the sugar, ½ cup water, the corn syrup, and butter. Cook over medium heat, stirring at first to dissolve the sugar, until the mixture is light caramel in color, about 12 minutes. Remove the saucepan from the heat and whisk in the baking soda, salt, and nuts.

4. Working very quickly with the buttered spatula, spread the mixture out onto the prepared baking sheet. The mixture will be very hot, so use caution when spreading it out. Let the brittle cool completely, then break it into pieces.

VARIATION

To make macadamia-nut brittle, simply substitute macadamia nuts for the pistachios.

SERVING SUGGESTION

· Serve with Chilled Rhubarb Soup (page 126) or Saffron Rice Pudding (page 170).

PECAN SANDIES

When pecans are toasted until very dark and combined with sugar, they take on a slight yet distinct maple flavor. These peerless cookies use well-toasted nuts, so not only do they have all those delicate, buttery, and melt-in-the-mouth qualities characteristic to a pecan sandy, they also have a compelling maple undertone. I like to cut these cookies really small, so that you can pop a whole one in your mouth. Or two. Or three . . .

Yield: About 24 dozen small cookies

1	cup pecans
2	cups all-purpose flour
1	cup (2 sticks) unsalted butter, softened
⅔	cup confectioners' sugar
2	teaspoons vanilla extract
1	teaspoon salt
½	teaspoon baking powder
2	tablespoons turbinado (raw) sugar

1. Preheat the oven to 350°F. Spread the nuts out in one layer on a baking sheet and bake them, stirring occasionally, until they are well browned, 10 to 13 minutes (they will smell toasted and nutty). Transfer the pan to a wire rack to cool.

2. In a food processor, grind the nuts with ¼ cup of the flour. Set aside.

3. Using an electric mixer, beat the butter and sugar until creamy and smooth, about 2 minutes. Add the vanilla and beat well. Sift together the remaining 1¾ cups of flour, the salt, and the baking powder, and add it to the dough, mixing until just combined. Stir in the nut mixture. Form the dough into a disk, wrap in plastic wrap, and chill for at least 3 hours.

4. Preheat the oven to 325°F. Roll the dough between two sheets of wax paper to ³⁄₁₆ inch thick (a rectangle approximately 10 × 14 inches).

Using a sharp knife, cut the dough into 1-inch squares, then cut the squares on a diagonal into triangles. Sprinkle the cookies with the turbinado sugar. Place them 1 inch apart on ungreased cookie sheets (do not reroll the scraps). Prick the cookies with a fork and bake until pale golden all over, about 10 minutes. Cool on a wire rack.

SERVING SUGGESTIONS
- Serve with Roasted Chestnut-Honey Pears (page 71).
- For a composed dessert, add Cream-Cheese Ice Cream (page 212).

ALMOND-MILK GRANITÉ

This granité was inspired by a Spanish recipe for an almond shake that I saw in *The New York Times*. I liked the idea of pairing a creamy almond-flavor component with another dessert, and I thought it would work well as a granité. It's a lovely paradox of icy and creamy, with an exceptional toasted-almond taste. Be sure to toast the almonds until they're very dark in color; otherwise you won't be able to achieve that special, deep almond flavor.

Yield: 1 quart

2 cups sliced blanched almonds
¼ cup plus 2 tablespoons sugar
1 quart milk

1. Preheat the oven to 350°F. Spread the nuts in a single layer on a baking sheet. Toast until very dark brown (just this side of burnt), 9 to 10 minutes. Transfer to a wire rack to cool completely.

2. Coarsely grind the nuts in a food processor with 2 tablespoons of the sugar.

3. In a medium, heavy saucepan, combine the ground almonds, milk, and remaining ¼ cup of sugar. Bring to a boil over medium heat, stirring to dissolve the sugar. Turn off the heat and allow the mixture to steep until cool.

4. Strain the mixture, discarding the solids, and pour it into a shallow metal pan. Freeze the granité for 45 minutes, then use a fork to stir it up (the aim is to break down any ice crystals). Make sure to stir around the sides of the pan. Repeat the stirring every 30 minutes until the granité has a texture between that of an Italian ice and a snow cone. It will take about 2½ to 4 hours, depending upon the size and depth of your pan and the temperature of your freezer.

SERVING SUGGESTIONS
- Serve with berries, cherries, or apricots.
- For something more complex, add candied almonds (see page 261).
- For a composed dessert, add Sour Cherry Sorbet (page 39).

HERBS AND FLOWERS

Summer is filled with an abundance of fresh herbs, which are the perfect warm-weather counterpart to the spices we bake with during cooler months. In July the idea of cinnamon is not nearly as appealing as the bright, clean flavor of basil, and the lovely licorice scent of fresh tarragon is far more refreshing than the wintry licorice taste of anise. Like spices, herbs add complexity and flavor to desserts. While spices are superb with dried fruit in the winter, nothing complements all the wonderful fruits of summer more than fresh herbs. (I don't recommend substituting dried herbs for the fresh in these recipes, since their vibrancy becomes earthy and musty when dried.)

Flowers, like herbs, are also excellent with fresh fruits. Used sparingly, flowers can subtly perfume a dessert with their ethereal, summery essence. The key word here, though, is sparingly. Flowers like lavender, rose, and chamomile have strong personalities and, when used with a free hand, can make a recipe seem more like a perfumed candle than a dessert. Many floral flavors are nicely balanced by the spark of an acid such as lemon, which sharpens them and keeps them from becoming cloying. The Lavender-Lemon Pound Cake is a perfect example of this terrific synergy.

Unlike herbs, some flowers, such as lavender and chamomile, can be used dried. Lavender is available in specialty shops or by mail order; see page 269. You can substitute a chamomile tea bag for the fresh chamomile according to the directions in the recipes. The downside is you won't have the pretty flowers for a garnish.

Since chewing on petals or leaves is not at all pleasant, the flavors of the herbs and flowers in this chapter are always infused. Cream is an ideal base for infusions, since it brings out the flavors of flowers and herbs while at the same time tempering them so they don't become overwhelming. Poaching liquids work beautifully, too. Nonetheless, use a light hand with these flavorings, since you don't want your ice cream to taste like a salad or potpourri.

While not abandoning the inherent fruit component, it is possible to locate wines that accentuate the earthy, floral tones necessary to match these desserts. Desserts made with honey can be paired with mead (a sweet fermented beverage made from honey) to accentuate their honeyed flavors.

It is important not to overwhelm the flavors of the rose and bay leaf desserts. In Alsace, late-harvest wines allow the food they are served with to shine, all the while providing support and the essence of greatness. Restraint is essential here.

Focusing on their four most respected varietals (Riesling, Pinot Gris, Gewürztraminer, and Muscat), the Alsatians have perfected the aspect of balance in a wine: sweet yet almost dry at the finish; rich but not cloying; fully flavored but still allowing for foods to make a mark. These wines, classified as *vendange tardive* (late-harvest) and *sélection de grains nobles* (individually selected, noble-rot-affected grapes), deserve a place on any table.

LAVENDER CRÈME BRÛLÉE

Lavender has a potent flavor, but that doesn't mean it has to be overpowering in a dessert. Here, it adds just a hint of its flowery perfume to crème brûlée. Since different varieties of lavender have different strengths, make sure to taste the cream as it infuses. When the lavender is subtle or strong enough to suit your taste, it's time to strain it, even if it's a few minutes more or less than the time frame I give in the recipe.

Yield: 6 servings

2   cups heavy cream
4   teaspoons dried lavender
6   tablespoons sugar
Pinch of salt
6   large egg yolks
½   teaspoon grated orange zest

1. In a heavy saucepan, combine the cream, lavender, 2 tablespoons of the sugar, and the salt; bring the mixture to a simmer over medium heat. Take off the heat and steep for 5 to 10 minutes, to taste.

2. Meanwhile, whisk 2 tablespoons of sugar and the egg yolks together until smooth.

3. Add a little of the cream mixture to the egg yolk mixture to warm it, whisking constantly to keep the yolks from curdling. Pour the egg yolk mixture into the hot cream mixture, stirring the cream constantly as you pour. Stir in the orange zest. Let the cream mixture cool completely. Strain through a fine sieve. Chill for at least 2 hours and up to 2 days.

4. Preheat the oven to 350°F. Pour the mixture into six 4-ounce glass or ceramic ramekins. Arrange the ramekins in a baking pan and place it on the oven rack. Pour enough very hot water into the baking pan to reach two-thirds of the way up the sides of the ramekins. Cover the baking pan with foil and pierce all over with a knife. Bake the custards for about 40 minutes, then lift off a corner of the foil to allow the steam to escape. Re-cover the pan and bake for 10 to 15 minutes longer, until the custards are set around the edges but still slightly jiggly in the center. Transfer the ramekins to a rack and let cool, then cover and refrigerate for at least 6 hours, or overnight.

5. Right before serving, sprinkle the remaining sugar in a thin, even coating on the surface of each custard, using 2 teaspoons for each one. Use a preheated broiler or a blowtorch to caramelize the sugar. It will take 1 to 2 minutes in a broiler, much less for a blowtorch.

SERVING SUGGESTION
• Serve with Citrus Lace Tuiles (page 90) and Blackberry Compote (page 18) or Spiced Red Wine–Fig Compote (page 52).

LAVENDER-LEMON POUND CAKE

In this rich, buttery pound cake, the vibrancy of lemon both brings out and helps temper the musky floral qualities of lavender. The flavors harmonize beautifully and make for a cake that manages to be at once plain and simple, as pound cakes are, but also much more interesting.

Using the traditional proportion of butter, sugar, and eggs, this pound cake is exquisitely light thanks to a modification in the technique. The classic recipe involves creaming the butter and sugar to beat air into the cake, whereas I incorporate air by beating the eggs and sugar until light and fluffy. Then I fold melted butter into the batter at the end. The resulting cake is meltingly tender, delicately scented with lavender, and refreshingly lemony.

Yield: 8 servings

1	cup (2 sticks) unsalted butter
4	tablespoons dried lavender
5	large eggs
1½	cups sugar
1½	cups plus 2 tablespoons cake flour
¼	teaspoon salt
1	tablespoon grated lemon zest
1	teaspoon vanilla extract
¼	cup strained fresh lemon juice

1. Preheat the oven to 350°F. Butter and flour a 9 × 5-inch loaf pan. In a small saucepan, melt the butter with 1 tablespoon of the lavender. Let the mixture steep for 10 minutes, then strain, discarding the lavender. Set aside to cool.

2. Using an electric mixer fitted with the whisk attachment, beat the eggs and 1 cup of the sugar until thick and pale, about 5 minutes.

3. In a bowl, sift together the flour and salt. Using a whisk, fold the lemon zest and a third of the flour mixture into the eggs until thoroughly combined. Fold in the rest of the flour in two batches. In a separate bowl, whisk 1 cup of the batter with the melted butter and the vanilla. Add this to the remaining batter and fold to combine. Pour the batter into the prepared pan.

4. Bake the cake until a tester inserted into the middle comes out clean, 40 to 45 minutes. If the top of the cake seems to be getting overly browned before the center is set, cover with foil and continue baking.

5. Meanwhile, in a medium saucepan, combine the remaining ½ cup of sugar, the lemon juice, ¼ cup water, and the remaining 3 tablespoons of lavender. Bring the mixture to a simmer and cook, stirring, until the sugar dissolves.

6. Transfer the cake to a wire rack. Using a cake tester or skewer, poke the cake all over. Brush the loaf with half the syrup and let cool for 10 minutes. Invert the cake onto the rack, remove the pan, and brush syrup over the bottom and sides of the cake. Reinvert the cake and brush with the remaining syrup. Let cool completely.

SERVING SUGGESTIONS
- Serve with Blackberry Compote (page 18).
- For something more complex, add Yogurt Sorbet (page 213).
- For a composed dessert, add whipped crème fraîche and Lemon Confit (page 261).

BAY LEAF FLAN

Although most people think of bay leaves as a dried herb to add to beef stew and pasta sauce, they are also beautifully suited to dessert. Bay leaves have a sweet, spicy flavor that, when used in small amounts, gives desserts a complexity. Cream is the perfect foil for this assertive herb, mellowing it and keeping it from taking over. Don't substitute dried bay leaves for the fresh in this recipe; they lack the bright, clean flavor that makes this flan both superb and unexpected.

Yield: 8 servings

2	cups heavy cream
2	cups milk
4	fresh bay leaves, roughly chopped
1¼	cups sugar
2	large eggs
6	large egg yolks
½	teaspoon light corn syrup

1. In a heavy saucepan, combine the cream, milk, bay leaves, and ½ cup of the sugar. Bring the mixture to a simmer.

2. Meanwhile, in a large bowl, whisk ¼ cup of the sugar with the eggs and egg yolks until smooth. Turn off the heat under the cream mixture and whisk a little into the egg mixture to warm it, whisking constantly to keep the eggs from curdling. Pour the egg mixture into the saucepan with the remaining cream, whisking the mixture constantly. Strain the mixture into a bowl and chill for at least 2 hours and up to 2 days.

3. Preheat the oven to 325°F. Place 2 tablespoons water in a small saucepan over medium heat, then add the remaining ½ cup of sugar and the corn syrup. Raise the heat to high and cook, swirling the pan occasionally, until the mixture becomes a deep amber caramel, about 7 minutes. Immediately pour the caramel into eight 4-ounce glass or ceramic ramekins, tilting to make sure the sides are well coated. If the caramel hardens, rewarm it over the stove.

4. Pour the custard mixture into the ramekins. Arrange them in a baking pan and place it on the oven rack. Pour enough very hot water into the baking pan to reach two-thirds of the way up the sides of the ramekins. Cover the baking pan with foil and pierce all over with a knife. Bake the flans for about 30 minutes, then lift off a corner of the foil to allow the steam to escape. Re-cover the pan and continue to bake until the flans are set around the edges but still slightly jiggly in the center, 10 to 15 minutes longer. Transfer the flans to a rack and let cool at room temperature, then cover and refrigerate overnight.

5. To unmold the flans, run a small knife around the sides of the ramekins, then invert the flans onto dessert plates.

SERVING SUGGESTIONS
- Serve with Cornmeal-Nut Biscotti (page 140) or Orange-Cornmeal Shortbread (page 88).
- For a composed dessert, add whipped crème fraîche and Roasted Pineapple with Pink Peppercorns (page 103).

LEMON VERBENA CUSTARDS

I think of lemon verbena as the pastry chef's perfect herb. It has both the fresh liveliness of lemon combined with the fragrant delicacy of a flower. Here, it lends its distinctive perfume to lush baked custards, adding a light, bright taste that keeps them from feeling too rich and heavy on the tongue. Lemon verbena is available from June to October, but don't be tempted to substitute dried verbena at other times. It just doesn't have that same compelling taste.

Yield: 6 servings

1 cup heavy cream
1 cup milk
1 ounce (1 cup packed) roughly chopped fresh lemon verbena leaves
½ cup plus 2 tablespoons sugar
1 large egg
3 large egg yolks

1. In a heavy saucepan, combine the cream, milk, lemon verbena, and ½ cup of the sugar. Bring the mixture to a simmer.

2. In a large bowl, whisk the remaining 2 tablespoons of sugar with the egg and egg yolks until smooth. Turn off the heat under the cream mixture and whisk a little into the egg mixture to warm it, whisking constantly to keep the eggs from curdling. Pour the egg mixture into the saucepan with the remaining cream, whisking the mixture constantly. Strain the mixture into a bowl and chill for at least 2 hours and up to 2 days.

3. Preheat the oven to 325°F. Pour the custard into six 4-ounce glass or ceramic ramekins. Arrange them in a baking pan and place it on the oven rack. Pour enough very hot water into the baking pan to reach two-thirds of the way up the sides of the ramekins. Cover the baking pan with foil and pierce all over with a knife. Bake the custards for about 30 minutes, then lift off a corner of the foil to allow the steam to escape. Re-cover the pan and continue to bake until the custards are set around the edges but still slightly jiggly in the center, 10 to 15 minutes longer. Transfer the custards to a rack and let cool at room temperature, then cover and refrigerate overnight.

4. To unmold, run a small knife around the sides of the ramekins, then invert the custards onto dessert plates.

SERVING SUGGESTIONS
- Serve with lightly sweetened raspberries and Raspberry Sorbet (page 20).
- For a composed dessert, add Citrus Lace Tuiles (page 90) or Vanilla Shortbread (page 191).

ROSE PARFAITS

This flowery and feminine frozen parfait has a lot going for it. It has a sophisticated taste that comes from the combination of rose water, which is bright and assertive, and rose preserves, which lend the mousse a subtle earthiness. The two different rose flavors marry to create a more nuanced, complex whole. When flavoring desserts with rose water, I always use a light touch, since the floral flavor can become overpowering. You can find it, and rose preserves, at Middle Eastern groceries and many specialty food stores.

Yield: 6 servings

3   tablespoons rose preserves
¾   cup crème fraîche
¾   cup heavy cream
½   teaspoon rose water
¼   cup plus 2 tablespoons sugar
2   tablespoons light corn syrup
3   large egg whites

1. Place the rose preserves in a small bowl and microwave on high power for 30 seconds, or until melted. Alternatively, melt the preserves in a small saucepan over low heat. Let cool to room temperature.

2. In a large bowl, using an electric mixer set on high speed, whip the crème fraîche, heavy cream, rose water, and rose preserves until the mixture holds soft peaks.

3. Place 2 tablespoons water in a small saucepan. Add the sugar and corn syrup and bring to a boil. Let the mixture cook without stirring until it reaches 248°F. (firm ball stage) on a candy thermometer, 8 to 10 minutes.

4. Meanwhile, when the sugar reaches 238°F., in the bowl of an electric mixer, whip the egg whites until they hold soft peaks. When the sugar syrup is ready, set the mixer on low speed and drizzle it into the whites in a slow and steady stream, avoiding the beaters. Once fully incorporated, increase the mixer speed and whip until the mixture is cool, about 5 minutes.

5. Using a spatula, fold in a third of the reserved whipped-cream mixture, then gently fold in the rest in two batches. Spoon the mixture into six 4-ounce molds or parfait glasses. Cover with plastic wrap and freeze for at least 6 hours.

6. Serve these directly from the parfait glasses, or turn them out if you are using molds. To unmold, dip the bottoms into a pan of very hot water, then run a knife around the inner edges of the molds. Dry the molds before turning over onto a plate. If the parfait doesn't easily slip out, firmly tap the bottom of the mold with the back of a knife, or dip it back into the hot water for another minute.

SERVING SUGGESTIONS
· Serve with Blackberry Compote (page 18).
· For something more complex, add Blood-Orange Sorbet (page 93) or Strawberry Sorbet (page 21).
· For a composed dessert, add Rose Meringues (page 157) and candied pistachios (see page 261).

FROZEN ORANGE–BLOSSOM HONEY MOUSSE

The combination of honey and orange blossoms is classically Middle Eastern. In this dessert these compelling flavors are suspended in a light, airy mousse. I add a touch of Grand Marnier to underscore the citrus flavor of the orange-flower water. This mousse is particularly creamy due to the honey in the sugar syrup. For the most intense flavor, make sure to use high-quality orange-blossom honey. It should taste like orange blossoms, not just sweet and syrupy.

Yield: 8 servings

1   cup heavy cream
¼   cup crème fraîche
2   teaspoons Grand Marnier
1   teaspoon orange-flower water
¼   cup plus 2 tablespoons orange-
    blossom honey
2   tablespoons light corn syrup
1   tablespoon sugar
3   large egg whites

1. Using an electric mixer, whip the heavy cream, crème fraîche, Grand Marnier, and orange-flower water until the mixture holds soft peaks.

2. In a small, heavy saucepan over medium heat, combine the honey, light corn syrup, and sugar. Cook without stirring until the mixture reaches 248°F. (firm ball stage) on a candy thermometer, 8 to 10 minutes.

3. Meanwhile, when the sugar reaches 238°F. in the bowl of an electric mixer, whip the egg whites until they hold medium peaks. When the honey syrup is ready, set the mixer to low speed and drizzle the syrup into the whites in a slow and steady stream. Once fully incorporated, increase the mixer speed and whip until the mixture is cool, about 5 minutes.

4. Fold a third of the reserved whipped cream into the egg white mixture, then fold in the rest in two additions. Gently spoon the mixture into eight 4-ounce molds or parfait glasses. Cover with plastic wrap and freeze for at least 6 hours.

SERVING SUGGESTIONS
· Serve with Blackberry Compote (page 18) or Caramel Blood Oranges (page 89).
· For something more complex, add candied pistachios (see page 261) or Citrus Lace Tuiles (page 90).

ROSE MERINGUES

With a sweet, melting crispiness that disappears as soon as you bite down, these thin, delicate meringues are like grown-up Necco wafers. My inspiration was the vacherin, a classic French dessert in which meringue is piped into the form of a bowl or tart shell and filled with sorbet or fruit. But my version is more delicate and modern—a vacherin pared down to its essence. Layer the wafers with berries to make a napoleon, serve them with a tart sorbet to cut their sweetness, or simply eat them as cookies.

To form these meringues, you can just spread the batter onto the baking sheets with the back of a spoon. Or, for something more refined, spread them into stencils, which are available at large kitchenware supply stores. Be advised that the rose flavor in these will soften when they bake, so be sure to flavor the meringue a little more strongly than you might initially think you need to.

Yield: 28 meringues

4   large egg whites
1½ cups confectioners' sugar
½ to 1½ teaspoons rose water
      (or to taste)

1. Preheat the oven to 200°F. Line 2 baking sheets with nonstick liners or parchment paper. In the bowl of an electric mixer, beat the egg whites until they hold soft peaks. Slowly add the confectioners' sugar and beat for 10 to 12 minutes, or until the mixture is very stiff. Add the rose water ½ teaspoon at a time to taste.

2. Drop tablespoon amounts of batter onto the baking sheets, leaving 3 inches of space between each. Using the back of the spoon, smooth each meringue into a flat disk. Bake for 2 to 2¼ hours, or until the meringues can be easily lifted off the liners and are completely dried out. Cool thoroughly and store the meringues in an airtight container for up to 2 days. They can be recrisped in a 200°F. oven if necessary.

SERVING SUGGESTIONS
· Serve with lightly sweetened fresh raspberries and sliced strawberries.
· For something more complex, add Goat Yogurt–Rose Mousse (page 207).
· For a composed dessert, add scoops of Yogurt Sorbet (page 213) or Raspberry Sorbet (page 20).

BASIL ICE CREAM

Basil is so abundant in the summer that it just begs to be used everywhere. With its sweet, bright, almost cinnamon-like flavor, it seemed like a natural for desserts. Like all herbs, basil shines when it's infused in cream, and here it really lends a delicious mix of cooling, fresh, and spicy flavors to this vibrant ice cream.

Yield: About 1 quart

2   cups packed fresh basil leaves (about 2 ounces)
¼   cup Simple Syrup (page 261)
3   cups milk
1   cup heavy cream
1   cup sugar
12 large egg yolks
½   tablespoon vanilla extract
Pinch of salt

1. Fill a small bowl with ice water and set aside. Meanwhile, bring a small saucepan of water to a boil and blanch the basil leaves for 30 seconds. Remove the basil with a slotted spoon and quickly plunge into the ice bath. Drain the leaves, lay them out on a paper towel, and blot to remove the excess water. Purée the basil in a blender with the Simple Syrup.

2. In a heavy saucepan, combine the milk, cream, and ¾ cup of the sugar. Bring the mixture to a simmer.

3. Meanwhile, whisk together the egg yolks and the remaining ¼ cup of sugar.

4. Remove the milk mixture from the heat and add a little to the egg yolk mixture to warm it, whisking constantly to keep the yolks from curdling. Pour the egg yolk mixture into the hot milk mixture, whisking the milk constantly as you pour.

5. Return the custard to the stove and cook it over low heat, stirring constantly with a wooden spoon, until it thickens enough to coat the back of the spoon. Let cool completely. Stir in the basil purée. Strain the custard, then stir in the vanilla extract and salt. Chill the custard until it's thoroughly cold, at least 4 hours.

6. Freeze in an ice-cream maker according to the manufacturer's instructions.

SERVING SUGGESTIONS
- Serve with Gingersnaps (page 176).
- For something more complex, add Sauté of Tomatoes and Plums (page 121).
- For a composed dessert, add basil syrup (see page 262).

BLACK MINT ICE CREAM

Black mint is a type of peppermint with a spicy, bracing flavor. It gives this ice cream a cool taste reminiscent of the center of a York Peppermint Pattie, or the cold, sweet, mentholated quality of peppermint schnapps. You can find black mint at farmer's markets in the summer, or use regular peppermint. But don't substitute spearmint. It has a completely different flavor.

Yield: About 1 quart

3   cups milk
1   cup cream
1¼ cups sugar
1   ounce fresh black mint leaves
    (about 1 cup, packed)
12 large egg yolks

1. In a heavy saucepan, combine the milk, cream, 1 cup of the sugar, and the mint; bring the mixture to a simmer.

2. Meanwhile, whisk together the egg yolks and the remaining ¼ cup of sugar.

3. Remove the milk mixture from the heat and add a little to the egg yolk mixture to warm it, whisking constantly to keep the yolks from curdling. Pour the egg yolk mixture into the hot milk mixture, whisking the milk constantly as you pour.

4. Return the custard to the stove and cook it over low heat, stirring constantly with a wooden spoon, until it thickens enough to coat the back of the spoon. Remove from the heat and pour it into a bowl. Let cool completely. Strain the custard, then chill until it's thoroughly cold, at least 4 hours.

5. Freeze in an ice-cream maker according to the manufacturer's instructions.

SERVING SUGGESTION
- Serve with Individual Chocolate Soufflé Cakes (page 217) or Chocolate Brownie Cookies (page 229) and/or a drizzle of mint syrup (see page 262).

LEMON VERBENA ICE CREAM

This floral and fragrant ice cream is a pure celebration of summer. As with the lemon verbena custards, don't try to replace the fresh lemon verbena with dried. It just doesn't have the same delightful flavor. Instead, serve this ice cream when you can buy bunches of aromatic verbena at farmer's markets. It's heavenly on top of a warm, seasonal fruit cobbler or crisp.

Yield: About 1 quart

3   cups milk
1   cup cream
1¼   cups sugar
1   cup packed fresh lemon verbena
     leaves (about 1 ounce)
12   large egg yolks

1. In a heavy saucepan, combine the milk, cream, 1 cup of the sugar, and the lemon verbena; bring the mixture to a simmer.

2. Meanwhile, whisk together the egg yolks and the remaining ¼ cup of sugar.

3. Remove the milk mixture from the heat and add a little to the egg yolk mixture to warm it, whisking constantly to keep the yolks from curdling. Pour the egg yolk mixture into the hot milk mixture, whisking the milk constantly as you pour.

4. Return the custard to the stove and cook it over low heat, stirring constantly with a wooden spoon, until it thickens enough to coat the back of the spoon. Remove from the heat and pour it into a bowl. Let cool completely. Strain the custard, then chill until it's thoroughly cold, at least 4 hours.

5. Freeze in an ice-cream maker according to the manufacturer's instructions.

SERVING SUGGESTIONS
· Serve with Nectarine-Blueberry Cobbler (page 31).
· For a composed dessert, serve with scoops of Raspberry Sorbet (page 20), Vanilla Shortbread (page 191), and lightly sweetened fresh raspberries.

TARRAGON ICE CREAM

I think of tarragon as the herbal equivalent of anise. It has a lively licorice flavor that's lighter and fresher than that of the spice. Made into ice cream, it becomes one of my favorite summer treats, one that pairs particularly well with the season's many fruits.

Yield: About 1 quart

1 ounce fresh tarragon leaves (about 1 cup, packed)
¼ cup Simple Syrup (page 261)
3 cups milk
1 cup cream
1 cup sugar
12 large egg yolks
½ tablespoon vanilla extract
Pinch of salt

1. Fill a small bowl with ice water and set aside. Bring a small saucepan of water to a boil and blanch the tarragon leaves for 30 seconds. Remove the tarragon with a slotted spoon and quickly plunge into the ice bath. Drain the leaves, lay them out on a paper towel, and blot to remove excess water. Purée the tarragon in a blender with the Simple Syrup.

2. In a heavy saucepan, combine the milk, cream, and ¾ cup of the sugar. Bring the mixture to a simmer.

3. Meanwhile, whisk together the egg yolks and the remaining ¼ cup of sugar.

4. Remove the milk mixture from the heat and add a little to the egg yolk mixture to warm it, whisking constantly to keep the yolks from curdling. Pour the egg yolk mixture into the hot milk mixture, whisking the milk constantly as you pour.

5. Return the custard to the stove and cook it over low heat, stirring constantly with a wooden spoon, until it thickens enough to coat the back of the spoon. Pour the custard into a bowl and let cool completely. Stir in the tarragon purée. Strain the custard, then stir in the vanilla extract and salt. Chill the custard until it's thoroughly cold, at least 4 hours.

6. Freeze in an ice-cream maker according to the manufacturer's instructions.

SERVING SUGGESTION
· Serve with Anise Shortbread (page 175) and sliced fresh strawberries.

HONEY–LEMON THYME SORBET

Lemon thyme is not a mix of thyme and lemon but an herb with a marvelous citrusy taste of its own. Lighter than thyme, brighter than lemon verbena, and without the sweetness of herbs like mint, basil, and tarragon, lemon thyme marries marvelously with the earthy sweetness of honey. And lemon and honey are a natural together, so this sorbet should make sense, even to those who don't expect to find herbs on their plate after dinner. You can also serve this sorbet as a palate-cleansing intermezzo.

Yield: 1 quart

¾ cup plus 2 tablespoons honey
1 cup fresh lemon thyme leaves (about 1 ounce)
⅛ vanilla bean, split lengthwise, pulp scraped (see page 180)

1. In a large saucepan, combine 1 quart water with all the ingredients. Bring the mixture to a simmer, stirring to dissolve the honey. Turn off the heat and allow to cool to room temperature.

2. Strain the mixture through a fine sieve and chill until it's very cold, about 3 hours. Freeze in an ice-cream machine according to the manufacturer's directions.

SERVING SUGGESTION
• Serve with whipped crème fraîche and/or Lemon Macaroons (page 85) or Pine-Nut Tart with Rosemary (page 134).

SPICES

Where would we be without spices? Everything would be plain vanilla. I use spices throughout this book to add texture, flavor, and the sensation of temperature, but this chapter is set aside for the adoration of spices. This is where their flavor is king.

Since a single spice on its own can often be too intense and overwhelming, spices are usually blended. But when using a combination of spices, their relative intensities have to be taken into account. For example, you can use cinnamon in larger quantities than cloves or more ginger than cardamom.

I like to borrow spices from the savory spice cupboard—after all, the spices that we think of as sweet spices are used in savory cooking all the time. If nutmeg is nice in a béchamel, why not put black pepper on a tuile? I particularly like to use black pepper with other, more traditionally sweet spices, such as cinnamon and star anise.

To truly appreciate their flavors, make sure you are getting fresh spices; the ones sitting in the cupboard for years have probably lost all of their personality. Ideally, you should try to buy whole spices and grind them yourself, in small quantities for short-term use. The flavor of a spice is in its volatile oils. Grinding exposes the oils to the air, which causes their flavor to begin to evaporate. If you do buy ground spices, buy small amounts, and store them in a dark place to preserve their flavor.

Some of my recipes call for toasting spices because heat releases their essential oils. Another way to flavor with spices, without grinding or toasting, is to infuse them in a liquid. For example, whole cinnamon sticks are simmered in the base for the Cinnamon Crème Brûlée, then strained out.

Although I use it in this chapter, fresh ginger isn't a spice but a rhizome. Still, it possesses a hot, spicy flavor that works well on its own, or in combination with the other spices in this chapter. Fresh gingerroot should be firm, plump, and shiny. The best way to grate ginger is to freeze it first. Buy extra ginger, cut it into 1-inch cubes, and stick it in the freezer for up to 6 months. Then whenever you need it, you'll have good-quality, fresh ginger on hand that you can grate up in a second.

Spices are great partners for beers and wines, depending upon their intensity. Guinness Stout Ginger Cake is perfectly matched by a big, rich beer, ideally an oatmeal stout to reinforce that flavor. The refreshing bitterness of an India Pale Ale is a surprising choice that might seem odd at first, but its play of textures and temperatures coalesces as you drink, making it a great counterpart to spice notes. Another excellent option is an aged rum from the Caribbean or South America. These offer all the deep notes of a cognac or brandy, with a bit more sweetness, which make it easy to enjoy with spiced desserts.

SUGAR-AND-SPICE DOUGHNUTS

A perfect after-school snack, these spicy little doughnuts are like warm, fluffy pillows. Since they are yeast-risen, they are light and soft, with a compelling buttery taste. The best way to enjoy these is right out of the fryer, tossed in sugar and spices. That way, the doughnuts are still warm enough to heat the spices and release their flavors. The addition of orange-flower water to the dough is a subtle nod to the Middle East that pairs beautifully with the cinnamon and cardamom, giving these doughnuts a slight fragrance and a little more complexity than the average type.

To make these ahead, follow the recipe up to the point of rolling out the dough and shaping them, then wrap them in plastic and refrigerate for up to 24 hours. Take the doughnuts out of the refrigerator 30 minutes before you want to fry them.

Yield: 5½ dozen doughnuts

DOUGHNUTS
½   cup milk
⅓   cup plus ½ tablespoon sugar
½   tablespoon active dry yeast
2½   cups all-purpose flour
⅛   teaspoon ground mace
½   teaspoon salt
1   large egg
1   tablespoon orange-flower water
4   tablespoons unsalted butter, melted
    Vegetable oil for frying

SUGAR-AND-SPICE TOPPING
1   cup sugar
1   teaspoon ground cinnamon
¼   teaspoon salt
⅛   teaspoon ground cardamom

1. To make the doughnuts, in a small saucepan, heat the milk until it feels warm, not hot, to the touch. Pour the milk into a small bowl and stir in ½ tablespoon of the sugar and the yeast. Set aside for 10 minutes, until the mixture is bubbly.

2. In the bowl of an electric mixer fitted with a paddle attachment, combine the flour, the remaining ⅓ cup sugar, the mace, and the salt. In a separate bowl, whisk together the egg, 3 tablespoons water, and the orange-flower water. On low speed, add the yeast mixture, egg mixture, and melted butter to the dry ingredients, mixing until just combined. Switch to a dough hook and knead the dough on medium speed until it begins to form a ball and pulls away from the sides of the bowl, 18 to 20 minutes. Place the dough in a large greased bowl and cover tightly with plastic wrap. Refrigerate overnight.

3. Roll the dough out on a lightly floured surface to ¼-inch thickness. Gently lift the dough up to allow it to contract slightly. Wrap it in plastic and chill it for 30 minutes to allow the dough to rest.

4. Meanwhile, combine all the ingredients for the topping in a large mixing bowl and set aside.

5. Line a baking sheet with parchment paper and spray the paper with cooking spray. Cut the dough into 1-inch squares and space them ½ inch apart on the prepared sheet. Spray a second sheet of parchment paper and use it to cover the doughnuts. Place the tray in a warm place and let rise for 30 minutes.

6. Fill a heavy, deep saucepan halfway with oil and heat over medium-high heat to 375°F. on a deep-frying or candy thermometer. Meanwhile, line a large platter or baking sheet with several layers of paper towels. Once the oil is at the proper temperature, carefully drop the doughnuts into the hot oil in batches, leaving enough space between them so they're not crowded. Fry for 1 to 2 minutes on each side, until lightly browned. Use

a slotted spoon to transfer the dough-nuts as they cook to the paper-towel-lined platter. Always check the temperature between batches to allow the oil to come back up to 375°F. Once the doughnuts are cool enough to handle, but still warm, toss with the spice topping in the mixing bowl. Shake off any excess and serve immediately.

SERVING SUGGESTION
• Serve with Orange-Cardamom Shakes (page 208) or Black and White Chocolate Malteds (page 226).

SAFFRON RICE PUDDING

Arborio rice and saffron make this pudding so luscious, creamy, and yellow that it seems like it must be enriched with eggs yolks. But it's not. The starch in the Arborio rice creates an instant eggless custard, while the sparing use of saffron adds a nutty spiciness. Although Arborio is the same rice used for risotto, there is no need to stir the pudding continuously; simply keep it at a low simmer and it will agitate the mixture, creating a creamy custard.

Yield: 6 to 8 servings

5   cups milk
½   cup plus 2 tablespoons sugar
1   tablespoon grated orange zest
¼   cinnamon stick (about 1 inch long)
¼   vanilla bean, split in half lengthwise, pulp scraped (see page 180)
Large pinch of saffron
¾   cup Arborio rice
1   cup crème fraîche

1. In a large, heavy saucepan, bring the milk, sugar, zest, cinnamon, vanilla pod and pulp, and saffron to a boil. Add the rice and allow to boil for 1 minute, then reduce to a low simmer. Stir occasionally to ensure that the rice is not sticking to the bottom, and simmer uncovered until the rice is tender, 45 to 50 minutes.

2. Fill a large bowl with ice water. Scrape the pudding into a medium metal bowl and submerge it halfway into the ice water. Stir the pudding gently with a spatula until it cools.

3. Using an electric mixer, whip the crème fraîche until it forms stiff peaks. Once it is cooled, fold the whipped crème fraîche into the rice. Either serve immediately or refrigerate until serving, up to 24 hours.

SERVING SUGGESTIONS
· Serve with Gingersnaps (page 176) and Macerated Dried Sour Cherries (page 265).
· For a composed dessert, make a napoleon by replacing the tamarind-glazed mango with the pudding (see recipe page 97), and serve with Caramel Blood Oranges (page 89) and candied pistachios (see page 261).

CINNAMON CRÈME BRÛLÉE

The oils in cinnamon bark give creamy cinnamon desserts an unbelievably silky texture. In this variation on a classic crème brûlée, the warm toasty qualities of the spice and the intense burnt-sugar topping complement each other perfectly.

Yield: 6 servings

2   cups heavy cream
1   cup milk
¾   cup sugar
5   cinnamon sticks
6   large egg yolks
Pinch of salt

1. Preheat the oven to 350°F. In a heavy saucepan, over medium heat, bring the cream, milk, ¼ cup of the sugar, and the cinnamon sticks to a simmer.

2. Meanwhile, whisk together the egg yolks and ¼ cup of the sugar.

3. Remove the cream mixture from the heat and add a little to the egg yolk mixture to warm it, whisking constantly to keep the yolks from curdling. Pour the egg yolk mixture into the hot cream mixture, whisking the cream constantly as you pour. Let the cream mixture cool completely. Strain through a fine sieve and stir in the salt. Chill for at least 2 hours and up to 2 days.

4. Pour the mixture into six 4-ounce glass or ceramic ramekins. Arrange the ramekins in a baking pan and place it on the oven rack. Pour enough very hot water into the baking pan to reach two-thirds of the way up the sides of the ramekins. Cover the baking pan with foil and pierce the foil in a few places with a knife. Bake the custards for 30 minutes, then lift off a corner of the foil to allow the steam to escape. Re-cover the pan and allow the custards to bake for 15 to 25 minutes longer, until they are set around the edges but still slightly jiggly in the center. Transfer the ramekins to a rack and let cool completely, then cover and refrigerate for at least 6 hours, or overnight.

5. Right before serving, sprinkle the remaining sugar in a thin, even coating on the surface of each custard, using 2 teaspoons for each one. Use a preheated broiler or a blowtorch to caramelize the sugar. In a broiler it will take 1 to 2 minutes, and it will take about 30 seconds with a blowtorch.

SERVING SUGGESTION
· Serve with Maple-Glazed Winter Squash and Apple Compote (page 125) and Cashew–Chocolate Chip Crisps (page 141) or Pecan Sandies (page 144).

GUINNESS STOUT GINGER CAKE

The recipe for this moist, dark, fragrant gingerbread pays tribute to Dona Abramson and Stuart Tarabour at the Bright Food Shop, a terrific little Mexican-fusion café in Chelsea where I spent some time. This was my favorite of their desserts, and it has since become a seasonal classic at Gramercy Tavern, though I've made a few adaptations and embellished a bit. My recipe has just a touch of cloves, and instead of just the ginger and cinnamon in a typical gingerbread, I use a panoply of spices, including cardamom, nutmeg, and a lot of fresh ginger, to give the cake a racy, intriguing flavor.

The most unusual thing about this recipe is that stout is substituted for the water or coffee used in most gingerbread recipes. I find it adds a lot of richness and underscores the spices. Since it is made with oil, this cake will stay moist for several days. Dress it up or simply enjoy it on its own, with coffee, tea, or a beer!

Yield: 8 servings

1   cup Guinness stout
1   cup molasses
½   tablespoon baking soda
3   large eggs
½   cup granulated sugar
½   cup firmly packed dark brown sugar
¾   cup grapeseed or vegetable oil
2   cups all-purpose flour
2   tablespoons ground ginger
1½ teaspoons baking powder
¾   teaspoon ground cinnamon
¼   teaspoon ground cloves
¼   teaspoon freshly grated nutmeg
⅛   teaspoon ground cardamom
1   tablespoon grated, peeled fresh gingerroot (see page 165)

1. Preheat the oven to 350°F. Butter a 9 × 5-inch loaf pan, line the bottom and sides with parchment, and grease the parchment. Alternatively, butter and flour a 6-cup Bundt pan.

2. In a large saucepan over high heat, combine the stout and molasses and bring to a boil. Turn off the heat and add the baking soda. Allow to sit until the foam dissipates.

3. Meanwhile, in a bowl, whisk together the eggs and both sugars. Whisk in the oil.

4. In a separate bowl, whisk together the flour, ground ginger, baking powder, cinnamon, cloves, nutmeg, and cardamom.

5. Combine the stout mixture with the egg mixture, then whisk this liquid into the flour mixture, half at a time. Add the fresh ginger and stir to combine.

6. Pour the batter into the loaf pan and bake for 1 hour, or until the top springs back when gently pressed. Do not open the oven until the gingerbread is almost done or the center may fall slightly. Transfer to a wire rack to cool.

SERVING SUGGESTION
· Serve with scoops of Ginger Ice Cream (page 178) and/or Caramel Blood Oranges (page 89).

MIXED-PEPPER TUILES

These tuiles have a lot of pep for a cookie. What is normally a dainty confection becomes positively piquant when sprinkled with two different types of peppercorn. The black pepper gives the cookies their hot spice, while the pink pepper adds a floral, piney note. The combination makes for a sophisticated cookie that is better suited to an after-dinner drink than a delicate cup of tea. Or serve them as an accompaniment to berry desserts and sorbets, since berries have a particular affinity for pepper.

Yield: 28 cookies

7 tablespoons unsalted butter, softened
1 cup confectioners' sugar, sifted
4 large egg whites (about ½ cup), at room temperature
½ cup all-purpose flour, sifted
Pinch of salt
½ teaspoon vanilla extract
2 tablespoons turbinado (raw) sugar
1 tablespoon pink peppercorns, crushed
1 teaspoon black peppercorns, crushed

1. In the bowl of an electric mixer fitted with a paddle attachment, beat the butter and sugar on medium speed until combined. Add the egg whites slowly until incorporated, scraping down the sides of the bowl with a spatula as necessary. On low speed, add the flour and salt. Add the vanilla and increase the mixer speed to medium. Beat until smooth, scraping the bowl once or twice. Cover and refrigerate for at least 4 hours and up to 5 days.

2. Preheat the oven to 350°F. Use nonstick baking sheets or line regular baking sheets with nonstick liners or parchment paper. For each tuile, drop a heaping teaspoon of batter onto the baking sheet, leaving 3 inches in between. Using a small offset spatula or the back of a spoon, gently pat each mound of batter into a very thin, very even 4-inch round.

3. In a small bowl, combine the turbinado sugar, pink peppercorns, and black peppercorns. Sprinkle each tuile with some of the pepper mix. Bake the cookies until they are golden brown all over, 5 to 6 minutes. Transfer the pans to a wire rack to cool for 1 minute. Using a plastic dough scraper or a spatula, carefully remove the tuiles from the pans and place them on a wire rack to cool completely.

4. Cool the baking sheets between batches, and continue making cookies until all the batter is used up.

SERVING SUGGESTION
• Serve with Cantaloupe Sorbet (page 56) and fresh cantaloupe.

ANISE SHORTBREAD

When my grandmother came to visit us, the most exciting things that she brought were fennel, pomegranates, and her packaged Italian anisette toasts, which I loved. I have taken that delicious anisette memory and translated it into a sweeter, richer cookie with that same compelling flavor. The result is a buttery shortbread with a lovely licorice taste.

Yield: 3½ dozen cookies

- 1 tablespoon anise seeds
- 1 cup (2 sticks) unsalted butter, softened
- ¾ cup confectioners' sugar
- 1 teaspoon vanilla extract
- ½ teaspoon anise extract
- 2 cups all-purpose flour
- ½ teaspoon salt

1. In a small skillet over high heat, toast the anise seeds, stirring, until fragrant, about 2 minutes. Transfer to a plate to cool.

2. Using an electric mixer, beat the butter and sugar until smooth. Add the vanilla and anise extracts and beat well. Beat in the flour, anise seeds, and salt until just combined. Form the dough into a disk, wrap in plastic wrap, and chill for at least 3 hours.

3. Preheat the oven to 325°F. Divide the dough in half and roll each piece between two sheets of wax paper to ¹⁄₁₆ inch thick (a 14 × 10-inch rectangle). Cut out rounds using a 2½-inch cookie cutter and arrange them on ungreased cookie sheets (do not reroll the scraps). Prick the shortbread with a fork and bake until light brown around the edges, 10 to 13 minutes. Cool on a wire rack.

SERVING SUGGESTION
- For a composed dessert, make a napoleon by layering the shortbread with Tarragon-Macerated Strawberries (page 12), Pernod Whipped Cream (page 124), and Strawberry Sorbet (page 21).

GINGERSNAPS

These gingersnaps are so snappy that when you break them it actually sounds as if you've snapped your fingers. The snap is not only in their texture but in the spicy fresh ginger flavor as well. Don't make these just around the holidays; they are too delightful to serve only once a year.

Yield: 6 dozen cookies

1¾ cups firmly packed dark brown sugar
1½ cups (3 sticks) unsalted butter, softened
1 large egg
1 tablespoon grated, peeled fresh gingerroot (see page 165)
1½ teaspoons grated lemon zest
3¾ cups all-purpose flour
2 tablespoons ground ginger
3 teaspoons ground cinnamon
1¼ teaspoons baking powder
½ teaspoon ground white pepper
¼ teaspoon ground cloves
2 tablespoons turbinado (raw) sugar

1. Using an electric mixer, beat the sugar and butter until smooth. Add the egg, gingerroot, and lemon zest and beat well.

2. In a bowl, whisk together the flour, ginger, cinnamon, baking powder, white pepper, and cloves. Gradually add the dry ingredients to the butter mixture, beating until well combined. Form the dough into a large disk, wrap in plastic, and chill for at least 4 hours, or overnight.

3. Preheat the oven to 350°F. Scoop out 1 teaspoon of the dough at a time and roll it between the palms of your hands to form a ball. Place the balls on a cookie sheet and press down hard with the base of a drinking glass that has been dipped in flour (to prevent sticking) to form thin rounds. Sprinkle the tops of the cookies with turbinado sugar and bake for 8 to 10 minutes, until crisp and browned. Transfer to a wire rack to cool.

SERVING SUGGESTION
• Serve with Concord Grape Parfaits (page 49).

GINGERSNAP ICE CREAM

Don't be misled; this is not ice cream with crumbled-up gingersnaps in it. This ice cream is a gingersnap in frozen form. To make it, gingersnap ingredients are added to a custard base rather than a cookie dough, then churned into one of the most aromatic ice creams around. With its intense fragrance and flavor, it's a terrific winter dessert that is frozen yet warming.

To crack the peppercorns and cardamom pods, hit them with the flat side of a knife.

Yield: About 1 quart

2   ounces peeled fresh gingerroot, sliced (about 16 quarter-size slices)
3   cups milk
1   cup heavy cream
⅓   cup granulated sugar
4   cinnamon sticks
1   tablespoon cracked black peppercorns
½   nutmeg, crushed
2   cardamom pods, cracked
12 large egg yolks
½   cup firmly packed dark brown sugar
2   tablespoons dark molasses
Pinch of salt

1. Fill a medium saucepan with water and bring to a boil. Add the ginger and let it blanch for 1 minute. Using a slotted spoon, transfer the ginger to a heavy saucepan. Add the milk, cream, granulated sugar, cinnamon, pepper, nutmeg, and cardamom and bring the mixture to a simmer over medium heat. Turn off the heat and allow the spices to infuse for 20 minutes.

2. Meanwhile, whisk together the egg yolks, brown sugar, and molasses.

3. Return the milk mixture to the heat and bring it to a boil. Turn off the heat and add a little of the hot milk to the egg yolk mixture to warm it, whisking constantly to keep the yolks from curdling. Pour the egg yolk mixture into the hot milk mixture, whisking the milk constantly as you pour.

4. Return the custard to the stove and cook it over low heat, stirring constantly with a wooden spoon, until it thickens enough to coat the back of the spoon, about 5 minutes. Remove from the heat, stir in the salt, and strain the custard through a fine sieve. Chill until thoroughly cold, at least 4 hours.

5. Freeze in an ice-cream maker according to the manufacturer's instructions.

SERVING SUGGESTIONS
· Serve with candied walnuts (see page 261).
· For something more complex, add Caramel Blood Oranges (page 89) or Maple-Glazed Winter Squash and Apple Compote (page 125).
· For a composed dessert, add Pumpkin Clafouti (page 123).

GINGER ICE CREAM

Subtler than my gingersnap ice cream, and without all the other spices, this is the pure essence of ginger. Its bright, crisp, clean, and spicy taste makes it a year-round favorite with tons of personality. It's superb on its own or served with just about anything.

Yield: About 1 quart

4 ounces peeled fresh gingerroot, roughly chopped (about 1 cup)
3 cups milk
1 cup heavy cream
1¼ cups sugar
12 large egg yolks
Pinch of salt

1. Fill a medium saucepan with water and bring to a boil. Add the ginger and let it blanch for 1 minute. Strain the ginger and place it in a blender or food processor. Process the ginger into a rough purée.

2. In a heavy saucepan, combine the milk, cream, 1 cup of the sugar, and the ginger purée; bring the mixture to a simmer.

3. Meanwhile, whisk together the egg yolks and the remaining ¼ cup of sugar.

4. Remove the milk mixture from the heat and add a little to the egg yolk mixture to warm it, whisking constantly to keep the yolks from curdling. Pour the egg yolk mixture into the hot milk mixture, whisking the milk constantly as you pour.

5. Return the custard to the stove and cook it over low heat, stirring constantly with a wooden spoon, until it thickens enough to coat the back of the spoon, about 5 minutes. Strain the mixture into a bowl, stir in the salt, and let cool completely. Chill the custard until it's thoroughly cold, at least 4 hours.

6. Freeze in an ice-cream maker according to the manufacturer's instructions.

SERVING SUGGESTION
· Serve with Pear Crisps with Dried Sour Cherries (page 62), or with Gingersnaps (page 176) and/or Chilled Rhubarb Soup (page 126).

BLACK PEPPER ICE CREAM

When I first started working at Gramercy Tavern, the chef, Tom Colicchio, asked me to put black pepper ice cream on the menu. At first I thought he was joking. But I soon learned what a fascinating flavor pepper is, with so many different qualities, and I became a quick convert. This unusual ice cream works because the pepper cuts through the richness of the cream, and its sharpness and slight heat give it a lot of sophistication. It's a versatile ice cream that pairs wonderfully with summer fruits like berries and peaches.

Yield: About 1 quart

3 cups milk
1 cup heavy cream
1¼ cups sugar
12 large egg yolks
1 tablespoon crushed
   black peppercorns
Pinch of salt

1. In a heavy saucepan, combine the milk, cream, and 1 cup of the sugar and bring to a simmer.

2. Meanwhile, whisk together the egg yolks and the remaining ¼ cup of sugar.

3. Remove the milk mixture from the heat and add a little to the egg yolk mixture to warm it, whisking constantly to keep the yolks from curdling. Pour the egg yolk mixture into the hot milk mixture, whisking the milk constantly as you pour.

4. Return the custard to the stove and cook it over low heat, stirring constantly with a wooden spoon, until it thickens enough to coat the back of the spoon, about 5 minutes.

5. Remove from the heat and strain into a bowl. Stir in the crushed peppercorns and the salt. Chill the custard until it's thoroughly cold, at least 4 hours.

6. Strain again and freeze in an ice-cream maker according to the manufacturer's instructions.

SERVING SUGGESTIONS
- Serve with scoops of Strawberry Sorbet (page 21) and Pistachio-Nut Brittle (page 142).
- For a composed dessert, serve with Passion Fruit–Pineapple Sorbet (page 111), Roasted Pineapple with Pink Peppercorns (page 103), Mixed-Pepper Tuiles (page 174), and macadamia-nut brittle (see Variation, page 142).

VANILLA BEANS

To get the most flavor out of a vanilla bean, it should be split in half lengthwise and scraped. To do this, use a small, sharp knife to split the pod, then use the tip of the knife to scrape out the pulp. In some recipes, just the pulp is called for, while in other recipes, the pod is used as well.

The pods contain a lot of flavor, and if you want, you can reuse them to make vanilla sugar. Rinse the pods first, then dry them thoroughly in a low oven (250°F.). Stick the pods in your sugar jar or bag. You'll be amazed at how much flavor they can impart.

SWEET ESSENCES

This book is arranged by ingredient, which, for the most part, means by season, since that's how I think about making desserts. I see what's at its most perfect ripeness at a given time of year, then create a dessert around it. But there are some compelling flavors that are available all year round, and these are an absolute boon for the pastry cook. Vanilla is the obvious perennial favorite and is a cherished taste that is equally good in winter and in summer. Others include coffee, maple syrup, spirits, and, my favorite, licorice. For lack of a better term, I call these sweet essences and have collected them in one chapter.

The beauty of this chapter is that you can make desserts from it any time of the year, without waiting for a fruit to ripen. While some of the desserts seem seasonal, like the Maple Flan in a Walnut Crust, others would be just as fitting served in the cold depths of winter as on a steamy summer night. For example, the Buttermilk Panna Cotta with Sauternes Gelée is light and cooling enough for summer but warming and festive enough for the holiday season because of the sophisticated addition of Sauternes. Chestnut-Honey Madeleines would pair just as well with fresh August raspberries as they would with Caramel Blood Oranges in February.

You will notice as you read through the chapter that sweet essences generally fall into two categories. Some of them are essentially drink flavors in dessert form, such as eggnog, espresso, Earl Grey, or Sauternes. Others are sweeteners that, unlike plain granulated sugar, have enough flavor to carry a dessert. This second category includes maple syrup, caramel, butterscotch, and chestnut honey. All of these essences enhance the desserts they're used in and give them a nuanced elegance that will pair well with seasonal fruits.

The desserts in this chapter run the gamut from sweet, creamy, and delicate to more tangy and robust. The more delicate, creamy choices, like Maple Flan in a Walnut Crust, Vanilla Shortbread, and Buttermilk Panna Cotta with Sauternes Gelée, can all be served with an upfront, fruity young Sauternes. The slightly more assertive flavors of Butterscotch Custards with Coconut Cream, Chestnut-Honey Madeleines, Caramel Ice Cream, and Eggnog Ice Cream can be paired with Madeiras made from the Bual or the Malvasia grape, which have a toasted-nut quality about them in their youth that goes well with the toasty flavors of these desserts. The coffee notes in LBV (late-bottled vintage) and ruby ports make them good options to serve with Espresso-Orange Panna Cotta Parfaits with Coffee Gelée and Espresso Shortbread.

BUTTERSCOTCH CUSTARDS WITH COCONUT CREAM

Yummy, rich, and satisfying, custards are the ultimate comfort food. This one has an added depth of flavor from the warm brown-sugar-and-caramel taste of butterscotch. If you need to substitute sweetened flaked coconut from the supermarket for the unsweetened, simply eliminate the sugar in the coconut cream.

Yield: 6 servings

BUTTERSCOTCH CUSTARD
4   tablespoons unsalted butter
1   cup firmly packed dark brown
     sugar
2½   cups heavy cream
3   tablespoons vanilla extract
1½   cups milk
½   teaspoon salt
8   large egg yolks

COCONUT CREAM
1   cup heavy cream
2   tablespoons sugar
½   cup grated unsweetened coconut

1. To make the butterscotch custard, in a small saucepan, melt the butter over medium heat. Add the brown sugar and stir until melted and smooth. Stir in 1 cup of the heavy cream and the vanilla and reserve.

2. In a medium, heavy saucepan whisk together the remaining 1½ cups heavy cream, the milk, salt, and reserved brown sugar mixture.

Bring to a simmer. Meanwhile, in a small bowl, whisk the egg yolks until smooth. Remove the brown sugar mixture from the heat and add a little to the egg yolks to warm them, whisking constantly to keep the yolks from curdling. Pour the egg yolk mixture into the brown sugar mixture, whisking the brown sugar mixture constantly as you pour.

3. Strain the custard through a fine sieve and chill for at least 2 hours and up to 2 days. Pour the custard into six 4-ounce glass or ceramic ramekins. Arrange them in a baking pan and place it on the oven rack. Pour enough very hot water into the baking pan to reach two-thirds of the way up the sides of the ramekins. Cover the baking pan with foil and prick all over with a fork. Bake the custards for 25 minutes, then lift off a corner of the foil to vent the steam. Re-cover the pan and continue to bake until the custards are set around the edges but still slightly jiggly in the

center, 10 to 15 minutes longer. Transfer the custards to a wire rack and let them cool at room temperature, then cover them and refrigerate overnight.

4. Preheat the oven to 325°F. To prepare the coconut cream, in a small saucepan, bring the cream and sugar to a simmer. Turn off the heat and add the coconut. Let the mixture infuse for 1 hour. Strain the coconut cream, discarding the solids, and chill until thoroughly cold, at least 2 hours.

5. Just before serving, use an electric mixer or a whisk to whip the cream until it holds soft peaks. Serve the custards topped with the coconut whipped cream.

SERVING SUGGESTION
· Serve with Coconut Tuiles (page 105), Gingersnaps (page 176), or Pecan Sandies (page 144).

CHESTNUT-HONEY MADELEINES

Tender honey madeleines are a classic French confection with a subtle taste. But substitute a more assertive honey, like the earthy chestnut variety I use in this recipe, and the whole character of the sweet changes. Now, these dainty, rich little cakes have verve. While they have much too much personality to dip in delicate lime-flower tea à la Proust, you might try them with a smoky Lapsang souchong, an espresso, or even hot chocolate.

If you can't find chestnut honey (which is available at specialty markets, or see page 269 for a mail-order source), try substituting another full-flavored honey such as lavender or wildflower. Or use regular honey for a more mellow-tasting madeleine.

Yield: 2 dozen madeleines

12 tablespoons (1½ sticks) unsalted butter, plus additional softened butter for the molds
4 large eggs
½ cup granulated sugar
2 tablespoons firmly packed dark brown sugar
¼ cup chestnut honey
1 cup all-purpose flour
½ cup cake flour
2 teaspoons baking powder
¼ teaspoon salt
Confectioners' sugar for dusting

1. In a small skillet over medium heat, melt the butter. Continue to let the butter cook until some of the white milk solids fall to the bottom of the skillet and turn a rich hazelnut brown, about 5 minutes. Strain the browned butter through a fine sieve into a small bowl.

2. In the bowl of an electric mixer fitted with the whisk attachment, beat the eggs, both sugars, and honey until pale and foamy, 2 to 3 minutes.

3. Sift both flours, the baking powder, and salt over the egg mixture and use a rubber spatula to gently fold in. Fold in the browned butter. Cover the batter and refrigerate for at least 8 hours, or overnight.

4. Preheat the oven to 400°F. Liberally butter the madeleine molds. Spoon or pipe the batter evenly into the molds. Bake for 5 to 7 minutes, until golden brown. Transfer the pans to a wire rack to cool for 5 minutes, then unmold the cakes and let them cool completely on the rack. Dust the madeleines with confectioners' sugar before serving.

SERVING SUGGESTION
· Serve with whipped crème fraîche, Roasted Chestnut-Honey Pears (page 71), and Chestnut Honey–Roasted Pine Nuts (page 262).

ESPRESSO-ORANGE PANNA COTTA PARFAITS WITH COFFEE GELÉE

This is a truly wintry dessert, perfect to make when fresh seasonal fruits are scarce. Two creamy layers of panna cotta, one scented with orange and the other with espresso, sandwich a jiggly, translucent band of espresso gelée. The visual effect of these three distinct tiers is striking, and the flavors are deep, rich, and inherently satisfying. After all, orange and coffee are a classic combination, as are coffee and cream.

Yield: 6 servings

ESPRESSO PANNA COTTA
1½ cups heavy cream
1   teaspoon unflavored powdered gelatin
3   tablespoons sugar
1   tablespoon finely ground espresso

ESPRESSO GELÉE
1   teaspoon unflavored powdered gelatin
1½ tablespoons finely ground espresso
3   tablespoons sugar

ORANGE PANNA COTTA
1½ cups heavy cream
1   teaspoon unflavored powdered gelatin
3   tablespoons sugar
1   tablespoon grated orange zest (about 1 orange, zested)

1. To prepare the espresso panna cotta, place ¼ cup of the heavy cream in a small bowl and sprinkle the gelatin over the top. Let the mixture rest for 5 minutes, until the gelatin softens. Meanwhile, in a small saucepan, combine the remaining 1¼ cups heavy cream, the sugar, and the ground espresso over medium-low heat. Bring to a simmer, then turn off the heat and let steep for 5 minutes.

2. Add the gelatin mixture to the saucepan with the espresso cream and place it over low heat. Warm the mixture, whisking, until the gelatin dissolves. Do not let it come to a simmer. Strain the mixture through a fine sieve lined with a double layer of cheesecloth, then pour it into 6 parfait glasses, dividing it evenly. Cover with plastic and refrigerate until set, about 1 hour.

3. To prepare the espresso gelée, place ¼ cup water in a small bowl and sprinkle the gelatin on top. Let the mixture rest for 5 minutes, until the gelatin softens. Bring an additional ¾ cup water to a simmer in a small saucepan. Add the ground espresso and sugar, turn off the heat, and let steep for 5 minutes.

4. Add the softened gelatin mixture to the espresso-sugar mixture and return the saucepan to low heat. Warm the mixture, whisking, until the gelatin dissolves. Do not let it come to a simmer. Strain through a fine sieve lined with a double layer of cheesecloth. Let the espresso mixture cool to room temperature. Gently pour it into the parfait glasses over the panna cotta layer. Cover with plastic and refrigerate until set, about 1 hour.

5. To prepare the orange panna cotta, place ¼ cup of the heavy cream in a small bowl and sprinkle the gelatin over the top. Let the mixture rest for 5 minutes, until the gelatin softens. Meanwhile, in a small saucepan, combine the remaining 1¼ cups heavy cream, the sugar, and the orange zest over medium-low heat. Bring to a simmer, then turn off the heat and let steep for 5 minutes.

6. Add the gelatin mixture to the saucepan with the orange cream and place it over low heat. Warm the mixture, whisking, until the gelatin dissolves. Do not let it come to a simmer. Strain the mixture through a fine sieve. Gently pour it into the parfait glasses over the espresso gelée, dividing it evenly. Cover with plastic and refrigerate until set, about 2 hours.

- Serve with Citrus Lace Tuiles (page 90), Cashew–Chocolate Chip Crisps (page 141), or Cornmeal-Nut Biscotti (page 140).
- For something more complex, add Caramel Blood Oranges (page 89) or Candied Kumquats (page 261).

BUTTERMILK PANNA COTTA WITH SAUTERNES GELÉE

Panna cotta, a traditional Italian dessert, is a silken, slightly wobbly custard made from lightly sugared heavy cream set with just a touch of gelatin. In my version, I cut the richness of the cream with tangy buttermilk and glaze the top with a thin layer of golden Sauternes gelée. The Sauternes—a dessert wine from the Bordeaux region of France—adds a sweetness that balances the acid of the buttermilk. The result is well rounded, luxurious, and highly complex. I like to serve tiny portions as a *dessert amuse,* or a pre-dessert, on the tasting menu at Gramercy. But here, I've increased the portion size to make this panna cotta an elegant dessert on its own.

Yield: 6 servings

1⅔ cups Sauternes or other white
    dessert wine, such as a muscat or
    late-harvest Riesling
¾   cup plus 1 tablespoon sugar
2-inch piece of vanilla bean, halved
    lengthwise, pulp scraped
    (see page 180)
2¼ teaspoons unflavored powdered
    gelatin
1¼ cups heavy cream
1¾ cups buttermilk

1. In a small saucepan, whisk together the Sauternes, 6 tablespoons of the sugar, and the vanilla bean pulp. Place the saucepan over medium-low heat and let the Sauternes reduce at a bare simmer (reducing the heat to low if necessary) until it measures 1 cup, about 45 minutes to an hour. Set aside.

2. Place 1½ teaspoons of the gelatin in a small bowl and add 1 tablespoon cold water. Let the gelatin sit for 5 minutes to soften.

3. Meanwhile, in a saucepan over medium-high heat, warm the cream with the remaining 7 tablespoons sugar, stirring until the sugar dissolves. Add the softened gelatin and stir until it dissolves. Turn off the heat and add the buttermilk. Strain the buttermilk mixture through a fine sieve into a measuring cup with a spout, then pour the mixture into six 6-ounce ramekins, bowls, or parfait glasses. Chill until firm, about 3 hours.

4. While the panna cottas are chilling, mix together the remaining ¾ teaspoon gelatin with ½ tablespoon cold water and let sit for 5 minutes to soften. Return the saucepan of Sauternes to the heat and bring to a simmer. Add the softened gelatin and stir until it dissolves.

5. Strain the mixture through a fine sieve into a clean heatproof glass measuring cup with a spout and let it come to room temperature. Check the Sauternes after 20 minutes. If you see gelatin crystals clinging to the sides of the measuring cup, place it in the microwave for 20 seconds, then stir well. (Alternatively, place the measuring cup in a pot filled halfway with simmering water and stir the Sauternes until the gelatin dissolves.)

6. When the panna cottas are set, stir up the cooled Sauternes mixture to redistribute the vanilla. Very gently pour a thin stream of the Sauternes down the sides of the ramekins to coat the tops of the custards (do this slowly; the creams are fragile). Chill until the Sauternes gelée is set, about 1 hour.

SERVING SUGGESTIONS
• Serve with Vanilla Shortbread (page 191).
• For a composed dessert, add Pear Sorbet with Poached Pear Compote (page 74).

MAPLE FLAN IN A WALNUT CRUST

Think custardy flan paired with crisp cookies. Add the compatibility of maple and walnut to the equation and you'll see how I came up with this unusual dessert. To make it, I unmold a maple-syrup-sweetened flan directly into a baked walnut tart crust. The buttery crust acts as a moat, containing and absorbing the caramel that slides off the flan, so that it doesn't have a chance to run all over your plate. Instead, you get all the rich, nutty flavors and creamy-crisp textures together in each bite. It's a completely satisfying dessert that takes flan to new heights.

There are a few things to keep in mind when making it. The first is to try to use grade-B maple syrup, which has a stronger taste than grade A and is generally better for cooking (you can buy it at specialty shops). The next is to simmer and reduce the maple syrup to concentrate it, which makes a richer, more satiny custard. And the last is to bake the crust in a quiche pan rather than a tart shell. A quiche pan is made in one piece, so if there are small tears in the dough and the caramel drips through, it won't leak out all over your serving platter. A tart pan with a removable bottom is a much riskier proposition.

If you'd rather forgo the tart shell, unmold the flan onto a platter and serve it with crisp cookies.

Yield: 8 servings

MAPLE FLAN
1   cup maple syrup, preferably grade B
3½ cups heavy cream
7   large egg yolks
⅛   teaspoon salt
½   cup plus 2 tablespoons sugar
½   teaspoon light corn syrup
Whipped crème fraîche for serving, optional

WALNUT CRUST
¼   cup walnuts
½   cup (1 stick) unsalted butter, softened
⅓   cup confectioners' sugar
1   large egg, lightly beaten
1½ cups all-purpose flour
½   cup plus 2 tablespoons almond flour
½   teaspoon salt

1. To prepare the flan, place the maple syrup in a large, heavy saucepan. Set it over low heat and let simmer until the syrup is reduced by a quarter (to ¾ cup), 15 to 20 minutes.

2. Add the cream to the syrup and stir until the mixture is smooth and comes back to a simmer.

3. In a large bowl, whisk the egg yolks until smooth. Add a little of the hot maple cream into the eggs to warm them, whisking constantly to keep the yolks from curdling. Pour the mixture into the saucepan, whisking the cream constantly. Strain the mixture into a bowl, stir in the salt, and chill for at least 2 hours and up to 5 days.

4. Preheat the oven to 300°F. Place ¼ cup water in a small saucepan over medium heat, then add the sugar and corn syrup. Raise the heat to high and cook, swirling the pan occasionally, until the mixture becomes a dark amber caramel, 7 to 10 minutes. Immediately pour the caramel into an 8-inch round nonstick cake pan, tilting to make sure the sides are well coated. Work quickly so the caramel doesn't harden. If it does, rewarm it over low heat.

5. Pour the maple custard into the caramel-coated cake pan. Place it in a baking pan and carefully move it to the oven rack. Pour enough very hot water into the baking pan to reach two-thirds of the way up the side of the cake pan. Cover the baking pan with foil and prick all over with a fork. Bake the flan for about 1 hour, then lift off a corner of the foil to vent the steam. Re-cover the pan and continue to bake until the flan is set

around the edges but still slightly jiggly in the center, about 45 minutes longer. Remove the flan from the baking pan and transfer to a rack. Let cool at room temperature, then cover and refrigerate overnight.

6. To prepare the walnut crust, preheat the oven to 350°F. Spread the nuts out on a baking sheet and toast them in the oven, stirring once or twice, until they smell nutty, about 10 minutes. Transfer the pan to a wire rack to cool.

7. Using a food processor, pulse the walnuts until they are finely ground, then reserve. In the bowl of an electric mixer fitted with the paddle attachment, beat the butter and confectioners' sugar until combined, about 1 minute. Beat in the egg. In a medium bowl, whisk together the flour, almond flour, walnuts, and salt. Add the flour mixture to the butter mixture in two batches, scraping down the sides of the bowl between additions. Mix until the dough just holds together. Scrape the dough onto a piece of plastic wrap and form it into a disk. Wrap it and chill for at least 1 hour, until firm.

8. Preheat the oven to 325°F. On a lightly floured surface, roll out the dough ⅛ inch thick to a 12-inch round. Fit the dough into a 9-inch quiche pan. Trim away any excess dough, then use a fork to prick the crust all over. Bake the tart crust until it's pale golden, about 25 minutes. Transfer the pan to a wire rack to cool. (The tart shell can be made 8 hours ahead and kept at room temperature or frozen; see page xxv.)

9. To unmold the flan, run a small knife around the sides of the cake pan, then invert the flan into the baked tart shell. Serve with whipped crème fraîche, if desired.

VARIATION

For individual flans without crust, divide the caramel and then the maple custard evenly among eight 4-ounce glass or ceramic ramekins. Bake as directed for 1 hour and 30 minutes, venting the steam after 45 minutes.

SERVING SUGGESTIONS
- Serve with whipped crème fraîche or sour cream.
- For something more complex, add Maple-Glazed Winter Squash and Apple Compote (page 125).

VANILLA SHORTBREAD

Simple and pure, golden, buttery shortbread is the original cookie. It is also extremely quick and easy, and most recipes will make an excellent cookie. But there are some ways to set your shortbread apart. Since the basic recipe uses a minimum of ingredients, make sure yours are the best. The butter should be fresh and unsalted, and the vanilla potent and fragrant. Try to handle the dough as little as possible, and chill it well before rolling it out. If you follow these guidelines, your shortbread will be melt-in-the-mouth tender and absolutely delicious.

Yield: 4½ dozen cookies

- 1 cup (2 sticks) unsalted butter, softened
- ¾ cup confectioners' sugar
- 2 teaspoons vanilla extract
- 2 cups all-purpose flour
- 1 teaspoon salt

1. Using an electric mixer fitted with the paddle attachment, beat the butter and sugar until creamy and smooth, about 2 minutes. Add the vanilla and beat well. Beat in the flour and salt until just combined.

Form the dough into a disk, wrap in plastic wrap, and chill for at least 3 hours or freeze for up to 2 months.

2. Preheat the oven to 300°F. Roll the dough between two sheets of wax paper to ¼ inch thick (a 9 × 12-inch rectangle). Using a sharp knife, cut the shortbread into 1 × 2-inch bars and place them 1 inch apart on ungreased baking sheets (do not reroll the scraps). Prick the shortbread with a fork and bake for 25 to 30 minutes, or until the bottoms turn lightly golden around the edges. Cool completely on a wire rack.

VARIATION

To make vanilla bean shortbread, add the pulp scraped from ½ vanilla bean (see page 180) to the dough along with the vanilla extract. Proceed with the recipe as directed.

SERVING SUGGESTION

- Serve with any ice cream, custard, or sorbet and/or a seasonal fruit dessert.

ESPRESSO SHORTBREAD

The slight bitterness of espresso is as perfect baked into sweet, buttery shortbread as it would be served alongside. Using ground espresso beans in the dough lends these cookies a lovely tan color, an intense coffee flavor, and a delicate crunch. Although the cookies are perfect as is, I don't think it would be gilding the lily to dip them halfway into melted chocolate (see Variation).

Yield: 2 dozen cookies

- 1 cup (2 sticks) unsalted butter, softened
- ⅔ cup confectioners' sugar
- 2 teaspoons vanilla extract
- 2 cups all-purpose flour
- ¼ cup ground espresso
- ½ teaspoon salt

1. Using an electric mixer fitted with the paddle attachment, beat the butter and sugar until creamy and smooth, about 2 minutes. Add the vanilla and beat well. On low speed, mix in the flour, espresso, and salt until just combined. Form the dough into a disk, wrap in plastic wrap, and chill for at least 2 hours.

2. Preheat the oven to 300°F. Roll the dough between two sheets of wax paper to ¼ inch thick (an 8 × 12-inch rectangle). Using a sharp knife, cut the shortbread into 2-inch squares and place them 1 inch apart on ungreased baking sheets (do not reroll the scraps). Prick the shortbread with a fork and bake until pale golden around the edges, 20 to 24 minutes. Cool completely on a wire rack.

VARIATION
To make chocolate-dipped espresso shortbread, melt 2½ ounces bittersweet chocolate, remove it from the heat, and add another 1½ ounces of chopped bittersweet chocolate. Stir continuously until the chocolate is at room temperature. (For tips, see page 216.) Dip each cookie halfway into melted chocolate, then place them on a wire rack and let stand undisturbed until the chocolate sets, about 2 hours. Store between sheets of wax paper in an airtight container.

SERVING SUGGESTION
- Serve with Pear Sorbet with Poached Pear Compote (page 74).

CARAMEL ICE CREAM

When I have a craving for ice cream, this is the flavor I reach for. I love its potent, bittersweet, nutty flavor and silken texture, all of which are the result of using a caramel cooked to the verge of burning. If you've never made caramel, letting it cook to the right color can be a little nerve-racking, since it goes from perfect to burnt in a millisecond. But if you watch carefully, you'll see the point at which the syrup turns from a golden amber to an almost foxy red-brown. That's when you should pull the pan away from the stove: the residual heat from the pan will cook it one shade darker, to an almost black hue just this side of burnt. Try to use a light-colored pan when making caramel. Or, if your pan is dark, test the syrup by spooning a little of it onto a white plate (make sure to take the pan away from the heat while you do this). Once it takes on a reddish, deeply brown cast and smells toasty, it's done.

Yield: About 1 quart

1½ cups sugar
1 teaspoon light corn syrup
1 cup heavy cream
3 cups milk
12 large egg yolks
1½ teaspoons vanilla extract
¾ teaspoon salt

1. Put ¼ cup water in a medium, heavy saucepan over medium heat. Add 1 cup of the sugar and the corn syrup and increase the heat to high. Cook, swirling the pan occasionally, until the mixture is dark amber brown and caramelized, about 7 minutes.

2. Add the heavy cream to the caramel—stand back, it may splatter.

Pour in the milk, bring the mixture to a simmer over medium heat, and cook, stirring, until the caramel dissolves and the mixture is smooth.

3. In a bowl, whisk together the egg yolks and the remaining ½ cup of sugar. Remove the caramel mixture from the heat and add a little to the egg yolk mixture to warm it, whisking constantly to keep the yolks from curdling. Pour the egg yolk mixture into the caramel mixture, whisking the caramel mixture constantly as you pour.

4. Return the custard to the stove and cook it over low heat, stirring constantly with a wooden spoon, until it thickens enough to coat the

back of the spoon. Remove from the heat and strain it into a bowl. Let cool completely. Add the vanilla and salt.

5. Chill the custard until it's thoroughly cold, at least 4 hours.

6. Freeze in an ice-cream maker according to the manufacturer's instructions.

SERVING SUGGESTION
· Serve with Citrus Lace Tuiles (page 90), Chocolate Brownie Cookies (page 229), or Earl Grey Chocolate Truffles (page 230).

EGGNOG ICE CREAM

Creamy, nutmeg-spiced eggnog is one of my favorite holiday indulgences, and has been since I was a child. It was something my dad was famous for. Every year at Christmas, he would stir together a big batch for the adults, but he was always sure to let me have a little nip. It was delicious!

Now I've turned my favorite holiday cheer into a compelling ice cream. It was easy to do. Since eggnog is essentially an egg custard spiked with brandy, rum, and sherry, all I did was reduce the amount of alcohol (which would prevent the ice cream from freezing) and pour the mixture into my ice-cream maker. I know my dad would approve.

Yield: About 1 quart

3 cups milk
1¼ cups sugar
1 cup heavy cream
12 large egg yolks
2 tablespoons sherry
2 tablespoons brandy
½ tablespoon vanilla extract
1 teaspoon Myers's Original
   Spiced Rum
¼ teaspoon freshly grated nutmeg
Pinch of salt

1. In a heavy saucepan, bring the milk, 1 cup of the sugar, and the cream to a simmer.

2. Meanwhile, whisk together the egg yolks and the remaining ¼ cup of sugar. Remove the milk mixture from the heat and add a little to the egg yolk mixture to warm it, whisking constantly to keep the yolks from curdling. Pour the egg yolk mixture into the hot milk mixture, whisking the milk constantly as you pour.

3. Return the custard to the stove and cook it over low heat, stirring constantly with a wooden spoon, until it thickens enough to coat the back of the spoon, about 5 minutes. Remove from the heat and strain it into a bowl. Let cool completely.

4. Stir the sherry, brandy, vanilla extract, rum, nutmeg, and salt into the custard. Chill until thoroughly cold, at least 4 hours.

5. Freeze in an ice-cream maker according to the manufacturer's instructions.

SERVING SUGGESTIONS

· Serve with Mixed-Pepper Tuiles (page 174), Gingersnaps (page 176), Vanilla Shortbread (page 191), or Pecan Sandies (page 144).
· For something more complex, add Roasted Dates with Sherry and Spices (page 101).

EARL GREY ICE CREAM

This is a frozen, sumptuous version of tea with milk and sugar. Since Earl Grey tea has such a smoky, fruity taste, I like to pair this ice cream with chocolate desserts, which I think possess some of those same nuances.

I always use loose tea leaves, which generally have the best, most complex flavor, but if you don't have any, substitute high-quality Earl Grey tea bags.

Yield: About 1 quart

3   cups milk
1¼   cups sugar
1   cup heavy cream
6   tablespoons Earl Grey tea leaves
     (or 2 tea bags)
12   large egg yolks
1½   teaspoons vanilla extract
Pinch of salt

1. In a heavy saucepan, bring the milk, 1 cup of the sugar, the cream, and the tea leaves or tea bags to a simmer.

2. Meanwhile, whisk together the egg yolks and the remaining ¼ cup of sugar. Remove the milk mixture from the heat and take out the tea bags if using. Add a little of the hot milk to the egg yolk mixture to warm it, whisking constantly to keep the yolks from curdling. Pour the egg yolk mixture into the hot milk mixture, whisking the milk constantly as you pour.

3. Return the custard to the stove and cook it over low heat, stirring constantly with a wooden spoon, until it thickens enough to coat the back of the spoon. Remove from the heat and strain it into a bowl. Let cool completely. Stir in the vanilla and salt.

4. Chill the custard until it's thoroughly cold, at least 4 hours.

5. Freeze in an ice-cream maker according to the manufacturer's instructions.

SERVING SUGGESTION
· Serve with a drizzle of Earl Grey Caramel (page 263) and Earl Grey Chocolate Truffles (page 230) or Vanilla Shortbread (page 191).

LICORICE ICE CREAM

Licorice, along with fennel and anise, is a flavor I have always adored. When I was a kid, all my friends saved their black jelly beans for me, and my mom and I shared all the black Chuckles from my father's big bag. So it was worth the trial and error it took to figure out how to flavor an ice cream like my favorite candy. First I tried licorice root, which is used in savory preparations, but the ice cream tasted like wood. So I tried licorice powder, which was hard to get and very sweet. Then I went back to where I had started, with licorice candy. I dissolved the candy in milk, cut back on the sugar in the recipe, and it worked like a charm. It is the creamiest ice cream ever, dense without being heavy, with the velvety texture of fudge and the taste that I cannot do without.

Yield: About 1 quart

3   cups milk
1   cup heavy cream
4   ounces Panda brand chewy
    licorice bars (about 2½ bars),
    cut into small pieces
12 large egg yolks
½   cup sugar
⅛   teaspoon salt

1. In a heavy saucepan, over medium heat, bring the milk, cream, and licorice to a simmer. Reduce the heat to very low and let the mixture cook below a simmer, stirring occasionally, until the licorice is mostly dissolved. This will take about 30 minutes. If the licorice isn't dissolving, mash it against the sides of the pot with the back of a spoon, or use a potato masher.

2. Meanwhile, whisk together the egg yolks and sugar. Remove the licorice mixture from the heat and add a little to the egg yolk mixture to warm it, whisking constantly to keep the yolks from curdling. Pour the egg yolk mixture into the hot licorice mixture, whisking constantly as you pour.

3. Return the custard to the stove and cook it over low heat, stirring constantly with a wooden spoon, until it thickens slightly, about 5 minutes. Transfer the mixture to a bowl and let it cool completely.

4. Strain the mixture through a fine sieve, stir in the salt, then chill until it's thoroughly cold, at least 4 hours.

5. Freeze in an ice-cream maker according to the manufacturer's instructions.

SERVING SUGGESTION
• Serve with Pear Crisps with Dried Sour Cherries (page 62).

CHEESE, MILK, AND CREAM

Dairy is one of the cornerstones of baking and dessert making, and dairy products can be incorporated into sweets in manifold ways. In this chapter I've tried to adapt and utilize a variety of products that go beyond the standard cream and milk.

Many versatile, mild cheeses are available, including cream cheese, triple-crème, and goat cheese. It's fun to experiment with new cheeses that appear on the market, and my aim is to expand the role of cheese beyond sandwiches, crackers, and the classic American cheesecake. Cheese and dairy desserts are a pleasant surprise, and they vary enough that you can find a recipe in this chapter to close any meal. These desserts run the gamut from rich and creamy, like Goat-Cheese Cheesecake, to much lighter and tangier, like Yogurt Sorbet. They pair very well with fresh or cooked seasonal fruit, and they make a great foundation for an unlimited number of composed desserts.

Of all the cheeses, I probably use mascarpone and goat cheese most often. Mascarpone is perhaps the most versatile of cheeses. Its texture is like sour cream, but thicker and denser, and it tastes like delicate, fresh-off-the-farm cream. The gentle flavor of mascarpone is sweet, but without the characteristics of sugar. It's quite fragile, however, and apt to break, so take care not to overwhip it. Fresh mild goat cheese has a nice tang and a lot of flavor, and because it's so dry, it flavors desserts without diluting them with excess moisture. I also love fresh ricotta cheese, which is creamy and luscious. It has its own place in desserts, lending a soft, rich, milky taste.

Crème fraîche is a great substitution for cream because it has the same smooth lushness, yet is denser and has a slight tang. When given the choice, I will always choose goat yogurt over regular yogurt because it has a more forward, pronounced flavor. If you don't like its tanginess, however, use plain yogurt instead.

The dairy desserts in this chapter are creamy and rich with varying degrees of acidity. For the cheese desserts, an accompanying beverage should have sweetness and enough alcohol and tannin to cut through their richness; serve a Banyuls or other *vin doux naturel*. (In essence, these wines are not "naturally sweet" but are unnaturally sweet; that is, a spirit is added to a fermenting wine, arresting the fermentation but creating a syrupy wine slightly higher in alcohol.)

Yogurt Sorbet and Goat Yogurt–Rose Mousse, both on the lighter side, are the only desserts in this chapter whose inherent acidity allows for a lighter wine. With these I would serve Austrian dessert wines by Kracher that are at least of Auslese level—these are light, but they still pack a punch that can take on the tang of goat milk.

TRIPLE-CRÈME TART

Triple-crème is a fresh, mild, very creamy cheese from France with a rich, salty flavor. Made into an airy dessert soufflé that's anchored in a crisp hazelnut crust, it is transformed into a compelling, billowy tart with sweet-savory flavor. Since pairing cheese and fruit is a classic way to end the meal, this tart is superb when served with fresh or dried fruit, or a fruit sorbet or compote.

Yield: 8 servings

HAZELNUT CRUST

- 5 tablespoons coarsely chopped hazelnuts
- ½ cup (1 stick) unsalted butter, softened
- ⅓ cup confectioners' sugar
- 1 large egg, lightly beaten
- 1½ cups all-purpose flour
- ½ cup plus 2 tablespoons almond flour
- ¼ teaspoon salt

TRIPLE-CRÈME FILLING

- 1 cup milk
- ¾ cup plus 3 tablespoons sugar
- 4 large eggs, separated
- 2 tablespoons cornstarch
- 10 ounces triple-crème cheese, such as Saint-André or Explorateur, rind removed and cut in pieces
- Pinch of freshly grated nutmeg
- 1 teaspoon light corn syrup

1. To make the crust, preheat the oven to 350°F. Spread the hazelnuts out on a baking sheet and toast them in the oven, stirring once or twice, until they smell nutty, about 7 minutes. Transfer the baking sheet to a wire rack to cool. Using a food processor, pulse the hazelnuts until they are very finely ground.

2. In the bowl of an electric mixer fitted with the paddle attachment, beat the butter and confectioners' sugar until combined, about 1 minute. Beat in the egg. In a medium bowl, whisk together the flour, almond flour, ground hazelnuts, and salt. Add the flour mixture to the butter mixture in two batches, scraping down the sides of the bowl between additions. Mix until the dough is well combined. Scrape the dough onto a piece of plastic wrap and form it into a disk. Chill for at least 1 hour and up to 3 days.

3. Preheat the oven to 325°F. On a lightly floured surface, roll the dough out to a 12-inch round. Fit it into a 10-inch tart pan with a removable bottom and trim away the excess dough. Use a fork to prick the crust all over. Bake the tart crust until it's pale golden, 20 to 25 minutes. Transfer to a wire rack to cool. (The tart shell can be made 8 hours ahead and kept at room temperature or frozen; see page xxv.)

4. To make the filling, preheat the oven to 350°F. In a heavy saucepan, combine ¾ cup of the milk and 2 tablespoons of the sugar; bring the mixture to a boil. Meanwhile, in a large bowl, whisk together the remaining ¼ cup milk, the egg yolks, cornstarch, and another 1 tablespoon of the sugar. Remove the milk mixture from the heat and add a little of the hot milk to the egg yolk mixture to warm it, whisking constantly to keep the yolks from curdling. Pour the egg yolk mixture into the hot milk mixture, whisking the milk constantly as you pour.

5. Return the custard to the stove and bring it to a boil. Let it boil for 1 to 3 minutes, whisking constantly, until it thickens. Add the cheese and whisk until smooth. Strain the custard through a fine sieve into a large bowl. Stir in the nutmeg and set aside.

6. Place 2 tablespoons water in a small, heavy saucepan. Add the remaining ¾ cup of sugar and the corn syrup. Cook over medium heat without stirring until the syrup reaches 242°F. (soft ball stage) on a candy thermometer, about 8 minutes.

7. Meanwhile, when the sugar syrup reaches 230°F., in the bowl of an electric mixer fitted with a whisk at-

tachment, whip the egg whites until they are very frothy. When the sugar syrup is ready, on low speed, drizzle it into the whites in a slow and steady stream. Once it is fully incorporated, increase the speed and whip just until the mixture holds stiff peaks. The meringue will still be warm.

8. Whisk a third of the meringue into the reserved triple-crème fillings. Fold the triple-crème mixture into the meringue in two additions. Mound the filling attractively in the tart shell and bake for 20 to 25 minutes, until puffed and golden brown. Let cool for 5 minutes before serving.

SERVING SUGGESTION
· For a composed dessert, serve with Raspberry Sorbet (page 20) and Lemon Thyme–Macerated Raspberry Compote (page 19), or with Concord Grape Sorbet (page 54) and Spiced Red Wine–Fig Compote (page 52).

MASCARPONE CREAM CANNOLI

In my interpretation of an Italian cannoli, a very simple tuile batter, baked and rolled into a tube, is used in place of the usual deep-fried dough. Tuiles are lighter and easier to handle, and they make a crunchy, citrusy contrast to the rich, smooth cream that fills them. To make the filling, I like to blend mascarpone, goat cheese, and goat yogurt to yield a fresh, off-sweet, and incredibly luscious cream. Not only delicious as a cannoli filling, it can also be used to garnish other desserts as an alternative to a dollop of whipped cream.

Yield: 2 dozen cannoli

LACE TUILES

- 1⅔ cups sugar
- 1 cup all-purpose flour
- 1 teaspoon grated orange zest
- ¾ cup plus 2 tablespoons fresh orange juice
- 14 tablespoons (1¾ sticks) unsalted butter, melted and cooled to room temperature

MASCARPONE CREAM FILLING

- 1 cup mascarpone cheese
- ¾ cup plus 2 tablespoons heavy cream
- ½ cup unflavored goat's-milk yogurt or plain yogurt
- ½ cup (4 ounces) plain goat cheese
- ¼ cup sugar
- 1 tablespoon Grand Marnier
- 1½ teaspoons grated orange zest

1. To make the tuiles, using an electric mixer fitted with the whisk attachment, mix the sugar, flour, and zest until smooth. With the mixer on low speed, drizzle in the orange juice, then the melted butter. Increase the speed to medium and mix until the batter is completely smooth. Refrigerate for at least 2 hours.

2. Preheat the oven to 350°F. Use nonstick baking sheets or line regular baking sheets with nonstick liners or parchment paper. For each tuile, drop a heaping teaspoon of batter onto the baking sheet, leaving 3 inches in between. Using a small offset spatula or the back of a spoon dipped in cold water to prevent sticking, gently pat each mound of batter into a very thin, very even 4-inch round. Bake the tuiles until they are golden brown all over, 9 to 11 minutes.

3. Transfer the baking sheets to a wire rack for 1 minute. Using a plastic dough scraper or a spatula, carefully remove the tuiles from the pans and wrap them around a clean broom handle or other cylinder of approximately the same diameter.

4. Cool the baking sheets between batches and continue making tuiles until all the batter is used up.

5. To prepare the filling, in a bowl of an electric mixer fitted with a whisk attachment, combine the mascarpone, cream, yogurt, goat cheese, and sugar and beat until stiff. Fold in the Grand Marnier and zest. Cover and refrigerate for at least 1 hour and up to 4 hours.

6. Using a pastry bag fitted with a large star tip (or a heavy-duty Ziploc bag with the corner snipped off), pipe the filling into the cooled tuile cylinders. Serve immediately after filling.

SERVING SUGGESTIONS

- Serve with scoops of Strawberry Sorbet (page 21).
- For a composed dessert, add Tarragon-Macerated Strawberries (page 12) and tarragon syrup (see page 262).

GOAT-CHEESE CHEESECAKE

Using a combination of mascarpone cheese for silky sweetness and fresh goat cheese for a slight tang, this ultra-creamy cheesecake is a bit more complex than most. For this recipe you should use the mildest goat cheese you can. I find that Coach Farms brand works beautifully, and it is nationally distributed. But if you can't find it, don't feel compelled to search out a fancy, artisanal cheese. Taste a few different available brands until you find one with a suitably mild, light taste. Avoid an aged cheese, which would be too strong and sharp for this recipe.

Yield: 8 servings

1¼ cups plus 2 tablespoons
    (11 ounces) cream cheese,
    at room temperature
8   ounces fresh goat cheese, at room
    temperature
½   cup sugar
½   vanilla bean, split lengthwise,
    pulp scraped (see page 180)
1½ cups mascarpone cheese
4   large eggs, at room temperature

1. Preheat the oven to 325°F. In the bowl of an electric mixer fitted with the paddle attachment, combine the cream cheese, goat cheese, sugar, and vanilla pulp and beat until smooth and creamy. Add the mascarpone and beat until smooth.

2. Add the eggs and mix well, scraping down the sides of the bowl with a rubber spatula as necessary. Strain the mixture into a bowl.

3. Wrap the outside of an 8-inch springform pan with foil. Spoon the mixture into the pan and place it in the center of a larger baking pan. Pour enough very hot water into the baking pan to reach two-thirds of the way up the side of the springform pan. Cover the entire baking dish with foil. Pierce the foil in several places with a knife. Bake the cake for 1 hour, then lift off a corner of the foil to allow the steam to escape. Re-cover the pan and bake for 50 minutes longer, or until the cake looks set around the edges but its still very slightly jiggly in the center.

4. Transfer the cake to a wire rack to cool completely before serving. The cake can be made up to 2 days in advance and kept covered in the refrigerator.

SERVING SUGGESTIONS
· Serve with a seasonal fruit dessert like Roasted Pineapple with Pink Peppercorns (page 103).
· For something more complex, add Passion Fruit–Pineapple Sorbet (page 111).
· For a composed dessert, add Pistachio-Nut Brittle (page 142).

CRÈME FRAÎCHE PANNA COTTA

Simple yet sublime, this variation on the classic Italian panna cotta gains depth and complexity from the slight acidity of crème fraîche and the almost imperceptibly fruity, floral qualities of Framboise liqueur. Though panna cotta doesn't contain eggs, it has the same silky, creamy texture as a custard. I use a minimal amount of gelatin so it's barely set—just enough to keep the cream from collapsing on the plate!

Yield: 6 servings

1   teaspoon unflavored powdered
    gelatin
2   cups heavy cream
1½ cups crème fraîche
⅓   cup sugar
1   tablespoon Framboise liqueur

1. Place 1½ tablespoons cold water in a small bowl and sprinkle the gelatin on top. Let the gelatin soften for 5 minutes.

2. Meanwhile, in a medium saucepan over medium-high heat, warm the cream and crème fraîche with the sugar, stirring until the sugar dissolves. Turn off the heat and add the gelatin mixture; stir until it dissolves. Strain the crème fraîche mixture through a fine sieve into a large measuring cup with a spout, and stir in the Framboise.

3. Pour the mixture into six 8-ounce ramekins, bowls, or parfait glasses, and cover with plastic wrap. Chill until firm, about 3 hours.

SERVING SUGGESTIONS
- Serve with scoops of Raspberry Sorbet (page 20).
- For something more complex, add candied almonds (see page 261).
- For a composed dessert, add small bowls of Apricot-Muscat Soup (page 33).

GOAT YOGURT—ROSE MOUSSE

The earthy richness of goat's-milk yogurt is uplifted by its pairing with the floral essence of rose water. It can be served on its own as a mousse, and it's superb when played off other desserts or fruits, particularly berries. Like many of the recipes in this chapter, this mousse is great as a topping, since it is essentially a more elegant and complex whipped cream.

Yield: 8 servings

2 cups unflavored goat's-milk yogurt or plain yogurt
1 cup plus 2 tablespoons heavy cream
½ teaspoon unflavored powdered gelatin
¾ cup confectioners' sugar
½ teaspoon rose water, or to taste

1. Line a sieve with a double layer of cheesecloth and suspend it over a bowl or sink. Place the yogurt in the lined sieve and let drain for 30 minutes.

2. Measure out 1 cup of the drained yogurt and save the remaining few tablespoons for another purpose. Place the yogurt in a medium bowl and whisk until smooth.

3. In a small saucepan, combine 2 tablespoons of the cream and the gelatin. Let sit for 5 minutes. Place the pan over low heat and gently stir until the gelatin is dissolved, about 5 minutes. Strain the gelatin mixture through a fine sieve into the yogurt and whisk well.

4. Using an electric mixer, whip the remaining cup of cream until it thickens. Whisk in the sugar and rose water. Whisk one third of the cream into the yogurt mixture, then fold in the remaining cream in two additions. Transfer the mixture to a serving bowl and chill the mousse until set, at least 3 hours.

SERVING SUGGESTIONS
- Use the mousse as an alternative filling for the Mascarpone Cream Cannoli (page 203) and garnish with fresh berries.
- Serve the mousse with Tarragon-Macerated Strawberries (page 12), Rose Meringues (page 157), and/or Pistachio-Nut Brittle (page 142).

ORANGE–CARDAMOM SHAKES

This fun drink was inspired by the women from the Dominican Republic, Anna, Argentina, and Iris, who do the prep work in the kitchen at Gramercy Tavern. They are incredible cooks, and they make a drink for every season. In the summer they mix up freshly squeezed orange juice, cream, ice, and lots of sugar, with spices like cinnamon and cloves, in huge batches for everyone in the kitchen to drink. I use cardamom and crème fraîche in my adaptation, and I blend it to make a frothy shake. Cardamom is wonderful with orange and makes this cooling shake taste almost like an Indian-spiced Creamsicle. The result is a shake that's less sweet than the original, but just as incredibly refreshing.

Yield: 2 servings

1 tablespoon cardamom pods
1 cup milk
½ cup sugar
Zest of ½ orange removed with a
    vegetable peeler
1 cup freshly squeezed orange
    juice, strained
¼ cup crème fraîche
½ cup ice

1. In a small skillet over high heat, toast the cardamom pods until they begin to color and are fragrant, about 5 minutes. Using a mortar and pestle or the back of a knife, crack open the pods and roughly chop or bruise them. Place the cardamom, milk, sugar, and zest in a small saucepan and bring to a simmer over medium-high heat, stirring until the sugar dissolves. Strain the mixture into a bowl and let cool to room temperature.

2. Place the milk mixture, orange juice, crème fraîche, and ice into a blender and blend until smooth. Serve immediately.

SERVING SUGGESTION
• Serve with Chocolate Brownie Cookies (page 229), Orange-Cornmeal Shortbread (page 88), Gingersnaps (page 176), or Citrus Lace Tuiles (page 90).

FROZEN RICOTTA—CHESTNUT-HONEY CREAM

Fresh ricotta—the kind you buy in an Italian specialty market rather than in the supermarket—has a wonderfully sweet, mild dairy flavor. Chestnut honey is intense and earthy. Mixed together in this unusual frozen dessert, the two play off each other to create something both full-flavored and delicate. Although this is made in an ice-cream maker, its texture is dense and rich. Take it out of the freezer about 30 minutes before you want to serve it; otherwise, it will be too firm to scoop. Or don't freeze it at all and use it as a sauce for fresh or roasted fruit.

Yield: 1 pint

1   pound ricotta cheese, preferably fresh
3   tablespoons chestnut honey
¼   cup Simple Syrup (page 261)

1. Place all the ingredients in the bowl of a watertight food processor or a blender, or use an immersion blender in a bowl. Pulse or blend the mixture until it is smooth. Strain through a fine sieve and chill until thoroughly cold, at least 4 hours.

2. Freeze in an ice-cream maker according to the manufacturer's instructions. Remove from the freezer 30 minutes before serving.

SERVING SUGGESTION
• Serve with Chestnut Honey–Roasted Pine Nuts (page 262), or with Blood-Orange Sorbet (page 93) and/or Caramel Blood Oranges (page 89)

BUTTERMILK ICE CREAM

This unusually refreshing ice cream is light, tangy, and not too sweet. Since I use buttermilk (a cultured skim milk) in place of whole milk in this recipe, it is much less rich than most ice cream.

Yield: 1½ pints

2 cups heavy cream
1¼ cups sugar
12 large egg yolks
2 cups buttermilk
2 teaspoons vanilla extract
Pinch of salt

1. In a large, heavy saucepan, combine the cream and 1 cup of the sugar. Bring the mixture to a simmer over medium heat.

2. Meanwhile, in a large bowl, whisk together the egg yolks and the remaining ¼ cup of sugar.

3. Remove the cream mixture from the heat and add a little to the egg yolk mixture to warm it, whisking constantly to keep the yolks from curdling. Pour the egg yolk mixture into the hot cream mixture, whisking the cream constantly as you pour.

4. Return the custard to the stove and cook it over low heat, stirring constantly with a wooden spoon, until it thickens enough to coat the back of the spoon, about 7 minutes. Transfer the custard to a bowl and let cool completely. Strain the mixture and stir in the buttermilk, vanilla extract, and salt. Chill the custard until it's thoroughly cold, at least 4 hours.

5. Freeze in an ice-cream maker according to the manufacturer's instructions.

SERVING SUGGESTION
· Serve with candied walnuts or pecans (see page 261) and Apple-Butter Crepes (page 63) or Maple-Glazed Bananas with Waffles (page 99).

CREAM-CHEESE ICE CREAM

This luscious, dense, and creamy dessert is essentially a frozen cheesecake, since a cheesecake is a baked custard made with cream cheese, and this ice cream is a frozen custard made with cream cheese. Like a really good cheesecake, it has some complexity and is not cloying. Cream cheese gives the ice cream an incredibly smooth texture and a slight tang that allows it to be really rich yet not over the top.

Yield: 1½ pints

2   cups milk
1¼ cups sugar
12 large egg yolks
1½ cups (12 ounces) cream cheese, at room temperature, cut into pieces
1½ cups sour cream
2   teaspoons vanilla extract
Pinch of salt

1. In a large, heavy saucepan, combine the milk and 1 cup of the sugar. Bring the mixture to a simmer over medium heat.

2. Meanwhile, in a large bowl, whisk together the egg yolks and the remaining ¼ cup of sugar.

3. Remove the milk mixture from the heat and add a little to the egg yolk mixture to warm it, whisking constantly to keep the yolks from curdling. Pour the egg yolk mixture into the hot milk mixture, whisking the milk constantly as you pour.

4. Return the custard to the stove and cook it over low heat, stirring constantly with a wooden spoon, until it thickens enough to coat the back of the spoon, about 7 minutes. Transfer to a bowl and add the cream cheese, sour cream, vanilla, and salt, whisking until the cream cheese melts. Strain the custard, then let it cool completely. Chill the custard until it's thoroughly cold, at least 4 hours.

5. Freeze in an ice-cream maker according to the manufacturer's instructions.

SERVING SUGGESTION
• Serve with Quince Thumbprint Cookies (page 68), Chocolate Biscotti with Pistachios and Sour Cherries (page 227), or Pecan Sandies (page 144).

YOGURT SORBET

Somewhere between a luscious ice cream and an icy sorbet, this frozen treat is made both refreshing and creamy by the dairy in the recipe. The yogurt is drained before it is churned into sorbet. This gets rid of any excess water, thickening it into a dense yogurt cheese that I then sweeten with simple syrup. Be sure to use high-quality, fresh, and preferably organic yogurt here. It will make a big difference in both the flavor and texture.

Yield: About 1 quart

4   cups plain yogurt
1½ cups Simple Syrup (page 261)

1. Line a sieve with a double layer of cheesecloth or a clean kitchen towel and set it over a bowl. Spoon the yogurt into the lined sieve and place in the refrigerator to drain overnight.

2. In a bowl, mix together the drained yogurt and the Simple Syrup.

Pour the mixture into an ice-cream machine and freeze according to the manufacturer's directions.

VARIATION
To make goat-yogurt sorbet, substitute unflavored goat's-milk yogurt for the regular yogurt. Or use half goat yogurt and half regular yogurt.

SERVING SUGGESTION
• Serve with Watermelon Granité (page 57), Maple Baked Apples with Dried Fruit and Nuts (page 70), or Maple-Glazed Winter Squash and Apple Compote (page 125).

TIPS FOR TEMPERING CHOCOLATE

Tempering chocolate involves melting it gently, then stirring it as it cools. This stabilizes the cocoa butter, and when the chocolate sets, it hardens with a dark, smooth, and beautifully glossy surface.

While there are lots of ways to temper chocolate, I recommend this simple method for the home cook. First, chop the chocolate. Then place approximately two thirds of it in the top of a double boiler, or in a metal bowl, and suspend it over a pot of water that is hot enough to steam yet not simmer. Let the chocolate slowly melt. Remove the double-boiler top or bowl from over the water and add the remaining third of the chocolate. Stir continuously so that the chocolate melts smoothly and cools evenly. The chocolate should be stirred until it feels neither hot nor cold when you touch a little to your lip. Use the tempered chocolate immediately

CHOCOLATE

Chocolate—the food of the gods. Anything made with chocolate is inevitably the most popular item on most dessert menus. I love its intense, robust taste and its incredibly rich, sensuous mouthfeel.

As with fruits and vegetables, the quality of the chocolate you use is of utmost importance and will dramatically affect the recipe you make. When I have an assertively flavored, high-quality chocolate, I can eat two or three pieces and I am sated, whereas I might go through a whole bag of waxy, poor-quality chocolate candies, waiting in vain to feel I've had my fill of chocolate flavor. In a dessert, good chocolate will add a robust vibrancy that can't be matched by lesser-quality chocolate. Valrhona and Scharffen Berger are two top-notch brands that are easily available to home cooks. You can find them at specialty shops, or see page 269 for a mail-order source.

There are four types of chocolate: unsweetened, bittersweet, milk, and white. Unsweetened chocolate has the most unadulterated flavor, since it has the highest percentage of cocoa solids, which is what makes chocolate taste like chocolate. It contains no sugar. Regular bittersweet (and semisweet) chocolate has anywhere from 35 to 60 percent cocoa solids, plus added sugar. At the restaurant, I use several types of extra-bittersweet chocolate (also called extra-bitter chocolate), which ranges from 66 to 80 percent cocoa, with much less added sugar than regular bittersweet and semisweet. I find it has a fuller, more powerful chocolate flavor, which is important since the butter and eggs in a recipe will decrease the chocolate's intensity. All the recipes here have been tested with extra-bittersweet chocolate unless otherwise specified, and it is worth seeking out. But in a pinch, you can use regular bittersweet chocolate, though the dessert might taste sweeter and not as chocolaty as it's meant to.

I also sometimes use milk chocolate, which is milder, sweeter, and extremely creamy. It contains less cocoa and more sugar than bittersweet chocolate, and also has added milk and milk fat. I love it in the Milk Chocolate Malted Ice Cream, where its sweet lusciousness helps temper the slight bitterness of the malt powder.

White chocolate contains no cocoa solids at all. Instead, it's made from cocoa butter that is sweetened and flavored with vanilla. Make sure that what you buy does indeed contain cocoa butter, since it is not always clear from the label, and some brands are made with vegetable fat instead. The delicate, velvety sweetness of white chocolate makes it an excellent base for stronger flavors like cocoa and espresso, as in the White Chocolate–Espresso Tart.

When cooking with chocolate, take care to respect its properties. Even though a block of chocolate seems indestructible, it actually is very fragile and it can burn easily, so it must be babied. Always melt chocolate in a double boiler, or a metal bowl suspended over (not in!) water that is hot enough to simmer, but not to boil. Chop a chunk of chocolate before melting it so it melts evenly and without burning. If I am melting butter with chocolate, I make a cushion of sliced butter on the bottom of the pan, then place the chopped chocolate on top.

If a small amount of moisture gets into a pot of melting chocolate, the chocolate will "seize," becoming hard, grainy, and dull. This happens because the dry cocoa content in the chocolate clumps together when moisture hits it, and separates out from the cocoa butter. For this reason, don't cover a pot of melting chocolate, since condensation may form inside the lid and drip into the chocolate. To avoid the risk of moisture from the steaming pot, make sure that the bowl you put over the pot of water is large enough to seal the pot, or that your double boiler fits together well.

You can also avoid the risk of steam causing your chocolate to seize by simply melting the chocolate in a microwave on medium power. Stir every 45 seconds until melted.

If you've noticed that none of my chocolate recipes call for fruit, don't think this is a random exclusion. Chocolate is special and complex, with a flavor that I prefer to savor uninterrupted. The high acid in chocolate clashes with the acidity of most fruit, so I prefer to enjoy chocolate with chocolate and fruit with fruit. However, if you like the combination, both chocolate with orange and chocolate with raspberry are classic pairings.

WINE NOTES: CHOCOLATE

For most of us, our first encounter with a perfect food and beverage pairing probably occurred when we were kids, and our moms served us chocolate-chip cookies with a glass of milk. But even now that I'm an adult, this is still one of the best pairings I know. For most chocolate desserts, milk has the perfect texture, temperature, and creaminess and makes an ideal partner. However, for something a little more sophisticated, you can match the sweet, dark complexity of chocolate with ruby and vintage ports or a sweet sherry or Madeira. Just make sure to adjust the level of the wine's sweetness to the chocolate dessert being served—remember that the sweeter the dessert, the sweeter the wine should be.

INDIVIDUAL CHOCOLATE SOUFFLÉ CAKES

With their dark, creamy centers topped by light, puffed caps, these potent little cakes have a texture that falls somewhere between a rich mousse and a soufflé. At the restaurant, I bake them in metal rings, which gives them an impressive stature on the plate. Here, I use ramekins surrounded by parchment-paper collars to extend their height. Cutting the parchment paper for the collars is probably the most time-consuming step in this recipe; whipping up the batter is quick and easy—not much more difficult than making brownies. But when these are served hot from the oven in all their souffléd glory, the payoff is much more satisfying.

Yield: 16 cakes

1   cup (2 sticks) unsalted butter, plus additional for ramekins
½   cup sugar, plus additional for ramekins
8   ounces extra-bittersweet chocolate, chopped (see page 215)
3   large eggs, at room temperature
3   large egg yolks, at room temperature
¼   cup cake flour

1. Preheat the oven to 325°F. Butter sixteen 6-ounce ramekins. Cut parchment paper into 3 × 8-inch collars for each ramekin and butter and sugar the collars on one side. Fit each parchment collar inside a ramekin, buttered side in, so it stands up above the rim and adheres to the buttered ramekin.

2. Place the butter in the top of a double boiler, or in a metal bowl suspended over a pot of simmering (not boiling) water, then add the chocolate on top. Heat until both the butter and chocolate are melted, about 5 minutes. Remove the chocolate mixture from the heat and stir the chocolate and butter until well combined. Cover and set aside.

3. In the bowl of an electric mixer, beat the eggs, egg yolks, and sugar on high speed until tripled in volume. Pour the chocolate mixture over the eggs. Sift the cake flour over the batter and carefully fold gently until just combined.

4. Fill each ramekin with ⅓ cup of the batter and place on a baking sheet. Bake the cakes until the tops are firm but the centers still soft and slightly spongy, about 16 minutes. Do not overbake. Cool the cakes on a wire rack for 5 minutes before serving. Or let cool completely and reheat in a 350°F. oven for 5 minutes, or until warm.

SERVING SUGGESTION
· Serve with whipped crème fraîche and/or scoops of Black Mint Ice Cream (page 159).

WARM CHOCOLATE GANACHE CAKES

Individual chocolate cakes that ooze a rich, liquid ganache when you cut them have become ubiquitous on dessert menus all over the country. My version is particularly luxurious, with a soft, tender cake barely enclosing its molten chocolate center. It's a chocoholic's dream come true.

Yield: 6 servings

GANACHE

4   ounces extra-bittersweet
     chocolate, finely chopped
     (see page 215)
¾   cup heavy cream

CAKES

3½   ounces extra-bittersweet
     chocolate, chopped
3   tablespoons unsalted butter,
     softened, plus additional for
     buttering the tins
3   large eggs, separated
¼   cup almond flour
¼   cup cake flour
¼   cup confectioners' sugar

1. Line an 8 × 4-inch loaf pan or 6-inch gratin dish with plastic wrap. To prepare the ganache, put the chocolate in a bowl. Bring the cream to a boil in a small saucepan and pour the hot cream over the chocolate. Let stand until the chocolate begins to melt, about 2 minutes, then whisk until smooth.

2. Pour the ganache into the loaf pan or gratin dish and refrigerate until firm, about 1 hour. When the mixture has set, unmold and cut out six 1½-inch rounds (you can use a knife or a cookie cutter). Refrigerate until ready to use (up to 5 days).

3. Preheat the oven to 350°F. Butter a muffin pan and set aside.

4. To make the cakes, in the top of a double boiler, or in a metal bowl suspended over a pot of simmering (not boiling) water, melt the chocolate. Whisk in the softened butter and turn off the heat. Let cool for 5 minutes, then whisk in the egg yolks one at a time.

5. Sift together the almond and cake flours and fold the flours into the chocolate mixture.

6. Using an electric mixer, beat the egg whites to soft peaks. Sift in the confectioners' sugar and continue beating to stiff peaks. Fold one third of the egg white mixture into the chocolate mixture, then gently fold in the remaining whites in two additions.

7. Scoop or pipe a ¼-cup measure of cake batter into each muffin tin.

8. Place a ganache round in the center of each muffin cup, then spoon in enough batter to cover. Bake the cakes for 20 minutes, or until the tops are firm. Allow the cakes to rest for 1 minute before serving.

SERVING SUGGESTION

• Serve with scoops of Earl Grey Ice Cream (page 195) or any of the spice ice creams.

WHITE CHOCOLATE–ESPRESSO TART

White chocolate may be creamy, silky, and luscious, but to my taste, it's much too sweet. This is why I tend to pair it with dark, assertive, slightly bitter flavors like espresso and cocoa. Here, a cloudlike white chocolate–espresso filling is anchored in a buttery chocolate cookie crust that provides great contrast in terms of color, texture, and taste. The resulting tart is light and fluffy, yet firm enough to cut. This dessert will pair well with any seasonal fruit.

Yield: 8 servings

WHITE CHOCOLATE–ESPRESSO FILLING
- 1 cup plus 2 tablespoons heavy cream
- 3 ounces white chocolate, chopped
- 1 tablespoon finely ground espresso beans

CHOCOLATE TART DOUGH
- ½ cup (1 stick) unsalted butter, softened
- ½ cup plus 1 tablespoon confectioners' sugar
- 1 large egg yolk
- ¾ teaspoon vanilla extract
- 1¼ cups all-purpose flour
- ¼ cup unsweetened Dutch-processed cocoa powder

1. To make the white chocolate–espresso cream, in a small saucepan, bring ½ cup of the cream to a simmer over medium heat. Place the white chocolate and espresso in a bowl. Pour the hot cream on top and whisk until the chocolate is melted and smooth. Cover and refrigerate overnight.

2. To prepare the tart dough, in the bowl of an electric mixer fitted with the paddle attachment, cream the butter and confectioners' sugar until combined, about 1 minute. Add the egg yolk and vanilla and beat until smooth. Sift in the flour and cocoa powder and beat on low speed until just combined. Scrape the dough onto a sheet of plastic wrap and form it into a disk. Wrap and chill until firm, about 1 hour, or up to 3 days.

3. On a lightly floured surface, roll the dough out to a 14-inch round, ⅛ inch thick. Fit it into a 10-inch tart pan with a removable bottom. Trim away the excess dough. Prick the dough all over with a fork. Chill the dough for 30 minutes. Preheat the oven to 325°F.

4. Line the tart dough with aluminum foil and fill with dried beans, rice, or pie weights. Place on a baking sheet and bake for 15 minutes. Remove the foil and weights, and bake for 10 to 15 minutes longer, or until the pastry looks dry and set. Transfer to a wire rack to cool.

5. Strain the white chocolate–espresso mixture through a fine sieve lined with a double layer of cheesecloth; discard the solids. In the bowl of an electric mixer, whip the chocolate-espresso mixture with the remaining ½ cup plus 2 tablespoons of cream until the mixture holds soft peaks. Scrape the filling into the cooled tart shell and smooth the top. Refrigerate for about 2 hours, or until set.

VARIATION
To make individual tartlettes, use a 2½-inch round cutter to cut out 24 rounds of dough and press them into mini muffin pans or 2-inch tart pans, trimming away any excess dough; prick the dough all over with a fork. Chill for 20 minutes. Line the tart shells with squares of foil and fill with dried beans, rice, or pie weights. Place the muffin or tart pans on a baking sheet and bake for 15 minutes. Remove the foil and weights, return the pans to the oven, and bake for 5 to 10 minutes more, until the pastry looks dry and is set. Transfer to a wire rack to cool. Divide the filling evenly among the tart shells and chill as directed.

SERVING SUGGESTION
- Serve with scoops of Extra-Bittersweet Chocolate Sorbet (page 233).

CHOCOLATE CARAMEL TARTS

Like a highly sophisticated Rolo candy, the caramel in these tarts oozes when you cut into them. Covered with a bittersweet chocolate glaze and nestled in a chocolate cookie crust, it's an exquisite combination that will speak directly to the kid in you.

At Gramercy Tavern, I serve this tart sprinkled with a few grains of sea salt. I find that salt rounds out the buttery sweetness of the caramel and makes the chocolate flavor really pop (think of chocolate-covered pretzels). If you're unsure whether or not to add the salt, why not make it a fun experiment to try with your guests? Ask them first to taste this tart plain, then to have a bite with a granule of salt and mark the difference. Pass around a little ramekin filled with sea salt, and encourage your guests to play with their food.

You can bake this as one large tart if you like, but expect a messier presentation, since the caramel begins to escape as soon as you cut into it.

Yield: 2 dozen tartlettes

CHOCOLATE TART DOUGH
½ cup unsalted butter (1 stick), softened
½ cup plus 1 tablespoon confectioners' sugar
1 large egg yolk
¾ teaspoon vanilla extract
1¼ cups all-purpose flour
¼ cup unsweetened Dutch-processed cocoa powder

CARAMEL FILLING
2 cups sugar
¼ cup light corn syrup
½ cup (1 stick) unsalted butter
½ cup heavy cream
2 tablespoons crème fraîche

CHOCOLATE GANACHE GLAZE
½ cup heavy cream
3½ ounces extra-bittersweet chocolate, chopped (see page 215)
Pinch of fine sea salt, such as fleur de sel (see page 269), optional

1. To prepare the tart dough, in the bowl of an electric mixer fitted with the paddle attachment, cream the butter and confectioners' sugar until combined, about 1 minute. Add the egg yolk and vanilla and beat until smooth. Sift in the flour and cocoa powder and beat on low speed until just combined. Scrape the dough onto a sheet of plastic wrap and form it into a disk. Wrap and chill until firm, about 1 hour, or up to 3 days.

2. Preheat the oven to 325°F. On a lightly floured surface, roll the tart dough to an 18 × 12-inch rectangle, ³⁄₁₆ inch thick. Using a 2½-inch round cutter, cut out 24 rounds of dough and press them into mini muffin tins or 2-inch tart pans, trimming away any excess dough; prick the dough all over with a fork. Chill the tart shells for 20 minutes.

3. Line the tart shells with foil and fill with dried beans, rice, or pie weights. Bake for 15 minutes. Remove the foil and weights and bake for 5 to 10 minutes longer, or until the pastry looks dry and set. Transfer to a wire rack to cool. (The tart shells can be made 8 hours ahead.)

4. To prepare the filling, place ½ cup water in a large saucepan. Add the sugar and corn syrup and cook the mixture over medium-high heat, swirling the pan occasionally, until you have a dark amber caramel, about 10 minutes. Carefully whisk in the butter, cream, and crème fraîche (the mixture will hiss and bubble up, so stand back), whisking until smooth. (The caramel can be made up to 5 days ahead and refrigerated.) Divide the caramel among the tart shells while still warm (or reheat the caramel in the microwave or over low heat until it is pourable) and let sit until the caramel is set, at least 45 minutes.

5. To make the ganache glaze, in a saucepan, bring the cream to a boil. Place the chocolate in a bowl. Pour the hot cream over the chocolate and let sit for 2 minutes, then whisk until smooth. Pour some of the glaze over each of the tarts while still warm. Let the glaze set at room temperature for at least 2 hours before serving. Sprinkle with salt, if desired, just before serving.

VARIATION

For a large tart, line a 10-inch tart pan with the pastry dough, then prick, weight, and bake as directed, adding 5 to 10 minutes to the baking time. When the tart shell is cool, spoon in the warm caramel filling. Allow the caramel to set before pouring the warm ganache onto the tart.

SERVING SUGGESTION

• Serve with scoops of Caramel Ice Cream (page 193) and/or Milk Chocolate Malted Ice Cream (page 232).

WARM CHOCOLATE SOUFFLÉ TARTS

Elegant, ethereal chocolate soufflés gain stability and crunch from a chocolate shortbread crust. Don't be dismayed when they fall once they're out of the oven; they end up tasting marvelously gooey and fudgy.

Yield: 2 dozen tartlettes

CHOCOLATE SOUFFLÉ FILLING

- 10 tablespoons (1¼ sticks) unsalted butter, cut into pieces
- 5 ounces extra-bittersweet chocolate, chopped (see page 215)
- 4 large eggs, at room temperature
- ¾ cup plus 2 tablespoons sugar
- 3 tablespoons all-purpose flour

CHOCOLATE TART DOUGH

- ½ cup (1 stick) unsalted butter, softened
- ½ cup plus 1 tablespoon confectioners' sugar
- 1 large egg yolk
- ¾ teaspoon vanilla extract
- ¼ cup unsweetened Dutch-processed cocoa powder
- 1¼ cups all-purpose flour

1. To prepare the filling, put the butter in the top of a double boiler, or in a metal bowl suspended over a pot of simmering (not boiling) water, and place the chocolate on top of the butter. Heat until the butter and chocolate are melted. Remove the boiler top from over the water and stir the chocolate and butter until well combined. Cover and set aside.

2. In the bowl of an electric mixer, beat the eggs and sugar on high speed for 5 minutes, until very light and thick. Fold a third of the egg mixture into the chocolate mixture to lighten it, then gently fold in the rest, taking care not to deflate the eggs. Sift the flour over the batter and carefully fold it in. Cover the filling and chill for at least 2 hours, or up to 2 days.

3. Meanwhile, prepare the tart dough. In the bowl of an electric mixer fitted with the paddle attachment, cream the butter and confectioners' sugar until incorporated, about 1 minute. Add the egg yolk and vanilla and beat until smooth. Sift in the flour and cocoa powder and beat on low speed until just combined. Scrape the dough onto a sheet of plastic wrap and form it into a disk. Wrap and chill until firm, about 1 hour, or up to 3 days.

4. Preheat the oven to 325°F. On a lightly floured surface, roll the tart dough to a 10 × 15-inch rectangle, ³⁄₁₆ inch thick. Using a 2½-inch round cutter, cut out 24 rounds of dough and press them into mini muffin tins or 2-inch tart pans, trimming away any excess dough; prick the dough all over with a fork. Chill the tart shells for 20 minutes.

5. Line the tart shells with foil and fill with dried beans, rice, or pie weights. Bake for 15 minutes. Remove the foil and weights and bake for 5 to 10 minutes longer, or until the pastry looks dry and set. Transfer to a wire rack to cool. Leave the oven on.

6. Divide the filling among the tart shells and return to the oven. Bake until the filling is puffed and cracked on top, 12 to 14 minutes. Slip a butter knife down along the side of the tarts and remove them from the pans. Serve immediately.

VARIATION

For a large tart, line a 10-inch tart pan with the dough and bake for 15 minutes with foil and weights, then 10 to 15 minutes without (until set). When the tart shell is cool, spoon in the filling and smooth the top. Bake for 20 minutes, or until the filling is cracked and puffed on top.

SERVING SUGGESTION

- Serve with scoops of Extra-Bittersweet Chocolate Sorbet (page 233) and/or whipped crème fraîche or Caramel Ice Cream (page 193).

CHOCOLATE ESPRESSO TERRINE

This intensely chocolaty flourless dessert has a marvelously light, mousselike texture. It is baked in a water bath until it is rich and creamy, like a decadent chocolate pudding, yet because it contains whipped eggs and whipped cream, it remains airy and melt-in-the-mouth smooth. A touch of espresso gives the chocolate a sophisticated flavor. Serve this in thin wedges.

Yield: 8 to 10 servings

6½ ounces extra-bittersweet
chocolate, chopped
(see page 215)
1 ounce unsweetened chocolate,
chopped
2 tablespoons freshly brewed
espresso
2 large eggs, lightly beaten
1 large egg yolk, lightly beaten
3½ tablespoons sugar
⅓ cup heavy cream

1. Preheat the oven to 325°F. Butter a 1-quart soufflé dish or other glass or ceramic baking dish and line with parchment or wax paper.

2. In the top of a double boiler, or in a metal bowl suspended over a pot of simmering (not boiling) water, warm both chocolates with the espresso and 1½ tablespoons water. When the chocolate appears melted, whisk well.

3. In the clean top of a double boiler, or in a metal bowl suspended over a pot of simmering (not boiling) water, heat the eggs, egg yolk, and sugar, whisking constantly, until it feels warm to the touch (do not heat it too much, or the eggs will curdle). Transfer the mixture to the bowl of an electric mixer and whip until the mixture triples in volume, about 5 minutes. Set aside.

4. In another bowl, beat the cream until it forms soft peaks.

5. Fold half of the egg mixture into the chocolate mixture, then gently fold in the remaining egg mixture. Gently fold in the cream.

6. Spoon the batter into the prepared dish and smooth the top. Set the dish in a larger pan and fill the larger pan with enough very hot water to come halfway up the sides of the dish. Cover the larger pan with foil and

pierce all over with a knife. Bake the terrine for 20 minutes, then lift off a corner of the foil to allow the steam to escape. Re-cover the pan and bake for about 30 minutes longer. The terrine is done when the center is set and feels foamy, not liquidy, when gently touched. Transfer the terrine to a wire rack to cool.

7. Cover the terrine and chill for at least 8 hours, or overnight (it will keep for up to 3 days in the refrigerator). To serve, run a small knife around the inside of the soufflé dish to loosen the terrine, then unmold it onto a serving platter.

SERVING SUGGESTIONS
· Serve with whipped crème fraîche.
· For a composed dessert, serve with scoops of Milk Chocolate Malted Ice Cream (page 232) or Yogurt Sorbet (page 213), Earl Grey Caramel (page 263), and candied hazelnuts (see page 261).

CHOCOLATE AND VANILLA MALTED CRÈME BRÛLÉE

What looks like a plain vanilla crème brûlée when you serve it is actually infused with barley malt syrup, which lends a complex, distinctly nutty-bitter flavor. Underneath is a hidden chocolate custard, just waiting for a spoon to unearth it. It may seem magical to your guests, but this sleight of hand is as simple as freezing the bottom layer of custard before pouring on the top.

Although I enjoy the added textural element of the crisp sugar cap, this dessert does not need to be brûléed. The custards can be made in advance, and the topping added if time allows. Otherwise, a crisp cookie will serve the purpose.

Yield: 6 servings

CHOCOLATE CUSTARD

3½ tablespoons sugar
1   tablespoon plus 1 teaspoon unsweetened Dutch-processed cocoa powder
1   cup heavy cream
¼   vanilla bean, halved lengthwise, pulp scraped (see page 180)
2   large egg yolks
Pinch of salt

VANILLA MALTED CUSTARD

1   cup heavy cream
¼   cup barley malt syrup (see Note)
2   tablespoons sugar
1   teaspoon vanilla extract
3   large egg yolks
Pinch of salt

TOPPING

3   tablespoons superfine sugar

1. To prepare the chocolate custard, in a small bowl, whisk together 2 tablespoons of the sugar and the cocoa. Place the cream and vanilla pod and pulp in a small saucepan and bring to a boil. Turn off the heat and whisk in the cocoa mixture until it dissolves.

2. Meanwhile, in a medium bowl, whisk the egg yolks with the remaining 1½ tablespoons of sugar until smooth. Whisk a little of the hot cream into the egg yolks to warm them, whisking constantly to keep the yolks from curdling. Pour the egg yolk mixture into the saucepan with the remaining cream, whisking constantly. Whisk in the salt. Strain the mixture into a bowl and divide among six 4-ounce ramekins or custard cups. Cover with plastic and freeze for at least 8 hours, or overnight.

3. Preheat the oven to 325°F. To prepare the vanilla malted custard, place the cream, barley malt syrup, sugar, and vanilla in a small saucepan and bring to a simmer. In a medium bowl, whisk together the egg yolks until smooth. Whisk a little of the hot cream into the egg yolks to temper them, whisking constantly to keep the yolks from curdling. Pour the egg yolk mixture into the saucepan with the remaining cream whisking constantly. Whisk in the salt. Strain the mixture, then pour it into the ramekins over the frozen chocolate custard.

4. Arrange the ramekins in a baking pan and place it on the oven rack. Pour enough very hot water into the baking pan to reach two-thirds of the way up the sides of the ramekins. Cover the baking pan with foil and pierce all over with a knife. Bake the custards for about 30 minutes, then lift off a corner of the foil to allow the steam to escape. Re-cover the pan and continue to bake until the custards are set around the edges but still slightly jiggly in the center, 15 to 20 minutes longer. Transfer the custards to a wire rack and let cool. Cover the ramekins and refrigerate for at least 4 hours, or overnight.

5. Right before serving, sprinkle a thin, even coating of the superfine sugar onto the surface of each custard (use ½ tablespoon for each). Use a

preheated broiler or a blowtorch to caramelize the sugar. This will take 1 to 2 minutes in a broiler and about 30 seconds using a blowtorch.

SERVING SUGGESTIONS
- Replace the caramelized sugar topping with a Citrus Lace Tuile (page 90) laid flat over each ramekin.
- Serve with Espresso Shortbread (page 192) or Cashew–Chocolate Chip Crisps (page 141).

Note: Barley malt syrup has a very distinct malt flavor. Look for it in health food stores.

BLACK AND WHITE CHOCOLATE MALTEDS

I associate chocolate malteds with childhood and summer—with stopping at Carvel on the way home from the beach. And since I love malteds and the memories they evoke, I wanted to re-create this timeless treat. Here is my favorite malted recipe, made with Ovaltine and a concentrated chocolate syrup. It's bolder and more luscious than Carvel's, and just as satisfying.

You can serve the malteds in tall glasses for sipping on their own, or consider the drink as part of a composed dessert and offer it in a smaller glass on the side. A beverage can enhance a dessert and add textural complexity in the same way a custard sauce or ice cream does. At Gramercy Tavern, I pour the malteds into tall shot glasses with little straws and present them as part of the chocolate tasting plate. I love the contrast between the cold, frothy chocolate drink and a warm, rich dessert like the chocolate soufflé tart.

Yield: 5 cups; 3 or 4 servings

⅓ cup sugar
1 tablespoon light corn syrup
6 tablespoons unsweetened Dutch-processed cocoa powder
2 cups heavy cream
12 ounces extra-bittersweet chocolate, chopped (see page 215)
1 cup plus 3 tablespoons original Ovaltine (not chocolate-flavored)
1 cup half-and-half (or ½ cup heavy cream plus ½ cup milk)
1⅔ cups vanilla ice cream

1. To make the chocolate syrup, in a saucepan, bring ½ cup water, the sugar, and the corn syrup to a boil, stirring to dissolve the sugar. Place the cocoa in a bowl and whisk in 3 tablespoons of the sugar syrup until smooth. Pour the cocoa mixture into the saucepan and whisk well. Let the syrup simmer gently for 5 minutes over low heat, stirring occasionally.

2. In another saucepan, bring ½ cup of the cream to a simmer. Place the chocolate in a bowl. Pour the hot cream over the chocolate and whisk until the chocolate is melted and the mixture smooth. Stir in the chocolate syrup and set aside.

3. Using an electric mixer, whisk together 1 cup of the Ovaltine and ½ cup of the half-and-half to make a very smooth paste. Add the remaining ½ cup of half-and-half, ½ cup of the remaining heavy cream, and the chocolate mixture and whisk well until smooth. Strain the mixture through a fine sieve into a bowl, cover with plastic wrap, and chill until very cold, at least 3 hours, and up to 3 days.

4. Just before serving, use an electric mixer or a whisk to whip the remaining cup of heavy cream until it forms soft peaks. Add the remaining 3 tablespoons of Ovaltine and whip until the cream holds stiff peaks.

5. To serve, combine the vanilla ice cream and the chocolate-Ovaltine mixture in a blender and blend until thick and creamy, like a milk shake. Serve the malteds immediately, garnished with the Ovaltine–whipped cream mixture.

SERVING SUGGESTION
- For a composed dessert, float scoops of Extra-Bittersweet Chocolate Sorbet (page 233) on top of the malted, and serve with Chocolate Espresso Terrine (page 223) and chocolate-dipped espresso shortbread (see Variation, page 192).

CHOCOLATE BISCOTTI WITH PISTACHIOS AND SOUR CHERRIES

These pretty, dark chocolate cookies are studded with red cherries and green pistachios, making them perfect for Christmas tins. As biscotti go, these are unusually rich, moist, and brownielike. And though I tend to shy away from pairing chocolate with fruit, the tart dried cherries here really match the intensity of the chocolate. If you prefer to have a soft, cakey cookie instead of crisp biscotti, don't bake them a second time. They will last for several days once-baked, and twice-baked will last at least 1 week in an airtight container.

Yield: 4½ to 5 dozen biscotti

1   cup dried sour cherries
2   cups shelled pistachio nuts
1¾ cups all-purpose flour
1¾ cups firmly packed dark brown
    sugar
½   cup granulated sugar
¾   cup unsweetened Dutch-
    processed cocoa powder
1   teaspoon salt
¼   teaspoon baking soda
3   large eggs
4   tablespoons unsalted butter,
    softened
1½ tablespoons coffee extract
1½ teaspoons vanilla extract
½   teaspoon almond extract
7½ ounces extra-bittersweet
    chocolate, cut into chunks
    (see page 215)

1. Place the cherries in a saucepan and cover with water. Bring to a simmer over medium heat, then turn off the heat and let cool. Drain the cherries (this can be done up to 1 week ahead; store the cherries in the refrigerator).

2. Preheat the oven to 325°F. Spread the pistachio nuts out on a baking sheet and toast them in the oven, stirring occasionally, until they are fragrant and lightly golden around the edges, 5 to 7 minutes. Transfer the pan to a wire rack to cool (keep the oven on).

3. Using an electric mixer fitted with the paddle attachment and set on low speed, mix together the flour, sugars, cocoa, salt, and baking soda. Add the eggs one at a time, mixing well after each addition. Add the butter and extracts and mix to combine. Stir in the pistachios, chocolate, and cherries. Let the dough rest for 5 minutes.

4. With wet hands, divide the dough and form it into 2 logs, each 2 inches in diameter. Place on a parchment-lined baking tray and bake until firm, about 30 minutes. Let cool completely on a rack.

5. Lower the oven temperature to 200°F. Using a serrated knife, slice each log on the diagonal into ¼-inch-thick slices. Arrange the biscotti on 3 parchment-lined baking sheets and dry them in the oven until firm and crisp, 1 to 1½ hours. Transfer to a wire rack to cool.

SERVING SUGGESTION

- Serve with Black Pepper Ice Cream (page 179), or serve the biscotti on a cookie plate with Gingersnaps (page 176) and Quince Thumbprint Cookies (page 68).

CHOCOLATE BROWNIE COOKIES

These are one of my signature cookies. They taste like miniature brownies—but oh, the texture! They're reminiscent of a meringue, with a soft, chewy, fudgy center and a crisp exterior that crackles appealingly. Since these cookies are smaller and less dense, they have an elegance that brownies lack. And they don't require the same commitment as a big, gooey bar. I can never eat just one of these. They are also a particular favorite of Gramercy Tavern owner Danny Meyer, who can't eat just one, either!

Yield: 5 dozen cookies

¼ cup all-purpose flour
¼ teaspoon baking powder
⅛ teaspoon salt
2 large eggs
⅔ cup sugar
½ tablespoon brewed espresso
1 teaspoon vanilla extract
2 tablespoons unsalted butter
5 ounces extra-bittersweet chocolate, chopped (see page 215)
2 ounces unsweetened chocolate, chopped
¾ cup mini chocolate chips

1. Preheat the oven to 375°F. Line 2 baking sheets with parchment paper.

2. In a small bowl, whisk together the flour, baking powder, and salt. Set aside.

3. In the bowl of an electric mixer, briefly whip the eggs to break them up. Add the sugar, espresso, and vanilla and beat on high speed for 15 minutes, until thick.

4. While the eggs are whipping, place the butter in the top of a double boiler, or in a metal bowl suspended over a pot of simmering (not boiling) water, and scatter the extra-bittersweet and unsweetened chocolate on top. Heat until the butter and chocolate melt. Remove the boiler top from over the water and stir the chocolate and butter until smooth.

5. Gently fold the chocolate mixture into the egg mixture until partially combined (there should still be some streaks). Add the flour mixture to the batter and carefully fold it in. Fold in the chocolate chips. If the batter is very runny, let it rest until it thickens slightly, about 5 minutes.

6. Drop the batter by heaping tea-spoonfuls onto the prepared baking sheets and bake until puffed and cracked, 8 to 9 minutes. Cool on a wire rack before removing from the baking sheets.

VARIATION

Substitute ½ cup chopped toasted nuts or dried sour cherries for an equal amount of the chocolate chips.

SERVING SUGGESTIONS

- To make ice-cream sandwiches, place scoops of ice cream, such as Milk Chocolate Malted Ice Cream (page 232) or Caramel Ice Cream (page 193), between two cookies and freeze until set.
- Serve with Black and White Chocolate Malteds (page 226).

EARL GREY CHOCOLATE TRUFFLES

I love the combination of bittersweet chocolate with bergamot, the orange oil that flavors Earl Grey tea. When you bite into one of these truffles, the first sensation you get is of intense chocolate, its bitterness heightened by the cocoa powder. Then you start to taste the brightness of the orange, which is tempered by the creamy ganache filling. I dip these candies in bittersweet chocolate for a thin, brittle coating, but you can also leave them undipped and just roll them in the cocoa powder as a finishing touch. These keep very well, so I make plenty for a party, then indulge in the leftovers, savoring one a night from my secret stash.

Yield: 2 dozen truffles

1¼ cups heavy cream
¼   cup Earl Grey tea leaves
      (not bags)
5   ounces extra-bittersweet
      chocolate, finely chopped
      (see page 215)
10 ounces bittersweet chocolate,
      coarsely chopped
1   cup unsweetened Dutch-
      processed cocoa powder

1. In a small saucepan, bring the heavy cream and tea leaves to a simmer. Turn off the heat and let the mixture infuse for 2 minutes.

2. Place the finely chopped extra-bittersweet chocolate in a bowl. Strain the hot cream over the chocolate, discarding the tea leaves. Let the mixture rest for 1 minute, then whisk until the chocolate is melted and smooth. Cover the chocolate and chill until the mixture is set, about 4 hours.

3. Using a teaspoon or a melon-baller, scoop out the truffles. Roll them in your hands to make rounded balls. Refrigerate the truffles for 15 minutes to firm them.

4. To make the coating, in the top of a double boiler, or in a metal bowl suspended over a pot of simmering (not boiling) water, melt two thirds of the bittersweet chocolate. Remove the boiler top from over the water and add the remaining chocolate. Stir continuously until the chocolate is melted and smooth and feels room temperature. (This tempers the chocolate—for tips, see page 214.)

5. Place the cocoa powder in a medium bowl. Drop the truffles one by one into the melted chocolate, turning them with a fork to coat them. Lift the truffles out of the chocolate and drop them into the cocoa powder. Roll the truffles in the cocoa until they are completely coated. They can be made up to 5 days in advance.

SERVING SUGGESTION
• Serve a petits fours platter with truffles, Chestnut-Honey Madeleines (page 184), and Citrus Lace Tuiles (page 90).

MILK CHOCOLATE MALTED ICE CREAM

This is the taste that a malted milk ball strives to attain. The sweetness of milk chocolate is tempered and made more complex by the malt, and together they achieve a rounder, fuller, earthier flavor. This ice cream is practically a chocolate malted in scoopable form, and since I have it on hand at Gramercy Tavern, I use it in place of vanilla to make super-intense chocolate malteds.

Yield: About 1½ quarts

3   cups milk
1   cup heavy cream
½   cup plus 2 tablespoons sugar
12 large egg yolks
3   ounces milk chocolate, chopped
1   ounce extra-bittersweet
    chocolate, chopped
    (see page 215)
1¼ cups original Ovaltine (not
    chocolate-flavored)

1. In a medium saucepan over medium heat, bring the milk, cream, and ¼ cup of the sugar to a simmer.

2. Meanwhile, in a large bowl, whisk together the egg yolks and the remaining 6 tablespoons of sugar. Place the chopped chocolates in a large, heatproof bowl.

3. Remove the milk mixture from the heat and add a little of the hot milk to the egg yolk mixture to warm it, whisking constantly to keep the yolks from curdling. Pour the egg yolk mixture into the hot milk mixture, whisking the milk constantly as you pour.

4. Return the custard to the stove and cook it over low heat, stirring constantly with a wooden spoon, until it thickens enough to coat the back of the spoon, about 7 minutes. Remove from the heat and pour it into the bowl with the chopped chocolates. Stir until the chocolate is melted and the mixture is smooth. Add the Ovaltine and stir until well combined. Let cool completely. Strain the custard through a fine

sieve, then cover and chill until thoroughly cold, at least 4 hours.

5. Freeze in an ice-cream maker according to the manufacturer's instructions.

SERVING SUGGESTIONS
· For a super-intense malted, use this ice cream in place of the vanilla ice cream called for in Black and White Chocolate Malteds (page 226).
· Serve with Individual Chocolate Soufflé Cakes (page 217).

EXTRA-BITTERSWEET CHOCOLATE SORBET

My aim in creating this recipe wasn't just to come up with the richest, boldest chocolate sorbet imaginable. It was also to re-create my childhood favorite, the Fudgsicle. If a Fudgsicle is supposed to be a chunk of frozen fudge on a stick, I think this sorbet mimics that (though without the stick). It's smooth, dense, and full of robust extra-bittersweet chocolate.

Yield: About 1 quart

¾ cup plus 2 tablespoons sugar
¾ cup unsweetened Dutch-processed cocoa powder
8½ ounces extra-bittersweet chocolate, chopped (see page 215)

1. In a medium saucepan, combine 2 cups water and the sugar and bring to a boil over high heat, stirring occasionally. Reduce the heat to low and gradually add the cocoa powder, whisking until smooth. Cook the mixture at a gentle simmer for 30 minutes, until syrupy.

2. Put the chocolate in a large bowl and add half the cocoa syrup, whisking until the chocolate is melted and the mixture is smooth. Add the remaining syrup and 2 cups water and whisk well. Strain the mixture through a fine sieve and let cool.

3. Chill the sorbet mixture, covered, until very cold, at least 4 hours, and up to 2 days. Freeze in an ice-cream maker according to the manufacturer's directions.

SERVING SUGGESTION
• Serve with Candied Kumquats (page 261) and Coconut Tuiles (page 105) or Citrus Lace Tuiles (page 90).

SIGNATURE COMPOSED DESSERTS

Of all the chapters in the book, this is the one that most truly reflects the desserts of Gramercy Tavern. In the other chapters, each dessert recipe stands alone, ready to be enjoyed as it is, or simply garnished. But at Gramercy Tavern I combine them, uniting the different components into something distinctive and unique, making each dessert into a perfect little composition. That's why at the restaurant, I call them composed desserts.

As you go through this chapter, you may begin to notice some trends. First of all, most of my desserts have three main components. I find that even numbers don't really work for me; visually they just aren't as striking on the plate. Since one component isn't special enough to serve at Gramercy, and five would be too busy, three seems perfect.

Using three elements gives me ample opportunity to integrate their flavors, textures, and temperatures, which is key to the final presentation. It makes sense to pair something sweet next to something tart, something crispy with something soft, and something hot near something cold. The contrast makes each experience all the more complete and balanced. For example, in the Peach Tartes Tatin dessert, although the focus of the plate is the hot tarte Tatin, adjacent to it is a cool, wobbly peach-rosé gelée, and next to that an icy peach sorbet. Therefore, it's not just a warm dessert; it's a warm dessert, a cool dessert, and a frozen dessert. In terms of flavor, this combination allows you to experience the taste of peach in myriad forms: cooked, tender, and caramelized in the tarte Tatin; as a gentle essence in the gelée; and fresh and tart in the sorbet. I like to think of each plate as its own complete, perfect sphere, as self-contained and considered as the entrées that came before. And most importantly, I strive to keep dessert elements simple and full of pleasing flavors.

When I'm creating the desserts, I like the challenge of playing with different flavor combinations and juxtapositions. I always try to breathe life into my flavor pairing, interpreting age-old favorites in new ways that still make sense—like serving a caramelized sauté of tomatoes and plums with basil ice cream, or putting an aromatic rose parfait into rhubarb soup. I have fun presenting people with something familiar, yet with a twist. To me, it's almost like a game. I'll think of an ingredient, and then say, "What can I do with this?" Cilantro has a fresh, green, herby taste, so why not mix it with coconut tapioca to both accentuate and cut its richness? It may be unexpected, but ultimately, it works because it's grounded in flavors that I both enjoy and understand. I can boil it down to a maxim as simple as this: if there's something you like, and you combine it with something else that you like, chances are that you're going to like the result.

That's the point of this chapter: to encourage you to have fun and experiment with dessert. Think of the composed desserts here as guidelines, not the gospel. They represent only a small portion of what I do at Gramercy Tavern, where I am constantly reworking the menu to follow a change in seasons, a new inspiration, or a shift in mood. These desserts are examples of combinations that work for me, but this doesn't mean you shouldn't put together others that might inspire you. Even if something doesn't come out exactly as you thought it would, it's probably still going to be delicious.

WAFFLES WITH MAPLE-GLAZED BANANAS AND MAPLE FLAN

This is a play on waffles with syrup. The warm, crisp waffles are topped with sweet maple-glazed bananas. The maple flavor is extended to a soft, creamy flan. Cool crème fraîche is just tangy enough to cut through the sweetness of the maple syrup, and candied pecans add a welcome crunch to complete the plate.

Yield: Serves 8

COMPONENTS
Maple-Glazed Bananas with
    Waffles (page 99)
Maple Flan, made in ramekins
    (see Variation, page 189)
Whipped crème fraîche
Candied pecans (see page 261)

DIRECTIONS
Slice the waffles in half on the diagonal. Place half a waffle on each plate. Top the waffle with the bananas, then lay another half waffle on top of the bananas. Unmold a flan onto the plate next to the waffles. Finish with a dollop of whipped crème fraîche and garnish with candied pecans.

WINE PAIRING
Château Pajzos Tokaji, 5 Puttonyos, 1993, Tokaji, Hungary
This classic dessert wine has exuberant toffee, caramel, and sweet fruit notes, along with enough acid and residual sugar, which harmonizes with the maple flavors of this dessert.

MASCARPONE CREAM CANNOLI WITH LEMON THYME—MACERATED RASPBERRY COMPOTE AND HONEY—LEMON THYME SORBET

The foundation of this dessert is the light, sweet, and crisp cannoli shell, filled with a smooth and sumptuous mascarpone cream. The sweet, juicy tartness of macerated berries acts as a vivid counterpoint to the rich cream, which is also underscored by the refreshing iciness and clean flavor of the sorbet. Lemon thyme adds an herbal undertone as it brightens the flavors around it.

Yield: Serves 8

COMPONENTS

Mascarpone Cream Cannoli
    (page 203)
Double recipe of Lemon Thyme—
    Macerated Raspberry Compote
    (page 19)
Honey—Lemon Thyme Sorbet
    (page 163)
Sprigs of fresh lemon thyme

DIRECTIONS

Using ½ teaspoon of batter for each tuile, bake as directed. Form the tuile cannoli shells around the handle of a thin wooden spoon and pipe the mascarpone cream into them. Place two cannoli crisscrossed on each plate and spoon the macerated raspberries around them. Finish with a quenelle of sorbet and a sprig of lemon thyme.

WINE PAIRING

Domaine Beaumalric Muscat de Beaumes-de-Venise, 1998, Southern Rhône Valley, France
The ever-so-slightly elevated alcohol level of the muscat will help to cut through the mascarpone cream, while the orange-blossom note will complement the raspberries and honey.

SAUTÉ OF TOMATOES AND PLUMS WITH BASIL ICE CREAM AND MIXED-PEPPER TUILES

The traditionally savory association of tomatoes dressed with basil and peppercorns is upended in this very untraditional dessert. The tomatoes are mixed with plums to create an exciting interplay of sweet fruitiness and acidity. Basil ice cream provides a cooling sweetness beside the jammy fruit, tasting creamy and mellow, and it is brightened by a drizzle of basil syrup. In case all these seductive, summery tastes lull you into laziness, the crisp tuiles add a spicy, peppery punch.

Yield: Serves 6

COMPONENTS
Sauté of Tomatoes and Plums
   (page 121)
Basil Ice Cream (page 158)
Basil syrup (see page 262)
Mixed-Pepper Tuiles (page 174)

DIRECTIONS
Place portions of the tomatoes and plums in shallow bowls and top with a scoop of basil ice cream. Drizzle the basil syrup over the top and serve mixed-pepper tuiles on the side.

WINE PAIRING
Giacomo Bologna Brachetto d'Acqui, 1999, Piedmont, Italy
To the textural, as well as flavorful, mélange of the dessert, this wine carries its own range of rose-petal and strawberry tones, buttressed by a very refreshing frizzante *sparkle.*

COCONUT TAPIOCA WITH COCONUT SORBET, PASSION FRUIT–PINEAPPLE SORBET, PASSION FRUIT CARAMEL, AND CILANTRO SYRUP

Of all the recipes in this book, this Thai-inspired dessert probably best illustrates my philosophy. The flavors of coconut, passion fruit, and cilantro form a harmonious trio of complementary tropical flavors. Without losing sight of this flavor foundation, I play with the textures of small and large pearl tapioca to create a soft yet thrilling explosion in the mouth. Then I add a drizzle of passion fruit caramel, which adds both a sweet and tangy counterpoint to the creamy coconut. Icy coconut sorbet plays a refreshing role that underscores the flavor of the tapioca, just as the tangy passion fruit–pineapple sorbet highlights the fruitiness of the caramel. Bright, sweet cilantro syrup forms a wreath around the whole, encircling and uniting the vibrant flavors. And finally, a coconut tuile tops it all off with a toasty crunch that completes this study in texture, flavor, and temperature.

Yield: Serves 6

COMPONENTS
Coconut Tapioca Soup (page 109)
Passion Fruit Caramel (page 263)
Cilantro syrup (see page 262)
Passion Fruit–Pineapple Sorbet
  (page 111)
Coconut Sorbet (page 107)
Coconut Tuiles (page 105)

DIRECTIONS
Ladle the coconut tapioca soup into shallow bowls and top with a generous tablespoon of the passion fruit caramel. Drizzle cilantro syrup around the perimeter of the bowl. Place 1 small scoop of passion fruit–pineapple sorbet and 1 of coconut sorbet directly onto the tapioca and top with a coconut tuile.

WINE PAIRING
Château de Suronde Quarts de Chaume, 1996, Loire Valley
Exotic, rich, mystifying flavors and textural nuance elevate this dessert; the combined elegance and lusciousness of this Loire Valley Chenin Blanc elevate the experience even more.

CORNMEAL CREPES WITH SWEET-CORN ICE CREAM AND BLACKBERRY COMPOTE

This is an example of highlighting a single ingredient—corn—in order to appreciate its many qualities. The steaming crepes have the gentle, earthy sweetness of cornmeal and a slight crunch, while the cool ice cream captures corn's fresher mellowness contained in a creamy base. Finally, nibs of candied corn express corn flavor at its sweetest, with a characteristic pop that is one of the most delightful textures corn has to offer. Blackberries enter into this equation via their seasonal connection, while their tartness balances the creaminess of the corn and highlights its sweetness. I find that the bright citrus note of the orange sauce unites the berries and corn and complements both flavors.

Yield: Serves 8

COMPONENTS

Cornmeal Crepes with Orange-Butter Sauce (page 116)
Double recipe of Blackberry Compote (page 18)
Sweet-Corn Ice Cream (page 127)
Candied Corn (page 264)

DIRECTIONS

As soon as all the crepes have been warmed in the orange-butter sauce (see recipe, page 116), place 1 folded crepe on each plate and spoon blackberry compote around the crepe. Drizzle the orange-butter pan sauce over all and place a scoop of sweet-corn ice cream beside the crepe. Sprinkle with candied corn.

WINE PAIRING

Yalumba Museum Muscat, NV, Barossa Valley, Australia
This is a "dig your heels in and lick the plate clean" type of dessert that demands a rich, unctuous wine that makes you want to "lick the glass clean."

ROSE MERINGUES WITH SUMMER BERRIES, RASPBERRY SORBET, AND GOAT YOGURT–ROSE MOUSSE

The seasonal compatibility of berries and roses inspires several of my desserts. Here, I explore classic combinations of temperature, taste, and texture by pushing them a little further than expected. The result is a playfully presented napoleon of sweet, crisp rose meringues, juicy berries, and tangy goat-yogurt mousse, set off by a refreshing berry sorbet.

Yield: Serves 8

COMPONENTS
Rose Meringues (page 157)

Fresh summer berries, such as raspberries, strawberries, and blackberries

Goat Yogurt–Rose Mousse (page 207)

Raspberry Sorbet (page 20)

DIRECTIONS
Place a meringue disk in the center of each shallow bowl and cover with fresh berries. Spoon a dollop of mousse over the berries, then repeat with another meringue layer, more berries, and more mousse, then finish with a meringue on top. Scatter more berries around the meringue napoleon and space three tiny scoops of sorbet evenly around the bowl.

WINE PAIRING
René Geoffrey Champagne Brut Rosé, NV, Champagne, France
While certainly dry, the Geoffrey Rosé may have the most extracted raspberry-strawberry fruit tone you have ever tasted. With its light effervescence, it will be the perfect partner for this glorious dessert.

ROASTED DATES WITH COCONUT SORBET AND CANDIED COCONUT

This dessert is deceptively simple, yet it has all the intrigue and complexity that a composed dessert needs. The warm and earthy spiced dates are lightened and refreshed by a cold and creamy coconut sorbet, and the sweet and crisp candied coconut is a lovely textural highlight. These combinations owe their success to the complex interplay of coconuts and dates—two tropical flavors that simultaneously underscore and complement each other.

Yield: Serves 6

COMPONENTS

Roasted Dates with Sherry and
    Spices (page 101)
Coconut Sorbet (page 107)
Candied Coconut (page 266)

DIRECTIONS

Place the dates in bowls and spoon the extra sauce from the pan over them. Top with scoops of coconut sorbet and sprinkle with candied coconut.

WINE PAIRING

Alvear Pedro Ximenez Sherry,
Abuelo Diego 27, Spain
The Pedro Ximenez mimics the richness of dates and candied coconut and the sweet, nutty tone of the coconut itself, with the addition of a coffee-toffee hint.

CHOCOLATE SOUFFLÉ TART WITH EXTRA-BITTERSWEET CHOCOLATE SORBET, MILK CHOCOLATE MALTED ICE CREAM, AND A CHOCOLATE MALTED

A true exploitation of chocolate in the very best sense, this dessert combines as many forms of chocolate as I could get onto one plate for the ardent chocolate lover. A crispy chocolate tart shell holds a warm, soft, soufflélike filling. The rich, fudgelike sorbet is simultaneously refreshing and decadent, while the mellow milk chocolate ice cream lends balance and delicate chocolaty flavor. Finally, I include a cool chocolate malted to nudge this dessert over the top!

Yield: Serves 20

COMPONENTS
Warm Chocolate Soufflé Tarts
  (page 222)
Extra-Bittersweet Chocolate
  Sorbet (page 233)
Milk Chocolate Malted Ice Cream
  (page 232)
Black and White Chocolate
  Malteds (page 226)

DIRECTIONS
Place a warm chocolate soufflé tart on each small plate. Place a small scoop of sorbet and one of ice cream beside the tart. Serve a small glass of chocolate malted on the side with a straw.

WINE PAIRING
Broadbent Vintage Port, 1994, Portugal
Because they're so pronounced and complex, chocolates are hard to match. The rich berry fruit and increased alcohol of a younger vintage port is a complementary partner that holds its own.

PEACH TARTES TATIN WITH BLACK PEPPER ICE CREAM, WHITE PEACH–ROSÉ CHAMPAGNE GELÉE, AND CHAMPAGNE–PEACH SORBET

This dessert presents peaches in myriad forms. A rich, buttery tarte Tatin crust contains earthy, caramelized peaches, which are complemented by clean-tasting, creamy pepper ice cream and a bright basil syrup. An elegant peach-champagne gelée, topped with icy-cold champagne-peach sorbet, is a refreshing counterbalance to the deep-flavored richness of the ice cream and tarte Tatin.

Yield: Serves 6

COMPONENTS
Basil syrup (see page 262)
Peach Tartes Tatin (page 32)
Black Pepper Ice Cream (page 179)
Freshly ground black pepper
White Peach–Rosé Champagne
    Gelée with Champagne-Peach
    Sorbet (page 36)
Baby or small sprigs of fresh basil

DIRECTIONS
Drizzle a small circle of basil syrup on one side of each large dinner plate. Place an individual tarte Tatin in the circle and a scoop of ice cream next to the tart. Garnish the ice cream with a grind of fresh black pepper. Spoon about 1 tablespoon of gelée onto the opposite side of the plate (alternatively, place a very small bowl of gelée onto the plate). Top the gelée with a scoop of sorbet and garnish with a sprig of baby basil.

WINE PAIRING
Carlo Hauner Malvasia delle Lipari, 1997, Sicily, Italy
The heat of the black pepper and the sweetness of the peaches will thrive with the addition of the ginger-spice-fig note of this southern Italian masterpiece.

CHILLED RHUBARB SOUP WITH ROSE PARFAIT, STRAWBERRY SORBET, CANDIED PISTACHIOS, STRAWBERRIES, AND RHUBARB CHIPS

This dessert features a fruit, a vegetable, and a flower, all with a natural affinity for one another. The rhubarb soup is sweet and tangy, softened by a delicate and creamy rose parfait. The crunchy pistachio nuts fit right in with these sweet, distinctive flavors, and the more delicate crispness of the rhubarb chips is a nice, tart contrast to the rich, nutty garnish. The warmth of the rhubarb, rose, and pistachio flavors is in pleasing opposition to the cool temperatures of the soup, parfait, and sorbet.

Yield: Serves 6

COMPONENTS

Chilled Rhubarb Soup (page 126)
Rose Parfaits (page 155)
Fresh hulled, quartered
  strawberries
Candied pistachios (see page 261)
Strawberry Sorbet (page 21)
Rhubarb Chips (page 264)

DIRECTIONS

Ladle the soup into shallow bowls. Place a rose parfait in the center of each bowl and scatter strawberries around the parfait. Sprinkle with candied pistachios. Top each parfait with a small scoop of sorbet and finish with a rhubarb chip.

WINE PAIRING

Domaine Marcel Deiss
Gewürztraminer, Bergheim,
Vendange
Tardive, 1994, Alsace, France
In this case, the wine does not have to be sweeter than the dessert, as the textural elements come to the fore; the off-dry level of residual sugar and the Gewürztraminer's inherent richness of spice-floral-honey tones will create a brand-new flavor profile.

SEMOLINA PUDDING WITH MINTED CITRUS SALAD, BLOOD-ORANGE SORBET, CANDIED KUMQUATS, AND MINT SYRUP

A warm, creamy pudding and icy, refreshing sorbet share the tart and sweet characteristics of citrus in this fresh, Middle-Eastern-inspired dessert. A minted salad of juicy citrus segments and bright mint syrup underscore the warmer citrus flavors, while candied kumquats round out the citrus palette with their own sweet, yet intensely zesty, flavor.

Yield: Serves 7

COMPONENTS

Semolina Pudding with Minted
    Citrus Salad (page 82)
Candied Kumquats (page 261)
Mint syrup (see page 262)
Blood-Orange Sorbet (page 93)

DIRECTIONS

Warm the puddings in a 300°F. oven for approximately 3 minutes. Un-mold the puddings onto plates and arrange the minted citrus salad beside the puddings. Top each pudding with a few candied kumquats, drizzle mint syrup onto the plate, and finish with a small scoop of blood-orange sorbet on top of the minted oranges.

WINE PAIRING

Inniskillin Vidal Icewine, 1998,
Niagara Peninsula, Ontario
With the kumquats and the oranges comes the need for a similar note in the wine and an exaggerated richness to hold up to the pudding. This "liquid dessert" from Canada will do the trick.

CHERRY NAPOLEON WITH ALMOND-MILK GRANITÉ, SOUR CHERRY SORBET, AND RED WINE–CHERRY SAUCE

In this napoleon, the crunchy layers of phyllo support a lovely combination of toasty, custardlike almond pastry cream and sweet, juicy Bing and white cherries drizzled with an earthy red wine–cherry sauce. The sweet creaminess of the napoleon is counterbalanced by a bright sorbet of sour cherries, while the almond-milk granité is a contradiction in itself of creamy and icy characteristics. Set beside the napoleon and sour cherry sorbet, it adds a lovely, sweet almond flavor and a pleasingly slushy texture. Candied almonds give the plate a final addition of crunch that makes a composed dessert well rounded and complete.

Yield: Serves 8

COMPONENTS

Bing Cherry and White Cherry
   Napoleons with Black Mint
   (page 27)
Red Wine–Cherry Sauce
   (page 264)
Almond-Milk Granité (page 145)
Sour Cherry Sorbet (page 39)
Candied almonds (see page 261)

DIRECTIONS

Make the cherry napoleons by placing a square of phyllo onto each dinner plate slightly left of center and topping it with Bing cherries. Spoon the almond pastry cream over the cherries, drizzle with red wine–cherry sauce, and cover with another phyllo layer. Spoon white cherries over this layer, top with almond pastry cream, and finish with a third phyllo square. Next to the napoleon, make a snowy mountain of granité, then drizzle with red wine–cherry sauce. Top the granité with a scoop of sorbet and sprinkle with candied almonds.

WINE PAIRING

Muller-Catoir Scheurebe Auslese, Haardter Mandelring, 1998, Pfalz, Germany
In another textural masterpiece, seemingly disparate flavors (cherries in the dessert and berries and citrus fruit in the wine) are combined to create another flavor altogether.

APPENDIX

SIMPLE SYRUP

Yield: 2½ cups

2   cups sugar

In a small saucepan over medium-high heat, combine the sugar and 1½ cups water. Bring the mixture to a simmer, stirring until the sugar dissolves. Let the syrup simmer for 1 minute, then turn off the heat and allow to cool. Simple Syrup will keep almost indefinitely in a tightly sealed bottle in the refrigerator.

LEMON CONFIT

This makes a delicious garnish for almost any citrus dessert. It's also great as a topping for a plain cake, like pound cake or angel food.

Yield: 8 to 10 servings

4   lemons, washed, trimmed, and sliced very thin
3   cups Simple Syrup (see above) or more to
    cover the lemons

Preheat the oven to 300°F. Lay the lemons in overlapping rows in a 9 × 12-inch baking pan and cover with the Simple Syrup. Place a sheet of parchment paper on top of the lemons, then cover the pan with foil; prick the foil all over with a fork. Bake the slices until they are translucent, about 1 hour. Remove the foil and continue to bake the lemons until the juices are thick and syrupy,

30 to 55 minutes longer. Cool completely before serving. The confit will keep, refrigerated, for several weeks.

CANDIED KUMQUATS

These sweet kumquats make an interesting addition to a winter fruit salad. Or try them stirred into plain yogurt, or even spread on your morning toast.

Yield: About 2 cups

2½ cups sugar
2   cups washed and sliced kumquats

In a medium saucepan, combine the sugar and 1½ cups water. Bring to a boil, stirring to dissolve the sugar. Add the kumquats, reduce the heat to low, and simmer for about 6 minutes, or until the kumquats appear translucent. Drain well before serving. The kumquats will keep, refrigerated, for several weeks.

CANDIED NUTS

Yield: 2 cups

2   cups nuts
3 to 5 tablespoons Simple Syrup (see above)
¼   cup turbinado (raw) sugar

1. Preheat the oven to 350°F. In a large bowl, toss the nuts with enough of the Simple Syrup to coat them well.

Some types of soft nuts, like cashews, macadamias, and pecans, may need a little more syrup since they will quickly absorb it. Harder nuts, like hazelnuts, may take less syrup. The nuts should be sticky and well coated with enough syrup so the sugar will stick.

2. Add the turbinado sugar to the nuts, tossing well. Work quickly so that the sugar doesn't melt. Spread the nuts out on a baking sheet and bake for 10 minutes, stirring the nuts after 5 minutes. Transfer the pan to a wire rack to cool completely.

CHESTNUT HONEY—ROASTED PINE NUTS

Yield: 2 cups
2 tablespoons chestnut honey
2 cups pine nuts
¼ cup turbinado (raw) sugar

1. Preheat the oven to 350°F. Place the honey in a small saucepan and warm it slightly over low heat. Alternatively, place the jar of honey in the microwave for 30 seconds to warm it (remove the lid first). Warming the honey liquefies it, making it easier to toss with the nuts.

2. In a large bowl, toss the nuts with the honey to coat them well. Add the turbinado sugar, tossing well. Spread the nuts out on a baking sheet and bake for 10 minutes, stirring the nuts after 5 minutes. Transfer the pan to a wire rack to cool completely.

HERB (CILANTRO, MINT, BASIL) SYRUP
These fresh, herby syrups are terrific drizzled on any summer fruit—from a bowl of berries to sliced apricots and peaches.

Yield: ⅓ cup
¼ cup tightly packed cilantro, mint, or basil leaves
⅓ cup light corn syrup

1. Bring a small saucepan of water to a boil. Fill a bowl with ice cubes and water. Plunge the herb leaves into the boiling water for 15 seconds, then drain and immediately plunge into the ice water. Remove from the water and pat dry.

2. Combine the corn syrup and herb leaves in a blender or food processor and purée. Let the mixture rest for 30 minutes, then strain the syrup, discarding the solids. The syrup will keep, refrigerated, for up to 1 day.

LEMON—GINGER SAUCE
This spicy, tart sauce can liven up any simple dessert like pound cake or ice cream. At the restaurant, we serve it with the Lemon-Lime Soufflé Tart and Ginger Ice Cream.

Yield: About 1 cup
Grated zest of 4 lemons
1 cup sugar
¼ cup chopped, peeled fresh gingerroot
2½ vanilla beans, split lengthwise, pulp scraped
   (see page 180)

1. Bring a small saucepan of water to a boil. Fill a bowl with ice cubes and water. Place the lemon zest in a fine strainer or a tea ball and plunge it into the boiling water for 30 seconds. Immediately drain and plunge into the ice water. Drain and set aside.

2. In a medium saucepan, bring the sugar and ½ cup water to a boil, stirring to dissolve the sugar. Turn off the heat and add the gingerroot and vanilla pods and pulp. Let the mixture infuse for at least 30 minutes. Strain through a fine sieve and stir in the reserved lemon zest. The sauce will keep, refrigerated, for up to 3 days.

caramelized, about 10 minutes. Remove the saucepan from the heat and carefully whisk in the tea (stand back, the caramel may splatter). Place the pan over low heat and whisk until the caramel is smooth. Transfer to a small bowl and let cool for at least 1 hour. The caramel will keep for up to 4 days in the refrigerator.

PASSION FRUIT CARAMEL

Indispensable for my coconut tapioca dessert, this sweet-tart caramel is also marvelous made into a tropical sundae with vanilla ice cream, passion fruit sorbet, and candied macadamia nuts or coconut.

Yield: ¾ cups
1   cup sugar
1   teaspoon light corn syrup
½   cup unsweetened passion fruit juice or purée
2   tablespoons unsalted butter
Pulp from 2 ripe passion fruits

1. Place ¼ cup water in a small saucepan. Add the sugar and corn syrup and simmer the mixture, stirring, until the sugar dissolves. Raise the heat to high and boil the mixture, swirling the pan occasionally, until it turns deep amber and caramelized, about 10 minutes. Remove the saucepan from the heat and carefully whisk in the passion fruit juice and butter (stand back, the caramel may splatter). Set the saucepan over low heat and whisk until the caramel is smooth. Transfer to a small bowl and let cool for at least 1 hour. The caramel will keep for up to 2 days in the refrigerator.

2. Just before serving, stir the passion fruit pulp into the caramel.

LEMON CURD

Sweet, tart, and silky, lemon curd is one of the nicest things to have on hand. It makes a great topping for pound cakes, filling for sandwich cookies or tart shells, or spread for toast.

EARL GREY CARAMEL

Smoky and sweet, this complex caramel is especially wonderful with chocolate desserts. But its citrus note also pairs well with citrus flavor—or use it to jazz up plain vanilla ice cream.

Yield: 1¼ cups
2   tablespoons Earl Grey tea leaves (not bags)
¾   cup sugar
1   teaspoon corn syrup

1. In a small saucepan, bring 1 cup water to a boil. Turn off the heat and stir in the tea leaves. Let sit for a few seconds (not longer than 10), then strain through a fine sieve, discarding the solids.

2. Place ¼ cup water in a small saucepan. Add the sugar and corn syrup and simmer the mixture, stirring, until the sugar dissolves.

3. Raise the heat to high and boil the mixture, swirling the pan occasionally, until it turns deep amber and

Yield: 2 cups

3 large eggs
3 large egg yolks
½ cup sugar
½ cup fresh lemon juice (about 3 to 4 lemons)
¼ cup grated lemon zest (about 2 to 3 lemons)
Pinch of salt
4 tablespoons unsalted butter, softened, cut into pieces

1. In a large, stainless-steel bowl, whisk together the eggs, egg yolks, and sugar. Whisk in the lemon juice, zest, and salt.

2. Place the bowl over (not in) a pot of barely simmering water and gently cook the curd, whisking constantly to avoid scrambling the eggs, until the curd thickens enough to coat the back of a spoon, about 10 minutes. Remove the bowl from the heat and whisk in the butter. Strain the mixture through a fine sieve and set the bowl in a larger bowl filled with water and ice. Whisk until cool. Cover the curd and refrigerate until it is thoroughly cold, at least 2 hours. The curd will keep for up to 3 days in the refrigerator.

CANDIED CORN

Yield: 1½ cups

3 ears fresh corn, husks and silk removed
1½ cups sugar
¼ vanilla bean, split lengthwise, pulp scraped
   (see page 180)

1. Using a sharp knife, cut the kernels off the corn.

2. In a medium saucepan over medium heat, bring the sugar, 1 cup water, and the vanilla pulp to a simmer, stirring to dissolve the sugar. Add the corn kernels and simmer until they are translucent, about 40 minutes. Turn off the heat and cool completely before serving. The candied corn will keep for up to 2 days in the refrigerator.

RHUBARB CHIPS

Yield: 20 chips

2 tablespoons sugar
¾ cup (about 4 ounces) chopped rhubarb

1. Preheat the oven to 250°F. In a small saucepan, bring the sugar and 1 tablespoon water to a boil, stirring to dissolve the sugar. Stir in the rhubarb and cook until the rhubarb breaks down and turns into mush, about 10 minutes. Stir the mixture over low heat until it is dry, 5 to 7 minutes. Push the mixture through a fine strainer, discarding the solids.

2. Spread the rhubarb evenly in a thin layer on a baking sheet covered with a nonstick baking liner. Bake until the rhubarb feels dry and leathery, 30 to 40 minutes. Transfer to a wire rack to cool completely.

3. Using a sharp knife, cut the rhubarb into long, thin strips, about ¾ × 2 inches. Store in an airtight tin for up to 2 days.

RED WINE–CHERRY SAUCE
Although the cherries that flavor this sauce are spooned out halfway through the cooking, don't throw them away. Use them over ice cream or stir them into yogurt for a sophisticated treat.

Yield: About 1¼ cups

2 cups red wine
2 cups pitted and halved red cherries
1 cup sugar
1 star anise

In a medium saucepan, combine all the ingredients and bring to a boil. Reduce the heat to very low and gently simmer the mixture until the cherries are soft and begin to fall apart, about 1 hour. Remove the cherries with a slotted spoon (you can reserve them for another use) and continue reducing the red wine syrup until it begins to thicken and becomes sticky, another 25 to 30 minutes.

Let cool completely before using. The sauce will keep for several weeks in the refrigerator.

MACERATED DRIED SOUR CHERRIES

These plumped-up dried cherries add a sweet-tart taste and soft-chewy texture to fruit crisps and cobblers, or to fresh fruit salads. I especially love to use them in the winter, when good fresh berries and cherries aren't available.

Yield: 1½ cups
½   cup red wine
½   cup sugar
¼   vanilla bean, split lengthwise, pulp scraped
     (see page 180)
1   cup dried sour cherries

In a small saucepan, combine the red wine, sugar, ¼ cup plus 2 tablespoons water, and the vanilla pulp and bring to a boil, stirring to dissolve the sugar. Stir in the sour cherries. Turn off the heat and let cool to room temperature. Refrigerate the cherries in the syrup overnight. They will keep for several weeks in the refrigerator.

GOLDEN RAISIN VERJUS

This assertive sauce makes a great accompaniment to mild cheese desserts, such as the Triple-Crème Tart or a cheesecake. It's also wonderful with roasted winter fruit and crème fraîche, or even spooned into yogurt for breakfast.

Yield: 1¼ cups
1   cup golden raisins
¾   cup white verjus (see page 269)
½   cup filtered apple juice
⅓   cup sugar
1-inch piece of vanilla bean, split lengthwise, pulp
     scraped (see page 180)

1. In a medium saucepan, combine the raisins, verjus, apple juice, sugar, and vanilla pulp and bring the mixture to a simmer over medium heat, stirring occasionally.

2. Immediately reduce the heat to low. Let the mixture slowly cook at a very low simmer until it is reduced by half, 35 to 40 minutes, stirring occasionally. Let cool for at least 15 minutes before serving. The verjus will keep, refrigerated, for several weeks.

VANILLA ICE CREAM

Yield: About 1 quart
3   cups milk
1¼ cups sugar
1   cup heavy cream
1½ vanilla beans, split lengthwise, pulp scraped
     (see page 180)
12 large egg yolks
1½ teaspoons vanilla extract
Pinch of salt

1. In a heavy-bottomed saucepan, combine the milk, 1 cup of the sugar, the heavy cream, and the vanilla pods and pulp and bring to a simmer over medium heat.

2. Meanwhile, whisk together the egg yolks and the remaining ¼ cup of sugar. Remove the milk mixture from the heat and add a little to the egg yolk mixture to warm it, whisking constantly to keep the yolks from curdling. Pour the egg yolk mixture into the hot milk mixture, whisking the milk constantly as you pour.

3. Return the custard to the stove and cook it over low heat, stirring constantly with a wooden spoon, until it thickens enough to coat the back of the spoon, about 5 minutes. Remove the custard from the heat and pour it into a bowl. Let cool completely.

4. Strain the custard through a fine sieve, then stir in the vanilla extract and salt. Chill until thoroughly cold, at least 4 hours.

5. Freeze in an ice-cream maker according to the manufacturer's instructions.

CANDIED COCONUT

This is just as delicious nibbled out of hand as it is sprinkled over ice creams, custards, or fruit desserts.

Yield: About 3 cups

1 coconut
2 tablespoons Simple Syrup (page 261)
2 tablespoons turbinado (raw) sugar

1. Preheat the oven to 400°F. Using a hammer or mallet, crack open the coconut and drain out the liquid. Place the coconut pieces on a baking sheet and bake until the coconut begins to dry out and the meat starts to pull away from the shell, 15 to 20 minutes. Remove from the oven and cool on a wire rack. Lower the oven temperature to 350°F.

2. When the coconut is cool enough to handle, slide a fork under the shell to loosen the coconut meat from the shell. Using a mandoline, cut the coconut meat into very thin slices. Place in a small bowl and toss with the Simple Syrup and sugar. Line two baking sheets with parchment paper or nonstick liner. Spread the coconut slices on the baking sheets in a single layer. Bake until they begin to lightly brown, 8 to 10 minutes. Transfer to a wire rack to cool.

BUTTERY BRIOCHE

Yield: 1 loaf

2 teaspoons active dry yeast
3 tablespoons warm milk (not hotter than 110°F.)
4 large eggs
1¾ cups plus 2 tablespoons all-purpose flour, plus additional if necessary
1½ tablespoons sugar
½ teaspoon salt
6 tablespoons unsalted butter, softened

1. Place the yeast in a small bowl and pour the warm milk over it. Stir and let dissolve for 5 minutes. Pour into the bowl of an electric mixer and add 1 egg and ½ cup of the flour. Stir to combine. Sprinkle ½ cup of the flour over the mixture without stirring. Cover the bowl tightly with plastic wrap and set aside in a warm place until the surface of the sponge cracks, about 30 to 40 minutes.

2. Add another 2 eggs and the remaining ¾ cup plus 2 tablespoons flour, the sugar, and the salt to the yeast mixture. Using the dough hook, mix on low for 1 to 2 minutes, until combined. Turn the mixer up to medium-high and mix until the dough wraps itself around the hook and is smooth, about 15 minutes. If the dough has not completely left the sides of the bowl, add a tablespoon or two of flour while the mixer is on. The dough should be shiny and sticky.

3. Reduce the mixer speed to medium-low and add the butter, 1 tablespoon at a time. Once all of the butter is incorporated, raise the mixer speed to medium-high and beat for another 3 to 5 minutes, until the dough is smooth and shiny.

4. Place the dough on a lightly floured surface and gather into a ball. Transfer to a large oiled bowl and cover tightly with plastic wrap. Set in a warm, draft-free place until doubled in size, 1½ to 2 hours.

5. Gently press the dough down and lay a piece of lightly greased plastic wrap on top of the bowl, leaving plenty of room for the dough to continue to rise. Refrigerate for 10 to 12 hours, or overnight.

6. Butter a 9 × 5-inch loaf pan and set aside. Knead the brioche dough for 1 to 2 minutes, until smooth, then gather it into a ball. Roll it out into a log shape, slightly smaller than the size of the loaf pan. Place it in the loaf pan. Beat the remaining egg with 1 tablespoon water until smooth, then brush the loaf with the egg glaze (cover and refrigerate the remaining egg glaze). Cover

the loaf with plastic and place it in a warm, draft-free place until doubled in size, 2 to 3 hours.

7. Preheat the oven to 350°F. Brush the loaf with the egg glaze once again before baking. Bake until the crust is a deep, golden brown and the bread sounds hollow when tapped on the bottom, about 45 minutes to 1 hour.

8. Unmold immediately and transfer to a wire rack to cool completely.

SOURCES

- ALMOND FLOUR is available in specialty food markets or by mail-order from the King Arthur Flour Company's Baker's Catalogue, 800-827-6836.

- HAZELNUT PASTE OR BUTTER, made from ground, unsweetened hazelnuts, is available at specialty food markets or by mail-order from Kalyustan's, 212-685-3451.

- TAMARIND CONCENTRATE, ROSE WATER, ORANGE-BLOSSOM WATER, AND ROSE PRESERVES are all available in Middle Eastern and some Asian specialty markets, or by mail-order from Kalyustan's, 212-685-3451.

- FLEUR DE SEL is a high-quality French sea salt with a very refined taste. It's available in specialty food markets or by mail-order from the King Arthur Flour Company's Baker's Catalogue, 800-827-6836.

- EXTRA-BITTERSWEET CHOCOLATE (also called extra-bitter chocolate) ranges from 66 to 80 percent cocoa. It has a fuller, more powerful chocolate flavor than regular bittersweet chocolate. Valrhona and Scharffen Berger are two top-notch chocolate brands that are easily available to home cooks. You can find them at specialty food markets or by mail-order from the Sweet Life, 212-598-0092.

- VERJUS ("green juice" in French) is the liquid extracted from unripe fruit, usually grapes or crabapples. White verjus is fruity and slightly acidic, though less acidic than wine (and it doesn't have any alcohol that would have to be cooked out). It is available at specialty food markets or by mail-order from Dean & DeLuca, 800-221-7714.

- DRIED LAVENDER is available at tea and spice shops or by mail-order from Dean & DeLuca, 800-221-7714.

- CHESTNUT HONEY AND CHESTNUT PASTE are available at specialty food markets or by mail-order from Dean & DeLuca, 800-221-7714.

- CANNOLI MOLDS, STENCILS, NONSTICK BAKING PAN LINERS (THE WELL-KNOWN BRAND IS SILPAT), PIPING BAGS AND TIPS, AND MANDOLINES are available at baking supply stores and by mail-order from J. B. Prince, 800-473-0577

CREDITS

—————

Page 9   Oval pewter tray: Distant Origin

Page 13   Teacup and plate: Ad Hoc

Page 29   Crinkle cups: Ad Hoc; kiriwood Japanese tray:
         Gordon Foster

Page 51   Linen placemat: Takashimaya

Page 67   Silver bowl by Stewart: Gordon Foster

Page 68   Medium plate: Nicole Fahri

Page 70   Serving plate by Stewart: Gordon Foster

Page 73   Brown bowl by Christiane Perrechone: Takashimaya

Page 87   Gold bowl by Stewart: Gordon Foster;
         curry linen napkin: Ad Hoc

Page 100   Oval cherry cutting board: Simon Pearce

Page 104   Bowls: Natasha David; bamboo spoon:
         ABC Carpet & Home

Page 119   Bowls: Global Table

Page 135   Glass and linen napkin: Ad Hoc

Page 138   Linen napkins: Ad Hoc; creamware plate: Aero Ltd.

Page 151   Square teak tray: Takashimaya

Page 153   Luster plate: ABC Carpet & Home

Page 160   Plate by Christiane Perrechone: Takashimaya;
         small footed bowls: Dean & Deluca

Page 169   Tray: ABC Carpet & Home

Page 170   Circular tray and spoon: Dean & Deluca

Page 197   Plate and porcelain bowls with rim: Ad Hoc

Page 209   Plate: ABC Carpet & Home; glasses:
         The Terence Conran Shop

Page 221   Bowl: Simon Pearce; kiriwood Japanese tray:
         Gordon Foster

Page 228   Wooden bowl: Dean & Deluca

Page 239   Rectangle tile: Shi; place mat: ABC Carpet & Home

Page 243   Plate: ABC Carpet & Home;
         Georg Jenson spoon: Shi

Page 244   Plate: Nicole Fahri; wineglass: Takashimaya

Page 247   Tray: Takashimaya

Page 248   Silver bowl by Stewart: Gordon Foster; wooden trivet:
         The Terence Conran Shop

Page 252   Oval point plate: Barneys New York; bowl:
         Global Table

Page 259   Celadon bowl (left): Dean & Deluca; melon bowl and
         nesting bowls: Shi; white platter by Maryse boxer:
         Barneys New York; oval plate by Christiane Perrechone:
         Takashimaya

Page 263   Plate: Ad Hoc

INDEX

Note: Italicized page numbers indicate recipes used in Signature Composed Desserts.

CLAUDIA FLEMING is the pastry chef of Gramercy Tavern restaurant in
New York City. She is the winner of the 2000 James Beard Outstanding Pastry
Chef Award and the 2000 and 2001 Best Dessert Award from *Pastry Art and
Design* magazine. She apprenticed at the prestigious Fauchon in Paris under
Pierre Hermé and returned to New York to work in pastry at Union Square Cafe,
Montrachet, Tribeca Grill, and Luxe. In 1994 Danny Meyer and Tom Colicchio
hired her as pastry chef at Gramercy Tavern. Her work has been celebrated
in publications such as *The New York Times, Bon Appetit,
Food and Wine, Saveur, Vogue,* and *Time.*

MELISSA CLARK writes about cuisine and is a regular contributor to
The New York Times, among other publications. A former professional caterer,
she earned an M.F.A. in writing from Columbia University and is the
author of twelve cookbooks. She lives in Brooklyn, New York.

ABOUT THE TYPE

This book was set in Bembo, a typeface based on an old-style
Roman face that was used for Cardinal Bembo's tract *De Aetna* in 1495.
Bembo was cut by Francisco Griffo in the early sixteenth century.
The Lanston Monotype Machine Company of Philadelphia brought
the well-proportioned letter forms of Bembo to
the United States in the 1930s.